D1824535

BEYOND THE CRISIS

BEYOND THE CRISIS

Korea's Emergence from
the Global Financial Storm of 2008

Jun Kwang-woo

Seoul Selection

BEYOND THE CRISIS
Korea's Emergence from the Global Financial Storm of 2008

Written by Jun Kwang-woo

Published by **Seoul Selection**
B1 Korean Publishers Association Bldg., 105-2 Sagan-dong,
Jongno-gu, Seoul 110-190, Korea
Tel: 82-2-734-9567
Fax: 82-2-734-9562
E-mail: publisher@seoulselection.com
www.seoulselection.com

ISBN: 978-89-91913-63-9 93320

Printed in Korea

To my loving family:

My wife, Jeonghwa and three wonderful children,
Eun-kyung (Esther), Hee-kyung (Hannah) and Jae-hak (Daniel)

CONTENTS

Preface   xi

Chapter I

LEADING UP TO GLOBAL FINANCIAL CRISIS

1. International Macroeconomic Environment   1
2. Microeconomic Factors   6
3. Effects on Emerging Market Economies   10
4. Korea's Road to Recovery   15

Chapter II

POLICY RESPONSES TO CRISIS

1. Stabilization of Financial Markets   19
2. Enhanced Capital Strength and Soundness of Financial   36
   Companies
3. Support for Corporate Funding   62
4. Intensified Corporate Restructuring Efforts   85
5. Greater Support to Low- and Middle-Income Population   102
6. BOK Monetary Policy in Response to Global Financial   107
   Crisis
7. Government Fiscal and Economic Policy Response to   113
   Global Financial Crisis
8. International Cooperation During Global Financial Crisis   120

Chapter III

LESSONS FOR CRISIS MANAGEMENT

1. Critical Importance of Preemptive and Decisive Stimulus   131
   Packages in Early Phase

2. Adhering to Principles and Discipline amid Crisis   140

3. Strong Leadership for Inter-Agency Cooperation and   148
   Public Support

4. Evolving Remedies for New Crises   152

Chapter IV

LESSONS FOR CRISIS PREVENTION AND
FUTURE AGENDA FOR SUSTAINABLE FINANCIAL
DEVELOPMENT

1. Rebalancing Financial Innovation and Prudential   159
   Regulation

2. Rebuilding Trust in Corporate and Financial Systems   171

3. Resetting Modern Financial Capitalism   181

4. Reshaping International Financial Regime   192

5. Rethinking Transition from Stimulus to Exit Strategy   208

Conclusion   217

Preface

Unprecedented financial turmoil erupted in the aftermath of the collapse of Lehman Brothers in September 2008, sending shock waves around the world and leaving behind a trail of economic, social, and political repercussions—the likes of which had not been seen since the Great Depression of the 1930s. Pessimists weighed in on the global crisis, predicting a long and painful road to recovery. Some questioned the likelihood of a recovery altogether, even going as far as to say that the crisis signaled the end of financial capitalism.

Dr. Christiaan Barnard, a pioneer in heart transplant surgery, once said, "Suffering isn't ennobling, recovery is." Working to facilitate recovery from suffering is indeed a noble mission, whether this is in medical science or the social science called economics or finance.

The global crisis required global solutions. The international community reacted quickly, and this time the G-20 Forum became the core consultative mechanism for coordinated policy responses to the crisis. Strong stimulus packages were implemented in fiscal, financial and monetary policies across countries and in every kind of economy, from emerging to advanced.

As the world is paying close attention to the ramifications the current financial crisis might bring about in its second year, there seem to be signs of a rebound. Although the story continues to unfold, economic circumstances have clearly brightened—and within a relatively short period of time—attesting once again to the resilient nature of the so-called "science" of finance. Shock has given way to relief more quickly than many had feared.

As relief often tends to give way to complacency, such optimism at this stage is premature at best. The long-term effects of the financial meltdown are still unclear, particularly in terms of the negative impact on growth in potential output and employment. Thus, even as the economy begins to expand, we remain wary that it may do so at a slower pace, while the vast deterioration in the fiscal positions of many countries also threatens a sustained recovery. Despite improved market sentiments, the financial sector remains weak and fragile, rendering its progress vulnerable to corporate distress and delayed restructuring.

As Martin Wolf, a renowned columnist and former World Bank economist argued in his Financial Times column of October 2009, we must avoid two fatal mistakes at this juncture, namely premature withdrawal of stimulus measures and failure to take the opportunities presented for reform. He is right on both counts.

On the flip side of the economic rebound is the exit strategy, historically plagued by the dilemma of timing and scope. That is, when implementing an exit plan, history suggests that a premature exit from accommodative fiscal and monetary policies could lead to the misinterpretation of the policy-induced rebound as a genuine recovery in private demand. At the same time, failure to exit in time presents the risk of a bubble effect recurring.

The principle of the exit strategy is similar to getting discharged from the hospital. Even when patients appear to have made a full recovery from their illness, doctors are still cautious about discharging them and insist on being absolutely certain of their ability to take care of themselves. Admitting a patient, however, is rarely second-guessed, in the assumption that a serious illness exists. Likewise, the basic principle in dealing with the crisis ought to be a "speedy and decisive" stance in the beginning stage, contrasted with a "slow and prudent" approach in the ending phase.

Stepping up to the task of economic reform is also critical in both the local and global contexts. Hasty optimism in a market known for its notoriously short memory must not be allowed to dilute the importance of the role of reform in further strengthening the financial systems in many countries. Otherwise, the ominous threat that "the end of one crisis is the beginning of the next crisis" looms exponentially closer.

This book is prepared to serve two objectives. One is sharing knowledge of effective crisis management, based on Korea's recent experience in overcoming its own turmoil during the global financial crisis. International organizations such as the IMF, OECD and the World Bank, as well as the international press, have given much coverage to Korea's economic comeback story. The Korean experience may shed some light for many emerging economies in dealing with such a financial crisis.

This book also endeavors to propose an agenda for a safer and more disciplined financial environment, leading to balanced and sustained growth of the world economy. While steps have already been taken, the global community must not lose momentum in continuing to improve the architecture of the international financial system. The present crossroads also coincides with Korea's assumption of the G-20 Forum chairmanship this year, under the auspices of which Korea stands ready to play an active role in promoting collective global efforts to these ends.

Niccolo Machiavelli wrote, "Never waste the opportunities offered by a good crisis." While one might argue the notion of a "good crisis," the message as its stands is inarguably wise, or pragmatic at a minimum.

This book is rarely academic but aims to generate policy implications from the experiences of Korean policymakers. The introductory chapter provides a brief overview of the background and factors directly contributing to the financial crisis, followed by a detailed discussion of specific policy measures showing how Korea has implemented crisis management under the leadership of President Lee Myung-bak. Emphasis is given to financial policies and market stabilization measures that fall under the purview of the Financial Services Commission (FSC), Korea's financial policy and supervisory authority.

The following chapter presents policy lessons, especially for emerging market countries, in dealing with a financial crisis. The final chapter discusses key issues and challenges facing the global economy and explores ways to move forward. The policy implications are aimed at helping to reduce risks and vulnerability to future shocks; creating a more resilient and equitable international economic paradigm; and promoting sustainable growth and shared prosperity for years to come.

To offer up another metaphor, the free market economy is like the incredibly resourceful yet unpredictable open sea, which from time to time may produce tremendous waves and disastrous storms, leading to inevitable casualties. In contrast, there is very little usefulness to be gleaned from the safe and confined waters of the Dead Sea. It is the responsibility of the international community to continue to foster openness as well as fairness in the world economy—even more so today than ever, given this current juncture in modern economic history, which will serve as a defining moment for future generations.

No one can complete a book without a great deal of help. This book is no exception and would not have been possible without the assistance of too many colleagues and supporters to name here.

First and foremost, I am deeply grateful to all the staff of the FSC and its related government branches, who have exhibited the highest standards of excellence throughout my tenure as the FSC chairman, and relentlessly and passionately pursued the goal of overcoming this recent and unprecedented financial crisis. It was my enormous privilege and a truly rewarding experience to navigate through this most turbulent period with such a skilled and devoted crew—whose members represent the very spirit that made Korea's dramatic turnaround from serious panic to ultimate sharp rebound possible during its own financial crisis.

The publication of this book would not have happened without the dedicated support of a number of scholars and industry analysts who made significant contributions with their economic insight and editorial ingenuity. Finally, I would like to extend my sincere appreciation to the staff of the National Pension Service (NPS) of Korea, who have provided outstanding assistance in the final phase of this publication and offered me tremendous support since I took on the role of its chairman recently.

Jun Kwang-woo

Seoul, Korea
January 2010

Chapter I

LEADING UP TO GLOBAL FINANCIAL CRISIS

When discussing the origins of the global financial crisis, there are two levels to consider: global macro policies affecting liquidity, and a severely inadequate overall regulatory framework. The policies affecting liquidity created a dangerous situation that may be considered somewhat akin to an overburdened dam, where stress against the dam wall had the result of ensuring the occurrence of asset bubbles and excess leverage. The cracks in the dam started forming as early as the beginning of the 2000s, leading to increased pressure in two highly sensitive areas: mortgage securitization and off-balance-sheet activity.

The turbulence caused by the financial crisis is further attributable to the negative influence that advanced economies exerted on emerging market economies (EMEs), mainly in the form of volatile capital flow movements.

1. International Macroeconomic Environment

The sub-prime mortgage sector in the U.S. was the proximate cause of the global financial crisis. At the fundamental level, however, the crisis could be ascribed to the persistence of large global imbalances, which, in turn, were the result of long periods of excessively loose monetary policy in major advanced economies during the early part of this decade. Global imbalances have been manifested through a substantial increase in the U.S. current account deficit contrasted with substantial surpluses in Asia—particularly China—and in oil-exporting countries in the Middle East and Russia. According to some academics, global macroeconomic imbalances were the major underlying cause of the crisis. Disproportionate savings-to-investment ratios and subsequent cross-border financial flows put enormous stress on the financial intermediation process. Global imbalances interacted with existing flaws in financial markets and instruments to generate specific crisis symptoms. Such a view, however, offers only a partial analysis of the global economic environment at the time. The role of monetary policy in major economies, especially the U.S., over the same time period requires a more balanced analysis.

The U.S. and other advanced economies (e.g., the Bank of Japan) aggressively eased their monetary policies in the aftermath of the bursting of the dot com bubble in the U.S. at the turn of the decade. Basking in record-low inflation and low inflationary expectations, central banks reverted to more intensive fine-tuning in a bid to obviate even an iota of risk of recession. As a result, the Fed aggressively reduced its benchmark rate three times over the preceding 10 years, starting with a series of crises in emerging markets (Mexico, Southeast Asia, Asia, Russia and the pre-crisis situation in Brazil) and the Long-Term Capital Management troubles in the U.S. at the end of 1998. The post 9/11 years of 2001-2002 witnessed drastic policy rate cuts that eventually brought the rate down to 1%, as well as the end of the dot com era. The benchmark interest rate in the U.S. subsequently dipped

Figure 1-1 **Federal Fund Rate in the U.S.**

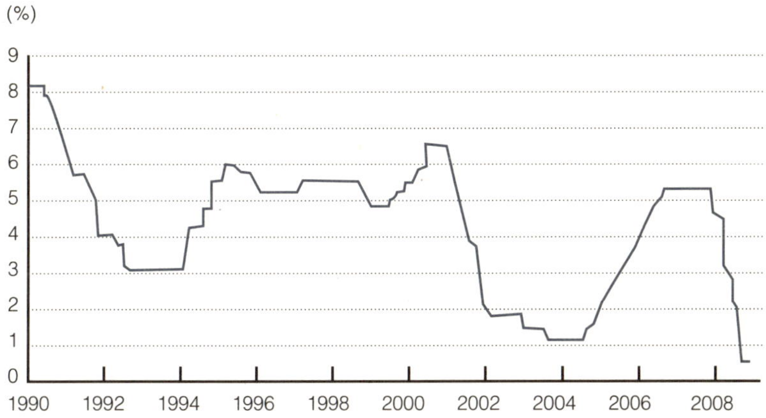

(%)

Source: Datastream

to one percent in June 2003 and remained at that level for an extended period of time (until June 2004).

In the period that followed, there did appear to be a gradual withdrawal of U.S. accommodative monetary policy; an empirical assessment of U.S. monetary policy actually indicates that the period from 2002 to 2006, and especially 2002 to 2004, was marked by a substantially looser policy than what a simple application of the Taylor rule would have required. Clearly, excessively loose monetary policy was implemented during this period.

The excessively loose monetary policy in the post-dot com period boosted consumption and investment in the U.S. and was the result of purposeful and careful consideration by monetary policy makers. Ultimately, the relatively low interest rates induced a prolonged period of excess global liquidity. As might be expected with such low nominal and real interest rates, asset prices also recorded strong gains, particularly in the housing and real estate sectors, providing further impetus to consumption and investment through wealth effects. Thus, aggregate demand consistently exceeded domestic output in the U.S. and, given the macroeconomic identity, this trend was mirrored in large and growing current account deficits in the U.S. over the period.

This large domestic demand in the U.S. was met by the rest of the world, especially China and other East Asian economies, which provided goods and services at relatively low costs, leading to growing surpluses in these countries. Furthermore, the availability of relatively cheaper goods and services from China and other EMEs also helped to maintain price stability in the U.S. and elsewhere, which might not have been possible otherwise. Thus, measured inflation in the advanced economies remained low, contributing to the persistence of accommodative monetary policy. The emergence of a dysfunctional global imbalance is essentially a post-2000 phenomenon that spiked after 2004.

Figure 1-2 **U.S. Current Account Balance**

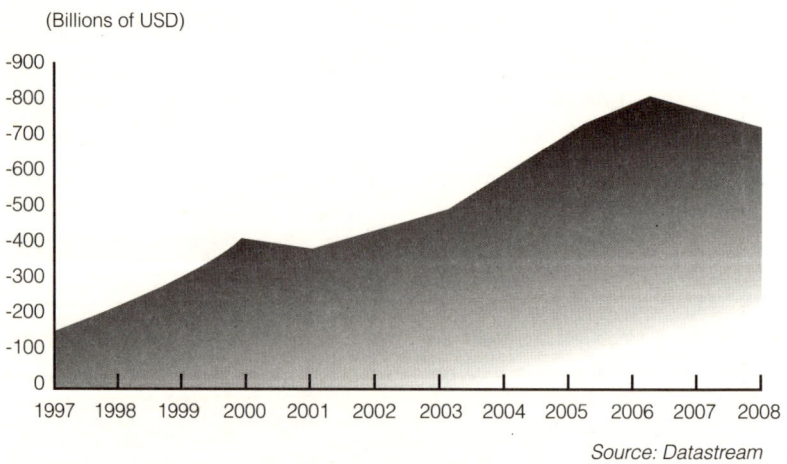

(Billions of USD)

Source: Datastream

Figure 1-3 **Current Account Surpluses of China, Newly Industrialized Asian Economies, and the Middle East (As Percentage of World GDP)**

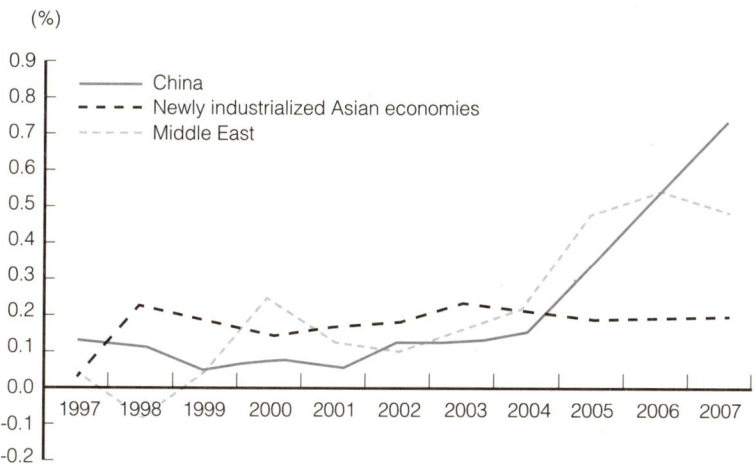

Source: IMF

Apart from creating large global financial surplus imbalances, accommodative monetary policy and extended periods of low interest rates encouraged a search for higher yields, as well as the easing of lending standards. Even as financial imbalances were building up, macroeconomic stability remained intact. Major advanced economies had seen relatively stable growth and low inflation since the early 1990s, known as the period of Great Moderation. The stable macroeconomic environment encouraged the underpricing of risk. Financial innovations, regulatory arbitrage, lending malpractices, excessive use of the originate-and-distribute model, securitization of sub-prime loans and their bundling into AAA tranches on the back of ratings all combined to create an environment for excessively leveraged financial market entities.

2. Microeconomic Factors

GENERAL PITFALLS IN FINANCIAL SUPERVISORY SYSTEMS

Monetary policy is not solely to blame for the crisis. Financial regulations and regulatory institutions lagged well behind rapid developments taking place in the financial market and therefore share responsibility for the economic fallout. Two major inconsistencies are particularly apparent from the perspective of regulatory and institutional weaknesses.

Whereas financial markets and major financial institutions are global in nature, financial supervisory institutions are predominantly country-specific. Also, financial conglomerates increasingly operate in various sectors of the finance industry as financial instruments continue to diversify. However, financial supervision remains strictly compartmentalized.

The blame should also be partly borne by the rating agencies and supervisory authorities that underestimated actual risk. These institutions failed to understand the nature of innovative financial instruments and provided excessively short-sighted risk assessments that did not sufficiently take into account the actual risk distribution in the long-run intermediation chain between final borrower and creditor.

Precautionary regulations in the form of capital adequacy ratio requirements (especially when assets are risk-weighted and mark-to-market priced) or tight accounting standards, such as required reserve provisions against expected losses, are traditionally intended to enhance the safety and credibility of financial institutions. In the case of the most recent crisis, however, these very regulations had the perverse effect of generating sudden credit freezes and massive asset selling.

PITFALLS OF U.S. FINANCIAL SUPERVISORY SYSTEM

Cracks in the regulatory system began to appear in 2004 in some very specific areas, namely mortgage securitization and off-balance-sheet activity.

Figure 1-4 shows the veritable explosion in residential mortgage-backed securities (RMBS) after 2004. As the surge in this class of assets coincides with the vortex of the crisis, any theory of causality must explain why it happened then and not at some other time.

The year 2004 was marked by four specific events: (1) the Bush Administration's "American Dream" zero equity mortgage proposals became operative, allowing low-income families to obtain mortgages; (2) the then regulator of Fannie Mae and Freddie Mac, the Office of Federal Housing Enterprise Oversight (OFHEO), imposed greater capital requirements and balance sheet controls on the two government-sponsored mortgage securitization

Figure 1-4 ABS Issuers, Home Mortgages and Other Loans

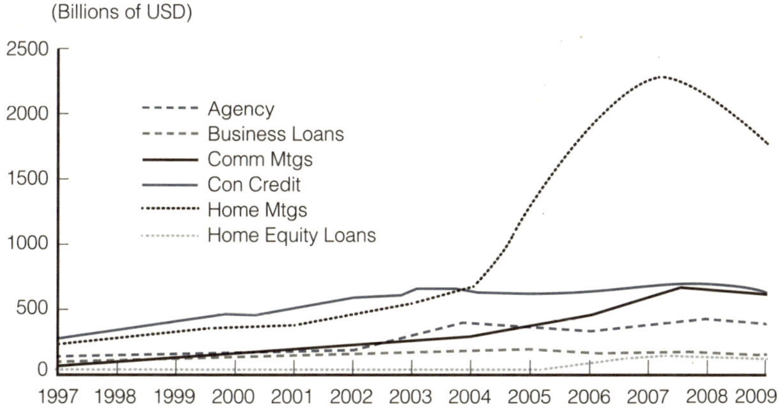

(Billions of USD)

Legend:
- ----- Agency
- ----- Business Loans
- —— Comm Mtgs
- —— Con Credit
- ·········· Home Mtgs
- ·········· Home Equity Loans

1997 1998 1999 2000 2001 2002 2003 2004 2005 2006 2007 2008 2009

Source: Federal Reserve

7

monoliths, opening the way for banks to move in on their ground with plenty of low income mortgages coming on stream; (3) the Basel II Accord on international bank regulation was published and opened arbitrage opportunities for banks that caused them to accelerate off-balance-sheet activity; and (4) the SEC agreed to allow investment banks to benefit from regulation changes and manage their risk using capital calculations under the "consolidated supervised entities program." (Prior to 2004, broker-dealers were supervised according to stringent rules and had to maintain a 15:1 debt-to-net equity ratio. Under the new scheme, investment banks could agree voluntarily to SEC consolidated oversight (not just for broker-dealer activities), but under less stringent rules that allowed them to increase their leverage ratio to 40:1 in some cases.) The combination of these four changes in 2004 caused banks to accelerate off-balance-sheet mortgage securitization as a way to drive up revenue and bank share prices.

When the OFHEO imposed greater capital requirements and balance sheet controls on Fannie and Freddie, the banks that had been selling mortgages to these companies suffered revenue gaps and an interruption in their earnings. Their solution was to create their own Fannie and Freddie lookalikes: the structured investment vehicle (SIV) and collateralized debt obligation (CDO). The next section will discuss in detail how this phenomenon virtually created a new business model in the financial sector.

CHANGED BUSINESS MODEL IN BANKING SECTOR

The business model for banks in the 1990s moved toward an equity culture focused on faster share price growth and earnings expansion. The previous model was based on balance sheets and old-fashioned loan spreads, which was not conducive to banks becoming "growth stocks." Hence, bank strategies began gravitating more toward activities based on trading income and fees via securitization, which enabled banks to grow earnings while at the same time economizing on capital by capitalizing on the Basel system. The motivation behind this particular application of the originate-to-distribute model and the securitization process was not to spread risk. Rather, the goal was clearly to ramp up revenue, return on capital, and share price. That is, the emerging strategy was more about taking risks and recognizing revenues up front. Under this approach, banks would issue loans with the primary intention of selling them to other financial institutions, which in turn would pool them together to issue asset-backed securities. The underlying rationale for these loan sales was a transfer of risk to the ultimate buyer of the security, backed by underlying mortgage loans. These securities could then be pooled again and new instruments created, and so forth. The mispricing of risk on mortgage-backed securities linked to subprime loans led the market to believe that there was an arbitrage opportunity. This market perception fueled demand for these instruments and contributed to banks lowering their underwriting standards in an attempt to increase the supply of loans in order to meet the demand for securitized instruments. Regulatory oversight missed the build-up of vulnerabilities induced by this process because risks were being transferred to an unregulated segment of the market. Banks, while heavily regulated, were only the originators, and the ultimate holders of the securities fell outside the purview of regulation. Regulators consequently also neglected the spillover effects and systematic risks, which resulted in the regulated segment inevitably being significantly affected.

Compensation schemes also evolved so that executives and sales staff at all levels could capture the benefits of this business model. Bonuses based on up-front revenue generation rose relative to salary, and substantial option and employee share participation schemes became the norm. These changes were argued to be in the interest of shareholders.

This business model based on securitization was most easily executed by investment banks, which were integral to the process of securitization and capital market sales. In Europe, universal banks had already been basking in the rewards that this model afforded. For these reasons, U.S. banks and/or IBs strongly supported and lobbied U.S. authorities first to remove Glass-Steagall in 1999, then to implement new SEC rules in 2004 and to adopt Basel II as soon as possible.

3. Effects on Emerging Market Economies

Emerging market countries were also being pulled into the unfolding turmoil, even though their direct exposures to impaired assets were limited. The fundamental reason for their vulnerability is an inherent byproduct of the increasingly borderless nature of the global economy.

Monetary policy developments in leading economies exert a profound impact on the rest of the world through changes in risk premiums and the search for yield, leading to significant diversions in capital flows. While the volatile quality of U.S. monetary policy, especially since the beginning of this decade, could have resulted from an internal compulsion to maintain employment and price stability, the consequent volatility in capital flows impinges on exchange rate movements and, more generally, the spectrum of asset and commodity prices. The dynamics of monetary policy thus entail sharp adjustments for EMEs.

Private capital flows to EMEs have grown rapidly since the

1980s, though with increased volatility over time. Large capital flows to the EMEs can be attributed to a variety of push and pull factors. The pull factors include strong growth in the EMEs over the past decade, reduced inflation, macroeconomic stability, the opening-up of capital accounts and buoyant growth prospects. The major push factor is monetary policy in the advanced economies. Periods of loose monetary policy and the quest for yield encouraged large capital inflows to EMEs. The opposite is true during periods of tighter monetary policy. Hence, depending on which way policymakers in these advanced economies decide, capital flows to EMEs are cyclical and volatile. Developments in information technology have also contributed to the expansion of capital flows. Overall, in response to these factors, capital flows to EMEs since the early 1980s have grown over time, but with large volatility.

After remaining nearly flat in the second half of the 1980s, private capital flows jumped to an annual average of USD124 billion in 1990-1996. With the onset of the Asian financial crisis, total private capital flows fell to an annual average of USD86 billion in 1997-2002. In 2003, with a low interest regime in place for the U.S. and major advanced economies and an ensuing search for yield, capital flows rose and varied to reach an annual average of USD285 billion in 2003-2007, peaking at USD617 billion in 2007.

Among the major components, while direct investment flows have generally seen a steady increase over the period, portfolio flows as well as other private flows such as bank loans have exhibited substantial volatility. Whereas direct investment flows largely reflect the pull factors, portfolio and bank flows reflect both the push and pull factors. It is also evident that capital account transactions have grown much faster than current account transactions, and gross capital flows are a multiple of both net

Figure 1-5 **Capital Flows to EMEs**

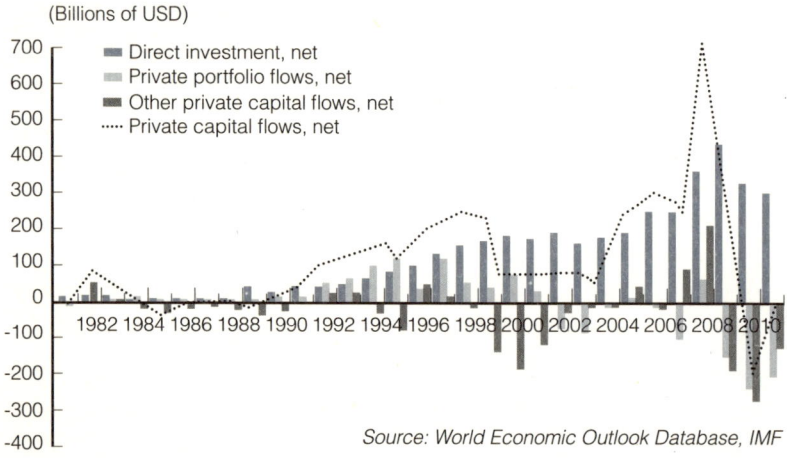

(Billions of USD)

- Direct investment, net
- Private portfolio flows, net
- Other private capital flows, net
- ····· Private capital flows, net

Source: World Economic Outlook Database, IMF

capital flows and current account transactions. Also, large private capital flows have taken place in an environment where major EMEs have been chalking up current account surpluses, leading to a substantial accumulation of foreign exchange reserves in many of these economies. As noted earlier, the benchmark rate in the U.S. reached extremely low levels during 2002 and remained at these levels for an extended period of time—through mid-2004. Low nominal interest rates were also witnessed in other major advanced economies over the same period. The extremely accommodative monetary policy in the advanced economies was mirrored by strong base money expansion during the 2001-2002 period. As the accommodating monetary policy was gradually withdrawn, base money growth underwent a correction beginning in 2004. However, unlike in the past when such developments would lead to a decrease in capital flows to EMEs, this particular period saw no change. There was also a delay in the expected reversal of capital flows from the EMEs, which finally appeared in 2008.

The global credit crunch and the liquidity problems of many transnational corporations led to net capital outflow from emerging markets, halting new investment projects. Furthermore, banks in many emerging market economies were vulnerable to a global liquidity crunch due to short-term international financing exposure and risky lending practices.

Reversals of capital flows from EMEs were quick, necessitating a painful adjustment in bank credit and leading to the collapse of stock prices. Such reversals also resulted in the contraction of the central bank's balance sheet, which might have been difficult to offset with an accretion of domestic assets given how quickly the reserves were being depleted. These developments then led to banking and currency crises, large output losses and huge fiscal costs, further attesting to how the boom and bust pattern of capital inflows resulted in macroeconomic and financial instability.

The speed at which the crisis impacted EMEs took many analysts by surprise. Since the Asian financial crisis, many Asian

Figure 1-6 **Global Foreign Exchange Reserves for EMEs**

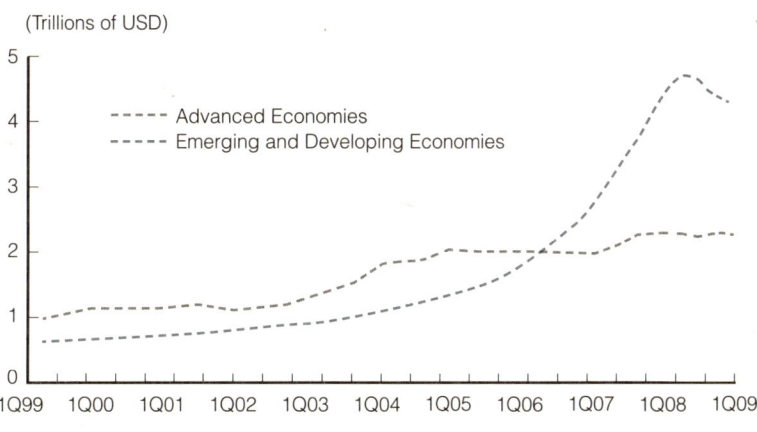

(Trillions of USD)

- - - - - Advanced Economies
- - - - Emerging and Developing Economies

Source: IMF

13

EMEs have embraced a policy of accumulating foreign reserves as a form of self-insurance should they once again be faced with the sudden disappearance of capital flows and the subsequent financial and balance of payments crises that follow a rapid tightening of international credit flows. These reserves provided a sense of financial security to EMEs. Some countries, like China and certain oil-exporting nations, also established sovereign wealth funds that invested the foreign exchange reserves in assets that promised higher yields.

Despite efforts to mitigate risk through reserve accumulation, the U.S. financial crisis and sharp contraction in credit and global capital flows affected EMEs on a par with their level of continued dependence on foreign capital flows. According to the Wall Street Journal, in the month of October 2009, Brazil, India, Mexico, and Russia drew down their reserves by more than USD75 billion in an effort to protect their currencies from depreciating further against a newly resurgent U.S. dollar.

A key to understanding why EMEs were so affected by the crisis is their high dependence on foreign capital flows to finance their economic growth. Even though several EMEs were able to reduce net capital inflows by investing overseas or by tightening the conditions for foreign investment, the large amount of gross foreign capital flows into EMEs remained a key vulnerability (see Figure 1-5).

In fact, up until the Lehman failure, losses had been driven largely by the implications of the crisis for export demand, both directly and through the impact of weakening demand on commodity prices. Following the Lehman collapse, emerging market assets weakened further on a broad basis as fears about the stability of banking systems in the major economies triggered a combination of concerns about collapsing global growth, lower commodity prices and the availability of external sources of funding.

That is, in addition to the immediate impact on growth resulting from the cessation of available credit, a downturn in advanced economies affected EMEs through several other channels. As advanced economies contracted, demand for emerging market exports slowed. The impacts of this trend were manifold for emerging and developing countries. For example, growth in larger economies such as China and India slowed as their exports decreased. At the same time, demand in China and India for raw natural resources from other developing countries also decreased, thus depressing growth in commodity-exporting countries.

4. Korea's Road to Recovery

Needless to say, the Korean economy has also been affected as severely as other EMEs by the global financial crisis. What is apparently different about Korea's case, however, is the pace of recovery compared to that observed in some other countries. Although there are uncertainties still facing the Korean economy, various data point to encouraging signs of a recovery phase in full swing.

GDP GROWTH

As shown in Figure 1-7, Korea's GDP growth was positive in the first quarter of 2009, growing 0.1% on a quarterly basis after a 5.1% contraction in 1Q 2008.

This outcome is quite impressive compared to other economies' performance, as shown in Table 1-1.

Figure 1-7 **Real GDP Growth Rate**

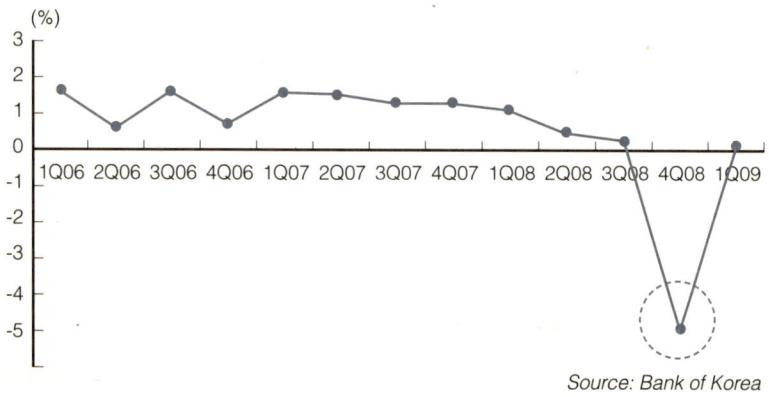

Source: Bank of Korea

Table 1-1 **Quarterly GDP Growth Rate**

(Unit: %)

	2007				2008				2009
	Q1	Q2	Q3	Q4	Q1	Q2	Q3	Q4	Q1
OECD Total	0.6	0.8	0.8	0.4	0.5	0.1	-0.3	-2.0	-2.1
US	0.8	0.8	0.6	0.9	0.3	0.0	-0.7	-1.6	-1.9
Japan	1.4	-0.2	0.2	0.4	0.8	-0.9	-0.6	-3.8	-4.0
EU	0.7	0.5	0.7	0.6	0.5	-0.1	-0.3	-1.5	-2.5
Korea	1.5	1.5	1.3	1.3	1.1	0.4	0.2	-5.1	0.1

Source: OECD Quarterly National Accounts

COMPOSITE LEADING INDICATOR

The CLI has drastically improved since last January after experiencing continued deterioration throughout 2008. This trend is a clear signal that the economy is on the right track to recovery.

Figure 1-8 **Growth Rate in CLI**

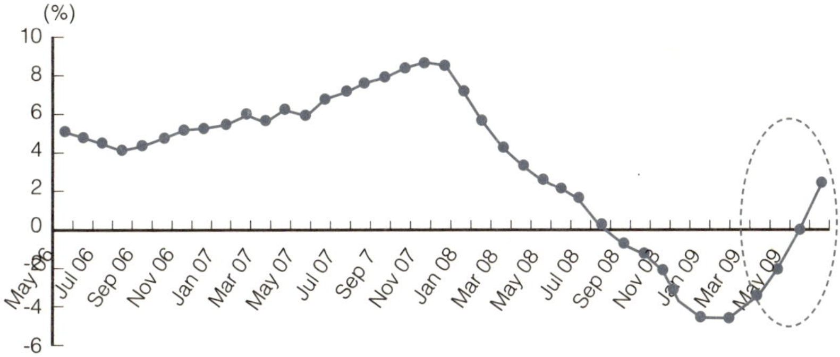

Source: Bank of Korea

FOREIGN EXCHANGE

The won-dollar exchange rate, after having experienced the most volatility in its history, soared to almost 1,600 in mid-February, hitting an 11-year high, and then dropped to below 1,300 by the end of June 2009. This trend may be interpreted as the foreign exchange market having entered a stage of gradual stabilization, even though potential factors for additional volatility remain.

STOCK MARKET

The stock market has also shown gradual improvement. Like the foreign exchange market, the stock market was severely affected by the global financial crisis, as was made evident in the KOSPI's plunge in 2008. The beginning of 2009, however, saw the KOSPI beginning to rally, signaling a recovery of the market.

What has driven this recovery process? In the next chapter, this question is explored in detail, with particular focus on various policies implemented by government authorities.

Figure 1-9 **USD/KRW Rate**

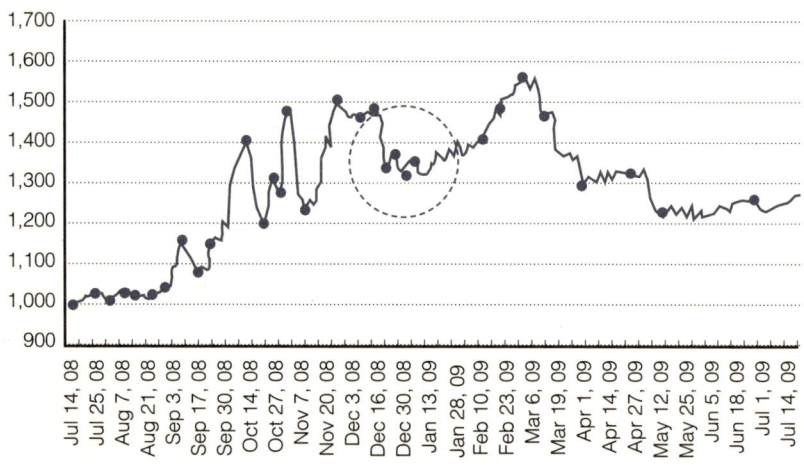

Source: Bank of Korea

Figure 1-10 **Korea Composite Stock Price Index (KOSPI)**

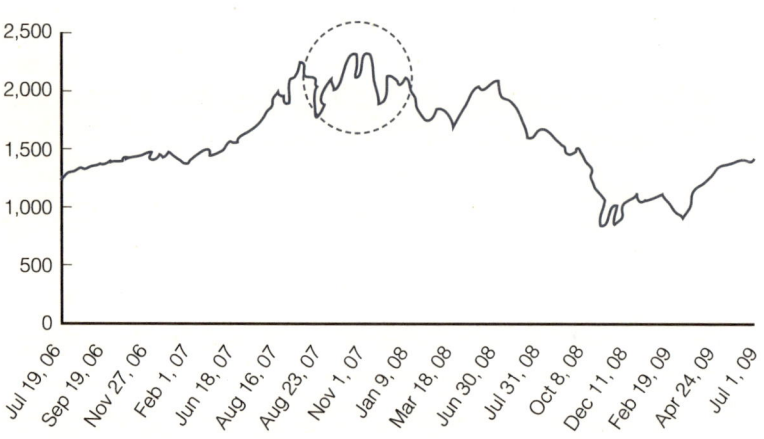

Source: Bank of Korea

Chapter II

POLICY RESPONSES TO CRISIS

The policy responses undertaken in Korea since the failure of Lehman Brothers in September 2008 fall into three categories: the financial policy of the Financial Services Commission (FSC), the liquidity policy of the Bank of Korea (BOK) and the fiscal-economic policy of the Ministry of Strategy and Finance (MOSF). Figure 2-1 illustrates Korea's policy responses aimed at tiding over the financial crisis.

1. Stabilization of Financial Market

BOND MARKET

Since the failure of Lehman Brothers in September 2008, credit spreads on bank debentures, corporate bonds, and other products widened significantly, and bond issuance slowed, leading to a credit crunch in the Korean bond market. As various securities firms increasingly exhibited risk-averse behavior and sold off bank debentures and other liabilities in large quantities to secure liquidity, the credit spread on bank debentures (3-year maturity) widened to 326bp at the end of October 2009 from 137bp at

Figure 2-1 Financial Crisis Policy Flowchart

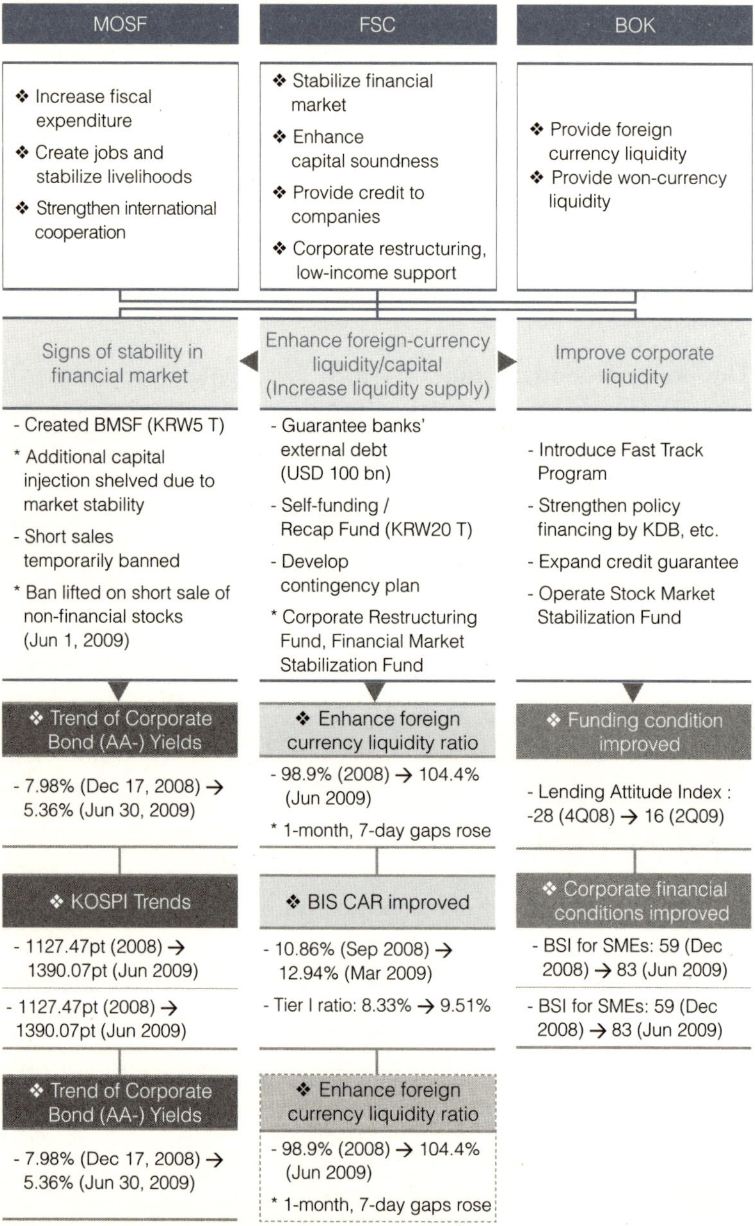

MOSF	FSC	BOK
❖ Increase fiscal expenditure ❖ Create jobs and stabilize livelihoods ❖ Strengthen international cooperation	❖ Stabilize financial market ❖ Enhance capital soundness ❖ Provide credit to companies ❖ Corporate restructuring, low-income support	❖ Provide foreign currency liquidity ❖ Provide won-currency liquidity

Signs of stability in financial market	◄ Enhance foreign-currency liquidity/capital (Increase liquidity supply) ►	Improve corporate liquidity
- Created BMSF (KRW5 T) * Additional capital injection shelved due to market stability - Short sales temporarily banned * Ban lifted on short sale of non-financial stocks (Jun 1, 2009)	- Guarantee banks' external debt (USD 100 bn) - Self-funding / Recap Fund (KRW20 T) - Develop contingency plan * Corporate Restructuring Fund, Financial Market Stabilization Fund	- Introduce Fast Track Program - Strengthen policy financing by KDB, etc. - Expand credit guarantee - Operate Stock Market Stabilization Fund

❖ Trend of Corporate Bond (AA-) Yields	❖ Enhance foreign currency liquidity ratio	❖ Funding condition improved
- 7.98% (Dec 17, 2008) → 5.36% (Jun 30, 2009)	- 98.9% (2008) → 104.4% (Jun 2009) * 1-month, 7-day gaps rose	- Lending Attitude Index : -28 (4Q08) → 16 (2Q09)

❖ KOSPI Trends	❖ BIS CAR improved	❖ Corporate financial conditions improved
- 1127.47pt (2008) → 1390.07pt (Jun 2009) - 1127.47pt (2008) → 1390.07pt (Jun 2009)	- 10.86% (Sep 2008) → 12.94% (Mar 2009) - Tier I ratio: 8.33% → 9.51%	- BSI for SMEs: 59 (Dec 2008) → 83 (Jun 2009) - BSI for SMEs: 59 (Dec 2008) → 83 (Jun 2009)

❖ Trend of Corporate Bond (AA-) Yields	❖ Enhance foreign currency liquidity ratio	
- 7.98% (Dec 17, 2008) → 5.36% (Jun 30, 2009)	- 98.9% (2008) → 104.4% (Jun 2009) * 1-month, 7-day gaps rose	

the end of August. Over the same period, the credit spread on corporate bonds (AA-) rose 209bp to 366bp from 157bp.

The BOK lowered the benchmark rate three times over the period of September-November 2008 (5.25% → 4.0%), injected short-term liquidity through repo transactions, and included bank debentures in the list of securities eligible for repo transaction.

These measures were limited in their ability to lower bank debenture yields and the CD rate—important lending indicators— because of the tight credit market. In particular, corporate bond yields went up, owing to the increased credit risk. These developments thwarted the efforts of supervisory authorities to mitigate the economic slowdown by easing the burden of interest payments on the part of households and SMEs.

Against this backdrop, on November 13, 2008, the FSC announced the creation of the Bond Market Stabilization Fund

Figure 2-2 **Policy and Market Rates Following Lehman Brothers Bankruptcy**

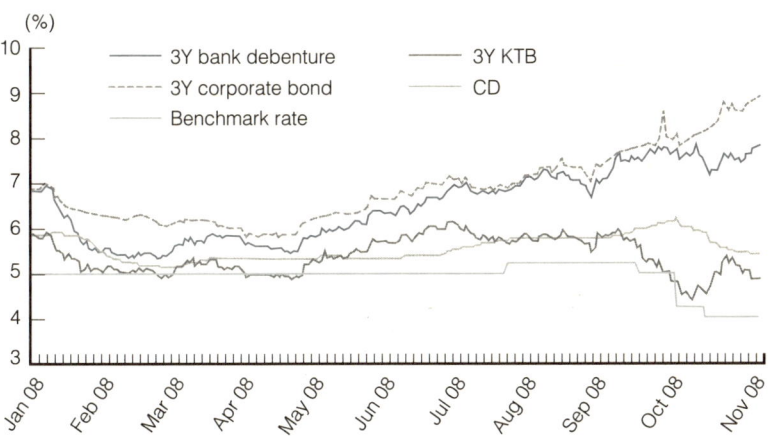

Source: Korea Financial Investment Association, BOK

(BMSF) to address the temporary dysfunctional elements of the bond market. This fund was created from contributions by financial institutions such as banks, insurance companies and securities firms as a vehicle for purchasing corporate bonds, credit-specialized financial company (CFC) bonds, P-CBOs, PF ABCP and the like. Since this fund was established from private capital, it only targets bonds rated above a certain level (e.g., BBB+ or above).

The initial plan was to launch the fund at KRW10 trillion. On December 17, 2008, however, the fund opened with KRW5 trillion, managed by the KDB Asset Management Co. Ltd., a subsidiary of the Korea Development Bank. KDB contributed KRW2 trillion to the fund, making it the fund's largest investor and overall manager. This fund is broken down into many sub-funds, including those for bank debentures, corporate bonds, PF-ABCPs and P-CBOs, bonds issued by credit-specialized financial

Figure 2-3 **BMSF Structure**

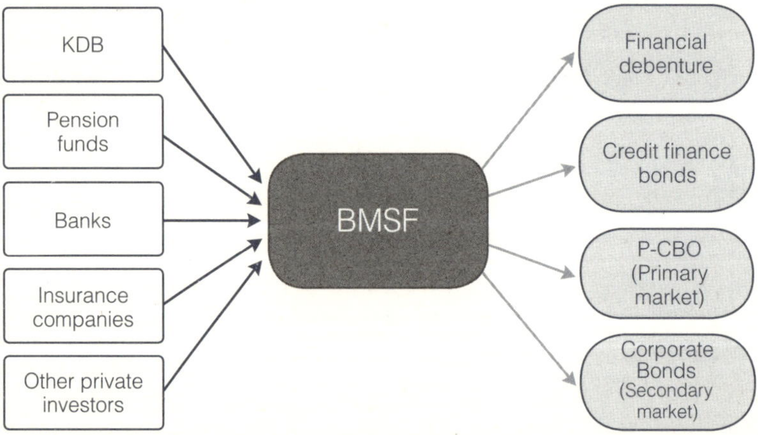

Source: FSC

companies and installment financing companies, and other groups. The fund matures in three years, and redemption is not allowed before maturity.

From the first batch of capital pooled into the BMSF, a total of KRW3,064.6 billion out of the KRW5 trillion was invested as of May 2009. By sub-fund, KRW562 billion was invested toward the bank debenture fund, KRW1,019.6 billion for the corporate bond fund, KRW1,047.9 billion for the PF-ABCP and P-CBO fund, and KRW435.1 billion for CFCs and IFCs. The remainder was invested into MMF and call loans. Of the investments made by the BMSF, KRW1,750 billion was invested into purchasing P-CBOs issued by KODIT (Korea Credit Guarantee Fund).

Overall, the BMSF is deemed to have had a positive impact, effectively easing some of the liquidity crunch felt by companies as a result of the financial crisis. In light of how the crisis prevented even creditworthy companies from accessing the debt market, the

Figure 2-4 **Corporate Bond Yields Since the BMSF**

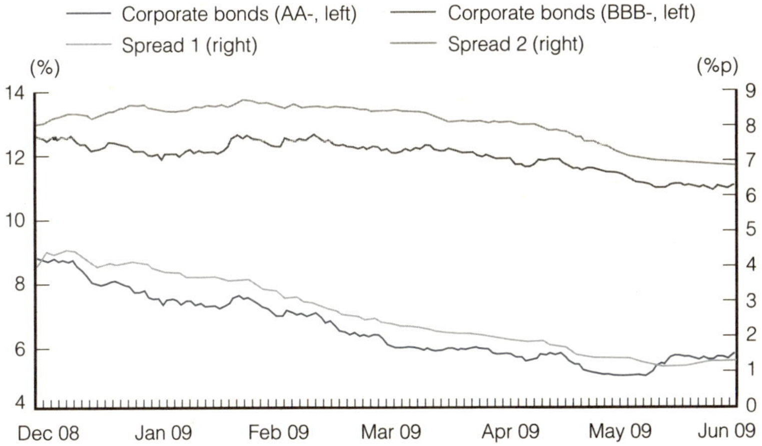

Source: Korea Financial Investment Association

BMSF relieved some of the associated market anxiety. As shown in Figure 2-4, corporate bond (AA-) yields, which stood at 7.98% at the time the BMSF was created, declined 262bp to 5.36% as of June 16, 2009, just six months after the fund's inception. Accordingly, the spread on KTBs (Korean Treasury Bonds) also dropped 303bp to 1.11% from 4.14% over the same period. Drops in the yields on corporate bonds with BBB- ratings were minimal on account of uncertainties over corporate restructuring. Although there were plans for a second round of fund contributions, with KRW4.5 trillion remaining, or 90% of the first round of capital contributions, an additional replenishment was put on hold in view of the continued stabilization of the bond market.

A case in point similar to this fund is the Bond Market Stabilization Fund (BMSF). As the likelihood of a mass redemption of investment trust funds containing Daewoo bonds increased exponentially during the financial crisis in 1999, the Korean government established the BMSF with a size of KRW10 trillion. This fund, which eventually grew to KRW30 trillion the following month, was intended to absorb the bonds sold off by the investment trust funds. The creation of the BMSF was successful in stabilizing market rates, and the fund was liquidated in April 2000, six months after its inception and one year ahead of schedule.

In the meantime, the FSC eased regulations pertaining to the won-currency liquidity ratio (100% or above), recognizing that greater bank debenture issuance by banks striving to meet the ratio could push up market rates and potentially bring about other negative side effects. As a consequence, the time horizon of assets and liabilities in terms of remaining maturity for calculating the won-currency liquidity ratio was shortened from "within three months" to "within one month" as of the end of October 2008.

STOCK MARKET

As anxiety lingered in the stock market, the Korean government responded with a temporary ban on short selling on September 30, 2008. The market had witnessed a sharp increase in the volume of short sales as the slide in stock prices continued in the period from January to September 2008. The daily average of short sales until June 2008 stood at KRW173.8 billion, up 59% compared to the KRW109.3 billion daily average recorded in December 2007. Beginning in the second quarter, the share of short positions to total stock transactions rose rapidly as stock prices started to drop, soaring to 5.1% in August from 3.2% in January 2008. The government's announcement of a prohibition on short selling was actually in line with that of many other countries, including the U.S. and U.K., which had begun

Table 2-1 **Daily Average Short Sales in 2008 by Month**

(Unit: Billions of KRW, %)

Year	Month	Short Sales (a)	Total Sales (b)	Share (a/b)
2007	Dec	109.3	4,945.1	2.2
2008	Jan	176.9	5,603.4	3.2
2008	Feb	113.6	4,768.8	2.4
2008	Mar	144.5	4,880.2	3.0
2008	Apr	151.5	5,777.7	2.6
2008	May	175.6	6,033.3	2.9
2008	Jun	170.7	4,746.8	3.6
2008	Jul	194.9	4,862.7	4.0
2008	Aug	201.0	3,921.8	5.1
2008	Sep	235.3	5,763.5	4.1
2008	Oct	35.0	5,171.1	0.7

Note: Based on stock market figures

Source: Financial Supervisory Service (FSS)

tightening their own short selling regulations.

On October 1, 2008 (October 2 for the KOSDAQ market), short sales, or the practice of selling borrowed stocks, were temporarily banned for all stocks listed on the KOSPI and

Table 2-2 **Restrictions on Short Selling in Major Countries**

Country	Action Step	Start Date	Expiration Date
US	Banned naked short selling of 19 financial stocks, including Fannie Mae	7/21/2008	8/12/2008
	Banned short selling of 799 financial stocks	9/19/2008	10/8/2008
	Ordered institutional investors to report their short positions	9/18/2008	8/1/2009
	Imposed an obligation to transfer stocks within the settlement date in the case of short selling	9/18/2008	7/31/2009
	Reintroduced a bill to reinstate the uptick rule (April 9, 2009)		
UK	Banned short selling of 32 financial stocks	9/19/2008	1/16/2009
	Imposed a disclosure obligation on investors holding short positions in excess of a certain percentage (0.25%) of issued and outstanding shares	9/19/2008	6/30/2009
France	Banned naked short selling of 15 financial stocks	9/22/2008	Undecided
Germany	Banned naked short selling of 11 financial stocks	9/20/2008	5/31/2009
Japan	Banned naked short selling	10/30/2008	7/31/2009
	Imposed a disclosure obligation on investors holding short positions in excess of 0.25% of issued and outstanding shares	11/7/2008	3/31/2009
Australia	Banned short selling of financial stocks	9/22/2008	5/31/2009
	Banned short selling of non-financial stocks	9/22/2008	11/19/2008
	Introduced an obligation to disclose short positions	9/22/2008	
Singapore	Banned naked short selling * A permanent ban on naked short selling is being considered.	9/22/2008	Undecided
Russia	Banned short selling altogether	9/30/2008	Undecided
Greece	Banned short selling altogether	10/10/2008	5/31/2009

Source: FSC

KOSDAQ markets. This restriction was originally only intended to be in effect until the end of 2008 but remained in place into 2009. In Korea, naked short selling, the sale of a stock that is not owned by the seller, is prohibited as a rule.

As stock prices stabilized, shown in Figure 2-5 as an upturn commencing in April 2009, the FSC lifted the ban on short selling of non-financial stocks on June 1. This decision, again, was in line with those of other major developed countries such as the U.S., U.K., and Canada, which had already lifted their short selling bans. Neighboring nations like Japan, Singapore and Australia were either banning the short selling of a limited number of stocks or naked short selling activities only. Given the uncertainties over financial markets at home and abroad, however, the government decided to retain the ban on short selling of financial stocks (listed on the KOSPI and KOSDAQ markets) indefinitely. In addition, financial authorities laid down a framework with which to supervise and

Figure 2-5 **KOSPI and KOSDAQ Trends**

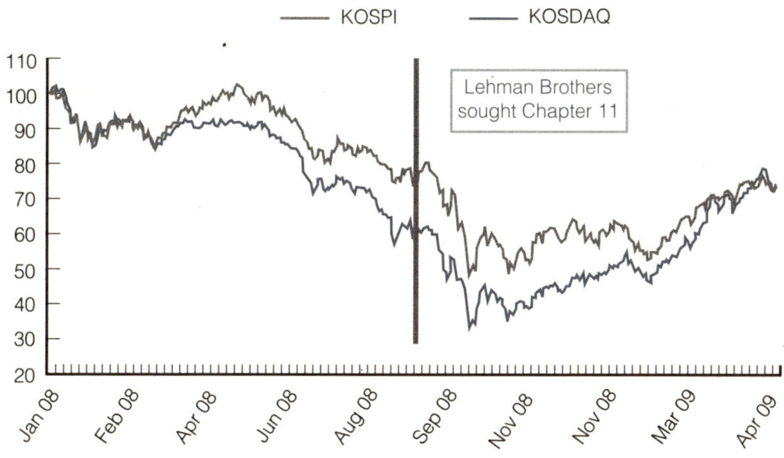

Note: Indices as of Jan 2, 2008 = 100

Source: KRX

monitor short selling. This effort included the introduction of the Short Selling Confirmation System (March 2009) and formulation of Short Selling Execution Guidelines (May 2009), designed to reinforce Korea's risk-mitigating financial policy.

FOREIGN CURRENCY FUNDING

As the failure of Lehman Brothers in September 2008 deepened the credit crunch in the global financial market, domestic banks faced severe difficulties in securing borrowings in foreign currencies. As the numbers in Table 2-3 indicate, prior to the onset of the financial crisis, domestic banks' foreign currency liquidity ratio, an indicator that represents the ability to make disbursements in foreign currencies, hovered above the minimum regulatory requirement. However, with anxiety in the international

Table 2-3 **Soundness of Korean Banks in Foreign Currency Prior to the Financial Crisis**

(Unit: %)

	May 2008	Jun 2008	Jul 2008	Aug 2008	Sep 2008
Foreign Currency Liquidity Ratio	104.4	101.7	101.2	101.7	101.1
One-Month Gap Ratio	1.2	1.1	1.3	0.9	1.3
Seven-Day Gap Ratio	2.8	2.3	2.5	2.9	2.3

Note: 1) The minimum required foreign currency liquidity ratio (liquid assets with a remaining maturity of no more than 3 months/liquid liabilities with a remaining maturity of no more than 3 months) is 85%.
2) The formula for calculating the one-month gap ratio is (assets in foreign currencies that mature within one month - liabilities in foreign currencies that mature within one month)/total assets in foreign currencies. The minimum required ratio is10%.
3) The formula for calculating the seven-day gap ratio is (assets in foreign currencies that mature within seven days - liabilities in foreign currencies that mature within seven days)/total assets in foreign currencies. The minimum required ratio is 0%.

Source: FSS

financial market spreading like wildfire, Korean banks found it difficult to roll over their maturing debt as foreign banks hurried to pull back their credit lines. Furthermore, borrowing conditions for Korean banks deteriorated as CDS (Credit Default Swap) premiums soared (520-580bp) more than tenfold over the CDS premiums (30-40bp) one year before the crisis.

Naturally, there were concerns that the financial crisis would spill over into the real economy if banks were compelled to curtail trade financing such as the negotiation of exchange bills. Withdrawing foreign currency credit lines would prolong the credit crunch, making it increasingly difficult for banks to secure foreign currency liquidity. There was also the likelihood that Korean banks would be at a disadvantage in the global debt market in terms of funding costs if the Korean government did not provide payment

Figure 2-6 **Movements in CDS Premiums Prior to Payment Guarantee for Banks' External Debt**

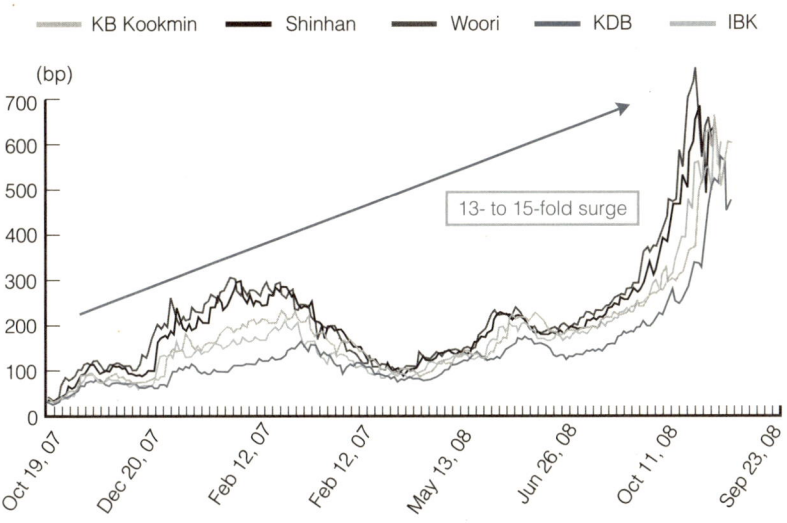

Source: International Finance Center

guarantees—which many other countries including the U.K., Germany, France, and Australia were already doing. That is, these countries were guaranteeing the repayment of inter-bank loans and enhancing the creditworthiness of their financial institutions.

Taking these circumstances into account, the Korean government announced its "Proposed Measures to Overcome Uncertainties in the International Financial Markets" on October 19, 2008. These measures provided payment guarantees for external debts incurred by banks prior to June 30, 2009, for a period of three years. The total payment guarantee was set at USD100 billion, which equated to 140% of the entire amount of all external debts among Korean banks maturing prior to June 30, 2009. This payment guarantee program was put forth before a Cabinet meeting (October 21), obtained approval from the National Assembly (October 30), and finally went into effect as the Financial Supervisory Service (FSS) executed an MOU with 18 banks in Korea on November 14. This set of MOUs is composed of MOU 1, which pertains to payment guarantees for external debts, and MOU 2, which relates to support for the real economy and corporate management rationalization. SC First Bank and Citibank Korea signed MOU 2 only. The first and second round payment guarantees for each bank's external debts are shown in Table 2-4.

With anxiety in the global financial market persisting, the Korean government announced a second payment guarantee program on April 7, 2009, which would extend the term for the payment guarantee until the end of 2009. In addition to the extended deadline, this program differed from its predecessor in terms of the types of liabilities covered by the payment guarantee, the term length, and the reference time point for determining the guarantee limit, among other details. For example, the previous program covered only non-resident foreign currency liabilities. The new program covered all liabilities (originating from both

Table 2-4 **Guarantee Limits for Banks**

(Unit: Millions of USD)

Bank	Debts maturing by June 2009(A)	Guarantee Limit		Change
		1st	2nd	
Shinhan	6,828	9,555	10,893	1,338
Woori	8,483	11,870	13,352	1,482
SC First	4,176	5,844	3,953	-1,891
Hana	8,431	11,797	8,438	-3,359
KEB	6,162	8,623	8,627	4
Citibank Korea	2,435	3,407	4,376	969
KB Kookmin	6,161	8,621	8,532	-89
Daegu	408	571	947	376
Pusan	621	869	1,719	850
Kwangju	296	414	679	265
Jeju	12	100	9	-91
Jeonbuk	45	100	271	171
Kyongnam	275	385	935	550
KDB	11,573	16,195	14,244	-1,951
KEXIM	6,713	9,394	9,421	27
IBK	5,010	7,010	7,441	431
NACF	3,439	4,812	5,238	426
NFFC	310	434	924	490
Total	**71,378**	**100,000**	**100,000**	**0**

Note: In the case of Hana Bank, the guarantee limit includes a USD1 billion global bond issued on April 2, 2009, which became the first to be guaranteed by the government under the new program.

Source: FSC, Strategy and Finance Committee of the National Assembly

residents and non-residents) denominated in foreign currencies. Also, guarantee terms were extended to three to five years as a way to encourage banks to borrow long-term and repay short- and medium-term debts. The new guarantee program also specified the reference time point for determining the guarantee amount as the date of guarantee issuance. Under the previous program, there was no clear way to calculate the guarantee amount for foreign currency-denominated borrowings given the exchange rate fluctuations. After the new guarantee program obtained approval from the National Assembly on April 29, the FSS signed a second round of MOUs with 18 banks in Korea on May 28. The new MOU retained much of the same framework of the previous version.

In addition to the payment guarantee provided by the Korean government, the signing of a currency swap arrangement between Korea and the U.S. (October 30) and the extension of existing currency swap deals between Korea and China and between Korea and Japan (December 12), among other measures, were immensely conducive to improving the environment for Korean banks to borrow in foreign currencies. Above all, the CDS premium (five-

Figure 2-7 Credit Spread on Mid- and Long-Term Debts of Domestic Banks

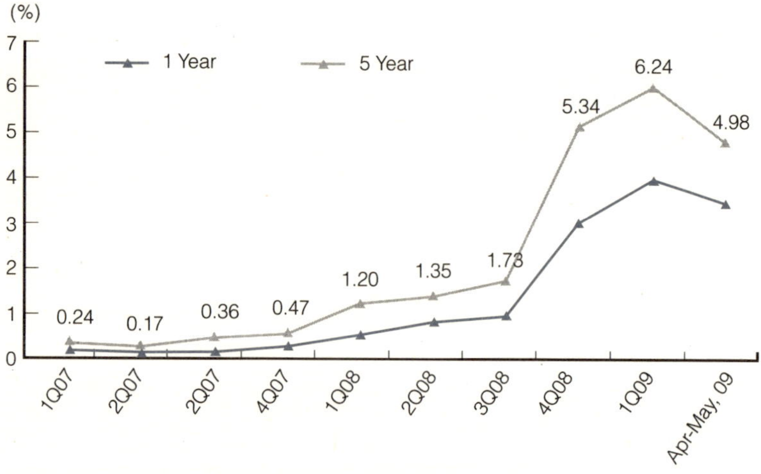

Note: Weighted average of credit spreads of ten domestic banks
(excluding SC First, Citibank Korea and regional banks)

Source: FSS

year) and the spread (maturing in September 2014) on Foreign Exchange Equalization Bonds, which serve as the benchmark rates for foreign currency borrowings, dropped back down to 135bp (June 2) and 233bp (June 8) in 2009, respectively, after soaring to 699bp and 791bp on October 27, 2008. As shown in Figure 2-7, the credit spread on mid- and long-term debts denominated in foreign currency also came down to 498bp in April-May from an average of 624bp in 1Q 2009. CDS premiums on Korea's major banks also declined to pre-crisis levels as borrowing conditions improved.

Overall improvements in funding conditions led to an actual increase in foreign-currency funding. As is shown in Table 2-5, mid- and long-term funding (exceeding one year) in foreign currency by domestic banks (excluding regional banks) during the January-May 2009 period (as of May 18) recorded USD12.06

Table 2-5 Trends in Mid- and Long-Term Funding by Domestic Banks

(Unit: Billions of USD)

		2007	2008					2009					
		2007	2008	1/4	2/4	3/4	4/4	2009	Jan	Feb	Mar	Apr	May
M-LT		22.45	15.63	3.31	7.47	2.45	2.40	12.06	4.71	0.58	0.39	3.30	3.08
Bank type	Commercial	11.30	6.23	0.91	3.04	0.76	1.52	4.25	0.27	0.13	0.29	1.32	2.24
	Special	11.15	9.40	2.40	4.43	1.68	0.89	7.80	4.43	0.45	0.10	1.98	0.84
Funding type	Bank Loan	7.43	5.50	1.07	2.29	0.66	1.48	2.75	0.33	0.22	0.27	0.66	1.27
	Bond Issue	15.02	10.13	2.24	5.18	1.79	0.92	9.31	4.38	0.36	0.12	2.64	1.81
Maturity	Below 5 year	12.47	10.23	1.53	4.65	2.08	1.97	5.09	0.71	0.40	0.39	1.91	1.68
	5 yrs. or more	9.98	5.40	1.78	2.82	0.37	0.43	6.97	4.00	0.18	-	1.39	1.40

Note: Based on borrowings with contractual maturities of more than 365 days secured by 12 banks (excluding regional banks) through May 18.

Source: FSS

billion (USD12.33 billion as of the end of May), up 148.7% from USD4.85 billion recorded in the latter half of 2008.

These improvements are attributable to the fact that commercial banks in Korea were able to conduct public offerings with ease following several successful public offerings by state-run banks such as KDB (USD2 billion) and KEXIM (USD2 billion) in early 2009, as well as successful foreign exchange equalization bonds (USD3 billion) offerings in April. By funding type, bond issuance amounted to USD9.31 billion, which represented 77.2% of the total funded amount of USD12.06 billion. By maturity, external debt with maturities of five years or more accounted for USD6.97 billion, or 57.8% of the total.

Improved conditions in foreign currency funding and the ensuing actual increase in the amount funded translated into an improvement in the soundness of domestic banks. As of the end of June 2009, the foreign currency liquidity ratio (104.4%), one-month gap ratio (1.5%), and seven-day gap ratio (3.0%) exceeded the minimum requirements and were quickly approaching pre-crisis levels. In particular, the foreign currency liquidity ratio, which had dipped to 98.9% owing to a severe credit crunch in the foreign-currency debt market in 4Q 2008, rose 5.5% in the first half of 2009.

In the meantime, the steady supply of foreign-currency liquidity also led to improvements in asset-liability ratios for Korean banks. Financial regulators currently require banks to maintain a minimum of 80% in mid- and long-term borrowings of total foreign currency debt to minimize mismatches between assets and liabilities. The mid- and long-term funding ratio dropped to 105.6% at the end of 2008 before increasing back to 124.7% as of the end of May 2009 (based on 15 banks, excluding Jeju Bank, Kyongnam Bank and Jeonbuk Bank), having topped 121.8% at the end of June 2008 immediately before Lehman Brothers went bankrupt.

Figure 2-8 **FX Soundness of Domestic Banks Following the Financial Crisis**

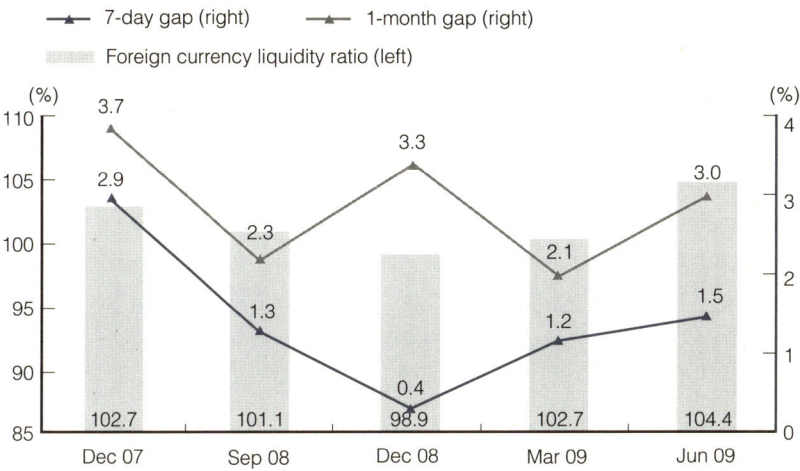

Note: Refer to the Note below Table 2-3 to see regulatory requirements for each ratio.

Source: FSS

Figure 2-9 **Mid- and Long-Term Foreign Currency Funding Ratios of Korean Banks**

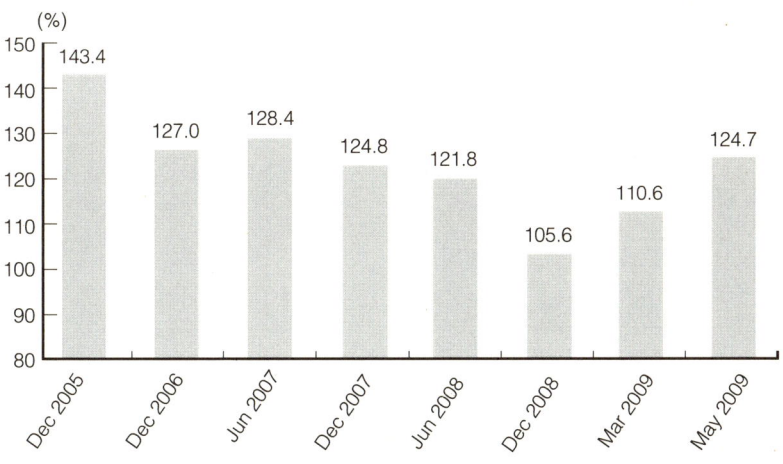

Note: The ratio for May 2009 is based on 15 Korean banks, excluding Jeonbuk, Kyongnam and Jeju Bank on a consolidated basis, including head offices and branches overseas.

Source: FSS

2. Enhanced Capital Strength and Soundness of Financial Companies

RECAPITALIZATION OF BANKING SECTOR

Capital Adequacy Levels of Domestic Banks at the Time of Financial Crisis

In 2006, the BIS capital ratios of domestic banks, which had marked 12.95% the year before, began to decline and hovered at the 10% level, marking 10.86% as of the end of September 2008. The leverage ratio (shareholders' equity/total assets), which is a leading indicator of capital adequacy alongside the BIS CAR, declined as well. The leverage ratio, which had been in the range of 4-5% in the early 2000s, recorded 6.9% at the end of 2007 before falling to 5.7% at the end of September 2008. Concerns

Figure 2-10 **BIS CAR and Leverage Ratio Trends of Domestic Banks**

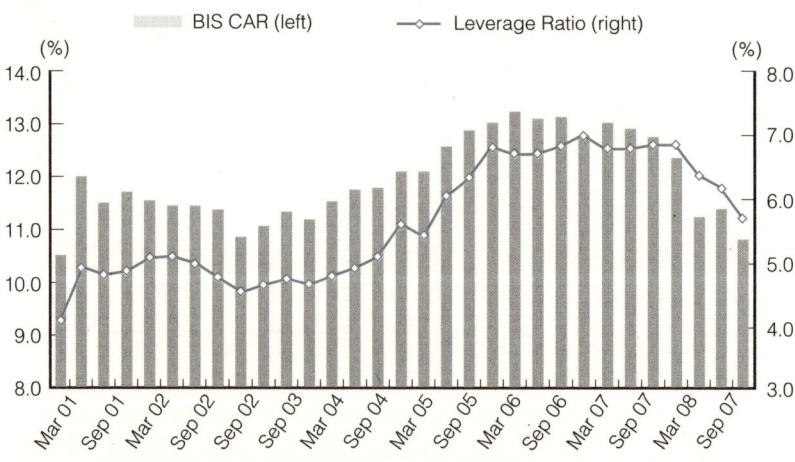

Note: The leverage ratio is (shareholders' equity/total assets)×100.

Source: FSS

regarding the capital strength of domestic banks grew as the possibility of worsening profitability and asset quality rose on account of the global financial crisis and deteriorating economic indicators at home and abroad.

A decomposition of the BIS capital ratio shows that movements of the primary Tier 1 ratio are consistent with those of the BIS capital ratio. Beginning in 2004, when the BIS capital ratio started appreciating, the Tier 1 ratio also witnessed an upward movement, whereas the Tier 2 ratio showed a downward trend. This trend indicates that Tier 1 capital contributed to enhancing the BIS capital ratio, and capital adequacy improved in terms of quality. However, the Tier 1 ratio, which had stood at the 9% level in 2006-2007, dipped to the 8% level in 2008, indicating a deterioration in capital adequacy in terms of quality.

Figure 2-11 **Decomposition of BIS Capital Ratio of Domestic Banks**

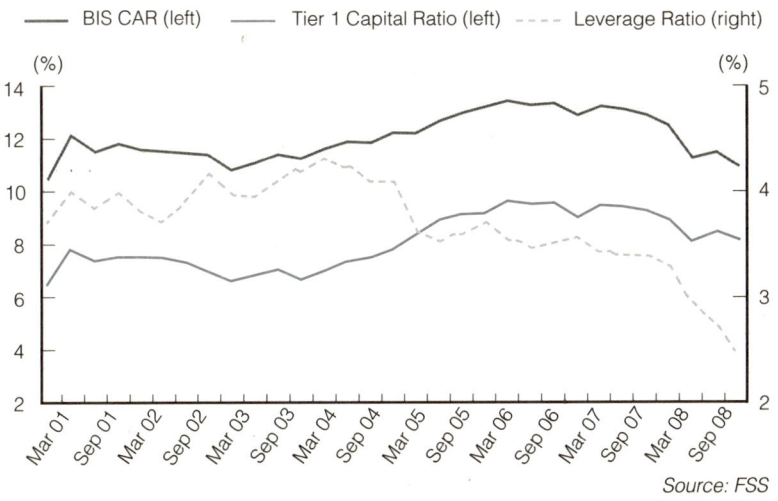

Source: FSS

Figure 2-12 Falling Stock Prices in Key Sectors, Sep 1 - Dec 31, 2008

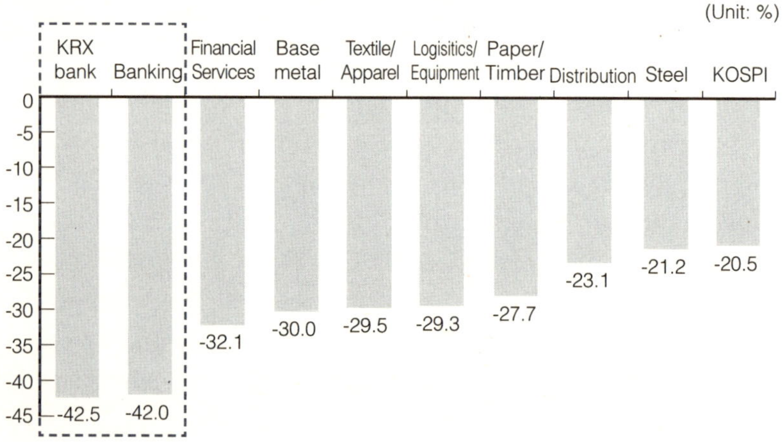

(Unit: %)

Note: KRX Banks are determined on the basis of the KRX Banks Index, and banks based on the Banking Index (including mutual savings banks).

Source: FSS, KOSCOM

Concerns about capital adequacy with the declining BIS capital ratios manifested themselves in the stock market. The KRX Banks Index, which had recorded 1,142.62 points in March 2007, dipped 33.0% to 765.74 points in September 2008. According to Figure 2-12, the banking sector registered the largest drop in stock prices during the last four months of 2008 as the global financial crisis unfolded. Over the same period, the KRX Banks Index slid 42.5%, recording more than a twofold slide compared to the KOSPI (-20.5%) index.

Amidst concerns about the capital adequacy of domestic banks following the financial crisis, there was also growing fear that the banks' weakened ability to absorb bad debts could in itself become a risk factor. The ratio of NPLs to total loans stood at a relatively stable level of 0.82%, although the total amount of non-

Figure 2-13 **Trends in Domestic Bank Coverage Ratios**

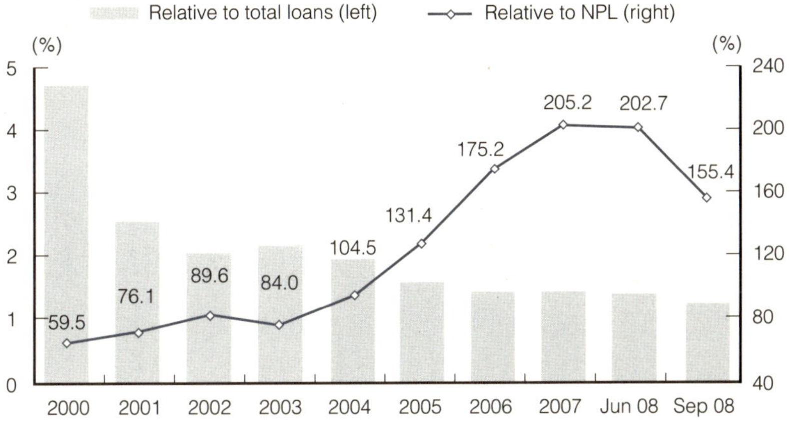

Source: FSS

performing loans at domestic banks grew to KRW10.4 trillion in September 2008 from KRW7.7 trillion at the end of 2007. However, the coverage ratio, which is the allowance for probable losses on non-performing loans divided by actual non-performing loans, plunged to 155.4% in September 2008 from 205.2% in 2007. These data reveal that banks were less able to absorb bad debts through bad debt allowance as the size of bad debts ballooned in the 3rd quarter of 2008—the culprit being corporate contractors of the risky foreign currency option product known as KIKO (knock-in knock-out) contracts.

In addition, asset quality deteriorated as the delinquency ratio for won-denominated bank loans witnessed an upswing. In particular, the delinquency ratios of those SMEs considered to be significant credit risks shot up 50% to 1.50% as of the end of September 2008, from 1% in 2007, as a result of hikes in exchange rates and raw material prices. Adding to this challenging business environment was the U.S.-sparked financial crisis that

Figure 2-14 **Delinquency Ratio for Won-Denominated Bank Loans by Business Segment**

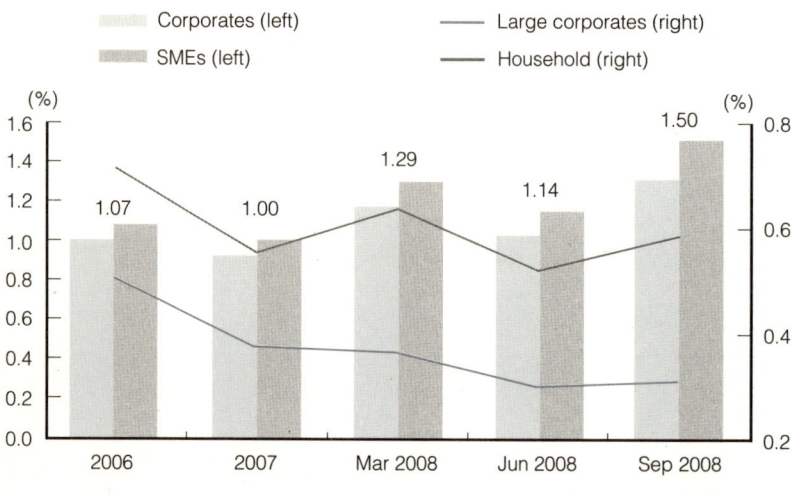

Source: FSS

further threatened the asset quality of SMEs.

Household and corporate debt repayment capacity also speaks to the asset quality of domestic banks and was considered to be quite weak during this period as well. The capital gearing ratio (financial debt/financial assets) for households, which represents the ability to repay debts without disposing of properties, appreciated 3.2% to 46.5% as of September 2008 from 43.3% in 2007—mainly because of the upward trend in mortgage loans. The growth in financial assets slowed noticeably, with dipping stock prices resulting from the sub-prime mortgage crisis and economic slowdown. The debt service ratio (DSR) of households possessing bank mortgage loans also rose to 20.7% at the end of June 2008 from 20.2% at the end of 2007.

The cash flow situation at corporations deteriorated rapidly as their debt-to-equity ratios and "total borrowings and bonds payable to total assets" climbed steadily. As of the end of September 2008, the debt-to-equity ratio of corporations jumped 18.6% over the end of 2007 to 104.3% as foreign currency-denominated liabilities increased with the KRW's depreciation

Table 2-6 **Debt Paying Capacity of Households with Mortgage Loans**

	End of 2005	End of 2006	End of 2007	End of June 2008
DSR (%)	15.3	19.3	20.2	20.7
Interest payment/ annual income (%)	10.2	12.0	13.2	13.1
Loan balance/annual income (multiple)	1.76	1.95	1.96	1.97
Interest burden (trillions of KRW)	19.3	22.7	25.9	26.7

Note: 1) Based on households with KRW20-100 million in annual income and a mortgage loan
2) Interest burden is based on the total number of households with mortgage loans and is calculated as follows: mortgage loan balance x lending rate on loan balance.

Source: BOK

Table 2-7 **Major Ratios of Domestic Corporations**

(Unit: %)

	2007		2008		
	End of Jun	End of Dec	End of Mar	End of Jun	End of Sep
Debt-to-Equity Ratio	86.2 (80.4)	85.7 (80.2)	92.5 (89.0)	95.4 (92.7)	104.3 (102.6)
Total Borrowings & Bonds Payable to Total Assets	21.2 (18.8)	20.4 (17.9)	21.7 (18.9)	22.4 (19.4)	23.4 (20.0)

Note: 1) Ratios in parentheses refer to those of the manufacturing industry. Debt-to-equity ratio is (total debt/equity capital) multiplied by 100; and total borrowings and bonds payable to total assets multiplied by 100.
2) Data provided by 1,624 companies required to submit quarterly financial statements pursuant to the Securities Exchanges Act

Source: BOK

Figure 2-15 **Free Cash Flow**

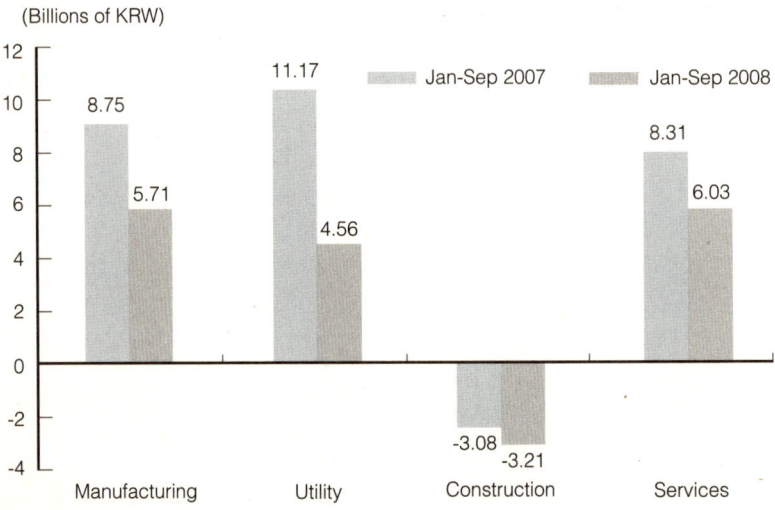

Figure 2-16 **Cash Flow Coverage Ratio**

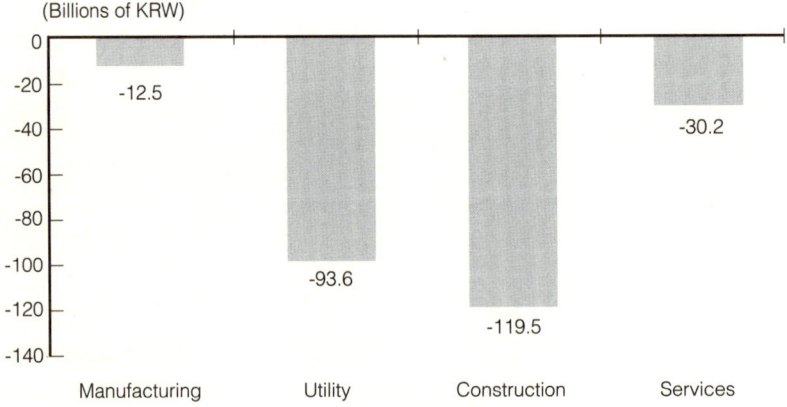

Note: 1) Free cash flow = cash from operating activities - net of cash used in investing
         activities
      2) Cash flow coverage ratio = (cash from operating activities + interest expense)/
         (short-term borrowings + interest expense)
      3) Data for the Jan –Sep 2008 period provided by 1,624 companies required to
         submit quarterly financial statements pursuant to the Securities Exchanges Act

Source: BOK

against the U.S. dollar. Furthermore, the debt-paying capacity of corporations weakened as major industries recorded free cash flows in the negative territory. In particular, the construction industry, which had seen a huge increase in bank loans over several years preceding the financial crisis, showed the poorest cash flow.

All in all, the capital adequacy of domestic banks and the debt-paying capacity of households and corporations at the time of the global financial crisis worsened compared to pre-crisis levels. Assets held by domestic banks were likely to worsen if the financial crisis spilled over into the real economy. Hence, a lack of fund flow into the real economy became a growing concern.

As shown in Figure 2-17, growth in KRW-denominated loans has slowed since the crisis hit in September 2008. In particular, loans to SMEs, which are particularly vulnerable to external

Figure 2-17 **Growth in Won Currency Loans by Business Segment**

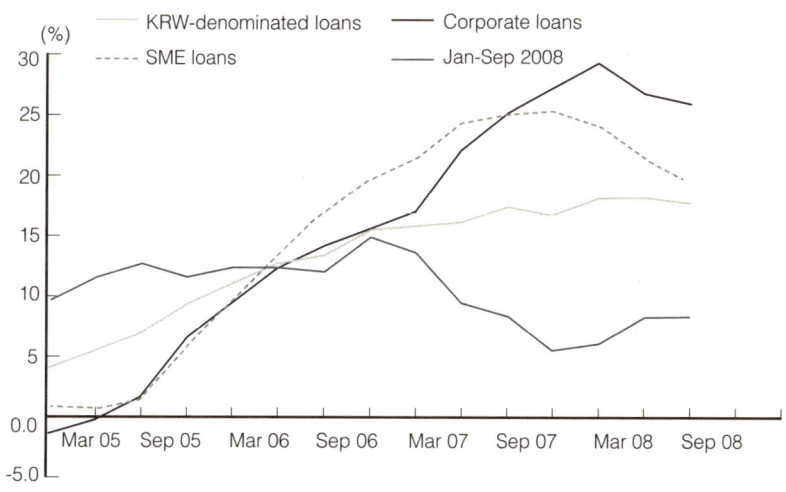

Note: Year-on-year basis

Source: FSS

shocks, have declined steadily since 2008. Because banks must comply with requirements in capital adequacy, asset quality and other areas, deterioration in these figures prevented banks from extending the loans necessary to alleviate the credit crunch affecting corporations and SMEs, in particular. The following section will analyze the measures undertaken by the government to minimize the credit crunch stemming from drastic declines in loan originations.

Heightening Self-Rescue Efforts: Independent Recapitalization

Beginning in the second half of 2008, the Korean government encouraged banks to increase their capital on their own in order to enhance their capacity to provide support to the real economy and absorb potential losses. Accordingly, domestic banks secured a total of KRW16.2 trillion in capital through a capital increase, issuance of sub-debts and Tier 1 hybrid securities to proactively cope with the potential risk of asset holdings going sour over the last two months of 2008. The capital raised breaks down into Tier 1 capital of KRW6.7 trillion and Tier 2 capital of KRW9.5 trillion. In particular, banks affiliated with holding companies raised relatively large amounts of capital as their holding companies participated in the rights offerings themselves. Aggressive sub-debt issuance also helped to raise capital. State-run banks such as KDB (KRW500 billion), IBK (KRW500 billion) and KEXIM (KRW650 billion) increased their capital through additional equity investment by the government.

In the meantime, the government strived to complement the efforts of these banks and reinforce their capital strength by improving its own regulatory policies. One prime example is the decision by financial supervisory authorities on December 23, 2008, to extend the cap on the amount of hybrid securities that could be converted into Tier 1 capital. The cap of 15% for Tier 1 capital remained intact with respect to innovative hybrids, which already enjoy a step-up provision. It was decided, however, that non-innovative hybrids that do not carry a step-up provision could also be regarded as Tier 1 capital. As a result, the cap on hybrid securities regarded as Tier 1 capital was effectively raised from 15% to 30% of Tier 1 capital. According to the FSS, this decision led to a large increase of KRW15.0 trillion—from KRW9.4 trillion to KRW24.4 trillion—in recapitalization funds via the offering of hybrid securities as of the end of September 2008.

Creation of Bank Recapitalization Fund

On December 18, 2008, the FSC announced the creation of the Bank Recapitalization Fund, worth KRW20 trillion and intended to encourage banks to increase their capital and engage actively in providing support to the real economy and corporate restructuring. On February 15, 2009, a workshop was held where financial supervisory officials and bank CEOs gathered to discuss their thoughts on how to maximize the benefits of the Bank Recapitalization Fund. On the corporate side, the CEOs agreed on the necessity of this fund in supporting the real economy and promoting corporate restructuring, as well as the importance of making full use of the fund. In connection with

---

✻ Capital Adequacy Ratios by Country

According to the FDIC, the BIS capital ratio of U.S. commercial banks as of the end of March 2009 stood at 13.31%, which is higher than the 12.94% of Korean banks. Given that the U.S. ratio includes those U.S. commercial banks that benefited from the Troubled Assets Relief Program (TARP), it can be said that Korean banks are performing well in terms of capital adequacy.

BIS CARs of Domestic and U.S. Commercial Banks

	2006	2007	2008				2008
	Dec	Dec	Mar	Jun	Sep	Dec	Mar
Domestic	12.75	12.32	11.20	11.36	10.86	12.31	12.94
US Commercial	12.37	12.23	12.27	12.36	12.37	12.75	13.31

Source: FDIC, FSS

Considering the TCE (Tangible Common Equity) ratio, which is the most conservative measurement of capital adequacy, domestic banks are more robust than those of developed countries. In Korea, the equity capital ratio is used similarly to the TCE ratio. As of the end of 2008, the equity capital ratio of domestic banks was 6.23%, higher by more than 2% than that of major developed countries—which generally fell below the 4% level. The equity capital ratio excludes the value of intangible assets from total equity, calculated as total equity minus intangible assets over real total assets minus intangible assets.

TCE Ratio by Country (as of the end of 2008)

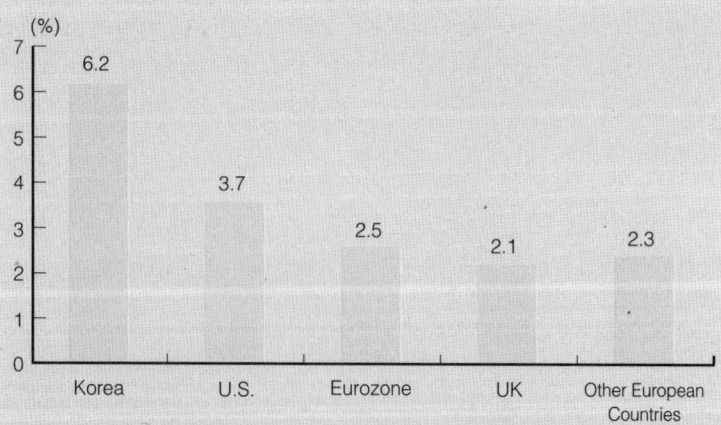

Note: "Other European Countries" includes Denmark, Iceland, Norway, Sweden and Switzerland.

Source: IMF

this, the CEOs also proposed that the Bank Recapitalization Fund be used based on the credit line approach, which was agreed to by the financial supervisory representatives. The workshop culminated in an agreement to research further how to fully take advantage of this fund and under what terms, based on the suggestions of the CEOs.

After the BOK decided who could participate in the fund following a meeting of the Monetary Policy Committee, the FSC announced how the Bank Recapitalization Fund would be operated on February 25, 2009. According to the announcement, the Bank Recapitalization Fund was to be created with KRW20 trillion, consisting of a BOK loan (KRW10 trillion), KDB loan (KRW2 trillion) and other contributions (KRW8 trillion) by institutional and retail investors. KDB's loan to the fund eventually

Figure 2-18 **Structure of Bank Recapitalization Fund**

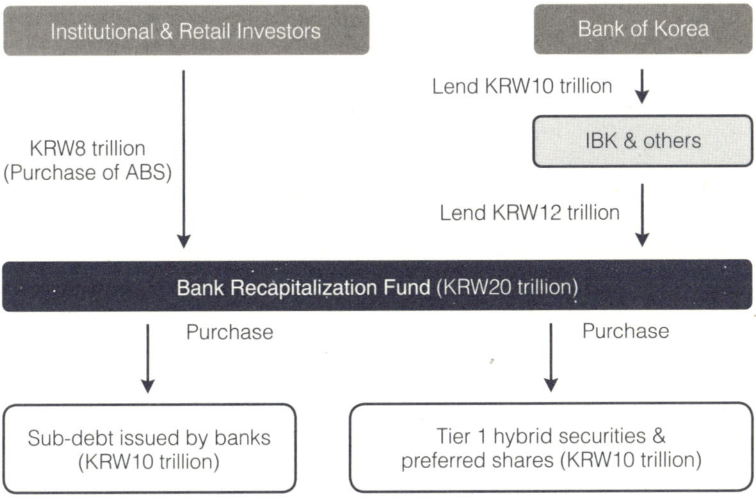

Source: FSS

47

amounted to KRW12 trillion. This fund is used to purchase hybrid securities, sub-debts, and other products issued by domestic banks, after which asset-backed securities (KRW8 trillion) based mostly on the sub-debts purchased are issued and sold to institutional investors.

The fund is to be operated is as follows: first, the basic principle is for the fund to serve as buffer capital for the banks that would support the real economy and corporate restructuring. To this end, use of the fund is restricted to supporting the real economy and corporate restructuring, and management intervention by the fund is prohibited.

Second, a method was adopted whereby applications would be received from commercial banks (or holding companies), IBK, NFFC or NACF, a credit limit would be set, and loans would be granted upon request from any of these institutions. It was decided that KRW12 trillion was to be provided at the outset for first-round support, and the size of second-round support would depend on the results of the first round. A credit limit was set for each institution so as to avoid a concentration of funds among certain financial institutions. More specifically, during the first round financial institutions were grouped according to their asset size. The size of support was then adjusted depending on the level of increase in BIS capital ratios, actual amount of loans granted to SMEs and other factors. Allocation limits during the second round of funding will be set based on the progress of each institution in terms of supporting the real economy, corporate restructuring and funding in foreign currency, among other performance metrics.

Third, it was decided that the terms under which institutions could obtain support from the fund, such as interest rates and the types of financial instruments purchased, should differ based on each bank's performance in support of the real economy, corporate restructuring, and actual foreign currency funds secured, among

Table 2-8 **Bank Recapitalization Fund Support Caps**

(Unit: KRW)

Group I (Asset: 200 tril. or less)	Group II (200-140 tril.)	Group III (140-50 tril.)	Group IV (below 50 tril.)
2 tril. limit	1.5 tril. limit	1 tril. limit	0.3 tril. limit
KB Kookmin, Woori, Shinhan	Hana, IBK, NACF	KEB, Citibank, SC First	NFFC, regional banks

Source: FSS

other factors. The terms for the first round of support, however, varied depending on the bank's level of performance in accordance with the MOU for guaranteeing external debt payments.

By February 27, 2009, the FSC received applications from 14 banks for credit lines from the Bank Recapitalization Fund totaling KRW12.3 trillion. Among the applicants, KB Kookmin, Woori and Shinhan Banks each requested KRW2 trillion; and Hana, IBK and NACF requested KRW1.5 trillion. On March 31, the Bank Recapitalization Fund completed the first-round purchase of securities worth KRW3.956 trillion. Hybrid securities amounted to KRW3.453 trillion, and sub-debts amounted to KRW503 billion, issued by eight financial institutions.

According to FSS data, a total of KRW23.7 trillion in capital was raised over the period of 4Q 2008-1Q 2009 owing to internal capital-raising efforts (KRW16.2 trillion) on the part of the banks, and securities purchases (KRW4 trillion) made through the Bank Recapitalization Fund and other such vehicles. As a consequence, the BIS capital ratios of domestic banks as of the end of March 2009 recorded 12.94%, up 2.08% from the 10.86% registered at the end of September 2008. The Tier 1 ratio returned to the 9% level or, more precisely, 9.51%, marking a 1.18% increase compared to the end of September 2008. This trend attests to an improvement in the capital strength of domestic banks in

Table 2-9 First-Round Applications by Bank

(Unit: KRW)

Group	Applications by Bank
Group I (Limit: 2)	KB Kookmin (2), Woori (2), Shinhan (2)
Group II (Limit: 1.5)	Hana (1.5), IBK (1.5), NACF (1.5)
Group III (Limit: 1)	KEB (0.5)
Group IV (Limit: 0.3)	Daegu (0.3), Pusan (0.3), Kwangju (0.17), Jeju (0.03), Jeonbuk (0.07), Kyongnam (0.23), NFFC (0.2)
Total	12.3

Source: FSS

Table 2-10 Purchase of Securities by Institution

(Unit: Billions of KRW)

	Woori Holdings	Woori	Kyong-nam	Kwangju	KB Kookmin	Hana	NACF	NFFC	Total
Hybrid Securities	-	1,000	116	87	1,000	400	750	100	3,453
Sub-Debt	300	-	116	87	-	-	-	-	503
Total	300	1,000	232	174	1,000	400	750	100	3,956

Source: FSC

Table 2-11 BIS Capital Adequacy and Tier 1 Ratios of Domestic Banks

(Unit: Billions of KRW)

	2006	2007	2008				2009
			Mar	Jun	Sep	Dec	Mar
BIS CAR	12.75 (12.31)	12.31 (11.95)	11.20 (10.97)	11.36 (11.16)	10.86 (10.66)	12.31 (12.72)	12.94 (13.40)
Tier 1	9.15 (8.52)	8.97 (8.45)	8.22 (7.89)	8.54 (8.24)	8.33 (8.24)	8.84 (9.01)	9.51 (9.72)

Note: 1) Basel I applied for 2006 and 2007, and Basel II for 2008 and 2009
2) Ratios in parentheses refer to general banks (commercial banks + regional banks).

Source: FSS

Table 2-12 **Additional Room for Lending Owing to Internal Capital-Raising and Securities Purchases Through Bank Recapitalization Fund**

(Unit: Trillions of KRW)

		Internal Capital-Raising (4Q 2008)	First-Round Securities Purchase[1] (1Q 2009)
Size		16.2	4.0
BIS CAR		10.86%	
BIS Capital	130.4	146.6	150.6
RWA	1,200.2	1,349.9	1,386.7
Additional Room for Lending		149.7	186.5

Note: 1) Indicates additional room for lending thanks to an increase in capital by KRW20.2
trillion: internal capital-raising (KRW16.2 trillion) by banks and first-round securities
purchases (KRW4 trillion) through the Bank Recapitalization Fund
2) BIS capital ratio, BIS capital and RWA for September 2008
3) Formula for calculating additional room for lending: [(Current BIS capital +
size of recapitalization)/Target BIS CAR (10.86% for the Table above)] - Current
RWA

Source: FSS

qualitative terms. This level of capital adequacy is evidence of the banks' ability to absorb, to a large degree, downward pressure on the BIS capital ratio stemming from the economic slowdown and corporate restructuring efforts. For general banks in particular, the BIS capital adequacy and Tier 1 ratios recorded 13.40% and 9.72%, respectively, far exceeding the levels needed to qualify for the composite CAMEL rating of "1" (BIS capital ratio 10%, Tier 1 ratio 7%).

These developments alleviated concerns that capital adequacy levels would lead to a sharp decline in lending by banks. Thanks to the KRW16.2 trillion in capital raised by the banks in 4Q 2008 and securities purchases amounting to KRW4 trillion through the Bank Recapitalization Fund in 1Q 2009, lending capacity as of March 2009 increased by KRW187 trillion compared to September 2008, at which time the BIS CAR recorded one of its lowest levels in recent history at 10.86%.

CAPITAL-RAISING OF NON-BANKING FINANCIAL INSTITUTIONS

The Korean government also induced non-banking financial institutions to adopt self-rescue measures by raising more capital. In the case of the insurance industry, both life and non-life insurance companies saw drastic declines in their solvency margin ratios (actual solvency margin/statutory solvency margin) as the valuation gains of long-term investment securities (AFS securities)—regarded as the solvency margin—dipped sharply due to aggravated market conditions such as a drop in stock prices and rise in interest rates. The solvency margin ratio of life insurance companies dropped to 184.4% in September 2008 from 237.1% in March 2008. The solvency margin ratio of non-life insurance companies dropped to 260.5% from 288.7% over the same period. Furthermore, as of the end of September 2008, the solvency margin ratios of the nine life insurance companies and six non-life insurance companies all recorded below 150%. Accordingly, the Korean government induced insurance companies to secure more capital on a proactive basis through capital increases, the issuance of sub-debts, and other measures under the purview of their large shareholders to ensure that the ratio would remain at or above 150%. As of the end of FY2008 (March 2009), the solvency margin ratio of life insurance companies stood

Table 2-13 **Solvency Margin Ratios of Insurance Companies**

(Unit: %)

	FY2003	FY2004	FY2005	FY2006	FY2007	FY 2008 (till Sep)
Life	217.0	230.0	229.9	232.9	237.1	184.4
Non-Life	280.0	290.0	294.0	281.6	288.7	260.5

Note: Accounts for insurance companies closed in March.

Source: FSS

at 216.3% and non-life insurance companies at 275.5%.

Beginning in 2008, the capital strength of securities firms also deteriorated slightly. A look at the net operating capital ratio (total net operating capital/total risk), which acts as a capital adequacy indicator for securities firms, shows that the ratio dipped 60.7% to 538.5% at the end of September 2008 from 599.2% at the end of 2007. Nonetheless, their capital adequacy is robust, as their net operating capital ratios are hovering well above 150%, the level that would trigger "prompt corrective action."

On October 24, 2008, however, the BOK engaged in repo transactions worth KRW2 trillion on an irregular basis with the Korea Securities Finance Corp. as the KOSPI dropped below 1,000 points and various securities firms faced a liquidity crunch. In addition, the maturity of such repo transactions was 28 days, the longest ever. Up until this point, the Korea Securities Finance Corp.—not independent securities firms—had been the counterpart to the BOK for repo transactions. Under this liquidity support program, the Korea Securities Finance Corp. would garner funds through repo transactions with the BOK against Korean Treasury Bonds (KTB), MSBs, bank debentures and other products, then turn around to provide liquidity to securities firms through repo transactions against KTBs, MSBs, bank debentures, etc., held by securities firms. Meanwhile, the net operating capital ratio and surplus capital of securities firms reached 615.7% and KRW20.5 trillion, respectively, at the end of March 2009.

As shown in Figure 2-20, mutual savings banks worsened in terms of capital adequacy and asset quality owing to the economic slowdown in the first half of 2008. Their BIS capital ratio, which had recorded 9.68% at the end of 2007, dropped to 9.10% at the end of June 2008, while their NPL ratio increased to 9.37% from 8.77% over the same period. In addition, mutual banks—largely consisting of low-income portfolios—recorded a net loss

Figure 2-19 **Net Operating Capital Ratios and Surplus Capital of Securities Firms**

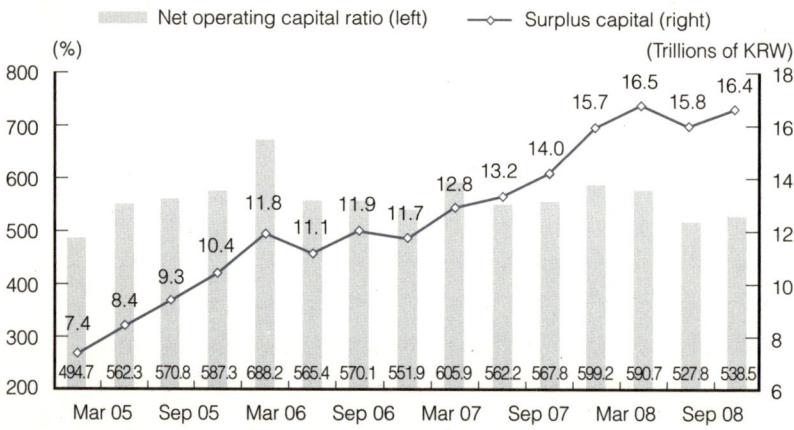

Note: Surplus capital is the net operating capital net total risk, and the net operating capital ratio = (net operating capital/total risk)×100

Source: FSS

in the first half of 2008. Given these dismal indicators, financial authorities encouraged mutual banks to increase their retained earnings and conduct rights offerings and other measures to prevent further deterioration in profitability as a result of the financial crisis. By the end of 2008, mutual savings banks saw improvements across major financial ratios compared to the end of June 2008.

Credit-specialized financial companies like installment financing companies also experienced liquidity shortages as anxiety in the market continued after September 2008. In particular, installment financing companies witnessed drastic declines in the issuance of corporate bonds, CPs, and other products, which had served as the core means of financing, owing to hikes in interest rates stemming from the uncertain financial environment. The monthly average issuance of debenture by installment financing companies up until September 2008 had reached approximately KRW900

Figure 2-20 **Management Status of Mutual Savings Banks**

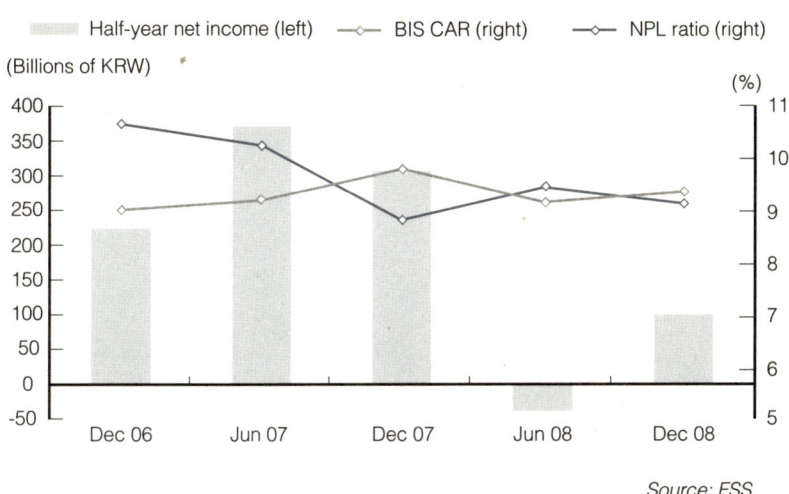

Source: FSS

billion but plunged sharply to KRW135 billion in October [FSS data]. Amid financing difficulties, installment financing companies were exposed to refunding risk, as the portion of corporate bond issuance in total financing had been on the rise (48.2% at the end of 2007 → 53.8% at the end of June 2008).

Financial authorities prepared an action plan to guard against potential insolvency while inducing the non-banking financial services industry to secure liquidity. With insurance companies, policies were formulated to ensure that existing insurance contracts remained in effect through the contract assignment.

As for securities firms, it was decided that their net operating capital ratios were to be closely watched. Ailing securities firms would be restructured through PCA, mergers, or other means. Securities firms with a net operating capital ratio of less than 150% were subject to Management Improvement Recommendations. Those with less than 120% fell under Management Improvement Requirements, and Management

Figure 2-21 **Trends in Debenture Issued by Installment Financing Companies**

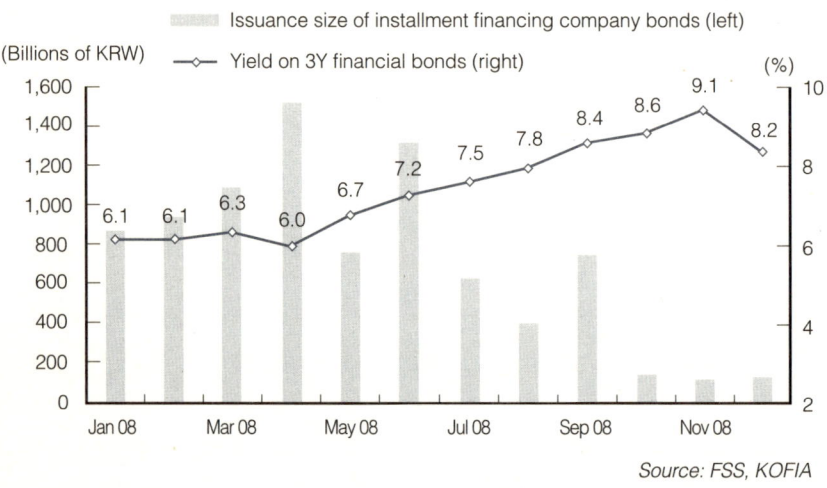

Source: FSS, KOFIA

Improvement Orders applied to those firms with less than a 100% capital ratio.

For mutual savings banks, a policy was put forth to motivate this group of institutions to successfully complete M&As that would lead to the normalization of ailing banks (to a BIS capital ratio of 8% or more) after their acquisition. In connection with this, supervisory authorities announced a reform measure intended to promote autonomous restructuring of mutual savings banks. The revision of the Enforcement Decree of the Mutual Savings Bank Act was completed on September 30, 2008, and contained several special provisions. According to this measure, once an ailing or potentially ailing mutual savings bank is acquired and successfully normalized, the acquirer, if qualified, would be allowed to establish up to five branches beyond its normal business units, depending on the amount of money invested into the bank toward its normalization. Furthermore, any investment that went toward the insolvency would be recognized as capital for a certain period of time, and the acquirer could extend the service coverage of lending offices. (The receipt of public dues and bills is also allowed.) In the meantime, in November 2008 the FSC approved the acquisition of shares in four mutual savings banks. This act was recognized as the first autonomous restructuring activity since the revision of the Enforcement Decree of the Mutual Savings Bank Act. According to the FSC, a PCA implementation was being shelved for three of these institutions, and all four were deficient in capital at that time.

As for CFCs, a measure that would allow the Bond Market Stabilization Fund (BMSF) to purchase debentures issued by CFCs with a certain grade or above was proposed. Between its launch and May 2009, the BMSF had purchased CFC debentures worth roughly KRW440 billion. Yields on financial debentures (excluding bank debentures), which had soared to the 9% level in November 2008, returned to the 5% level at the end of May 2009.

FORMULATION OF A CONTINGENCY PLAN

In accordance with the current Depositors Protection Act and Financial Industry Restructuring Act, only ailing or potentially ailing financial institutions may receive fiscal investments. This condition gave rise to concerns that the continued economic slowdown would cause households and businesses to become insolvent, while financial institutions—for fear of compromising their asset quality—would tighten credit lines, thereby accelerating the economic slowdown further. As the debt-paying capacity of households and businesses weakened owing to the precipitous declines in the economy at home and abroad, bad debts surged KRW10.4 trillion (164.9%) to reach KRW31 trillion over the

Table 2-14 **Approval of Acquisition of Shares in 4 Mutual Savings Banks**

(Unit: Billions of KRW, %)

| Acquirer | Status of Acquirees | | | | | | |
| | Name | Stake Sold | Total Assets | Shareholders' Equity | | BIS CAR | |
				Before Approval	After Approval	Before Approval	After Approval
Savings Bank A, etc. + PEF B	AAA	99.9	792.3	-80.9	31.1	-13.42	8.08
Savings Bank A, etc.	BBB	100	215.8	-22.4	12.6	-13.95	9.60
Savings Bank C	CCC	72.9	130.2	-28.5	7.5	-27.28	8.88
5 Affiliates of D Group	DDD	90.0	382.4	-94.1	3.9	-20.30	8.84

Source: FSS

Figure 2-22 **SBLs in Financial Services Industry**

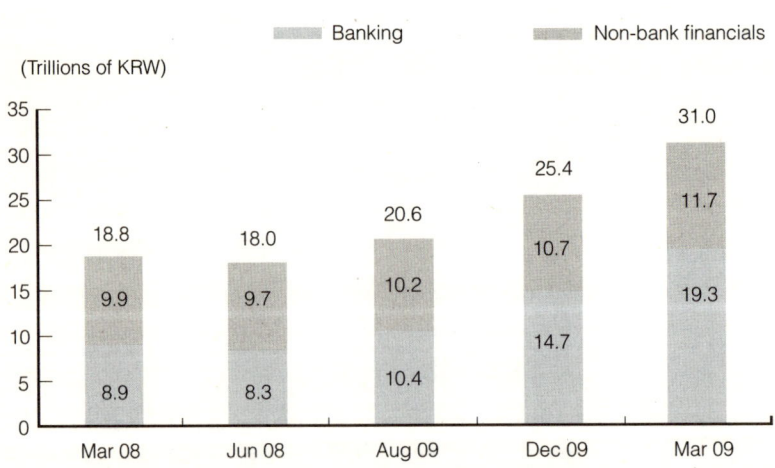

Note: Non-banking financial sector includes mutual savings banks, insurance companies, securities firms, CFCs, merchant banks and credit unions.

Source: FSS

period of September 2008-March 2009, further exacerbated by growing SBLs (Substandard or Below Loans) resulting from corporate restructuring.

Given that corporate restructuring is still under way, substandard or below loans are likely to increase further. The Korean government responded by announcing "proactive measures aimed at enhancing the asset quality of financial institutions," containing policies for supporting the real economy, implementing early warning systems, and preventing the spread of system risk (March 13, 2009). The core of the measures pertains to the creation of a "Restructuring Fund" and "Financial Stabilization Fund." Figure 2-23 shows the schematics for providing financial support to financial institutions according to these measures.

KAMCO Restructuring Fund

The Act on the Effective Treatment of Financial Institutions' SBLs and the Establishment of KAMCO (KAMCO Act) is to be revised to allow the creation of a "Restructuring Fund" within KAMCO. According to a draft of the revised act, the Restructuring Fund is to be financed through the issuance of bonds and other products, guaranteed by the government up to a maximum of KRW40 trillion. The fund's capital will be spent on purchasing substandard or below loans held by financial institutions and assets of corporations undergoing the restructuring process. This fund will be in operation until 2014, and residual assets, including profit, will revert to the national treasury.

After this revised bill passed the National Assembly on April 29, 2009 (going into effect on May 13), the Restructuring Fund was created within KAMCO in June and is currently in operation. In accordance with the investment plan for the 2009 Restructuring Fund, the total size of investment for 2009 stands at KRW20.2 trillion. Of this amount, KRW20 trillion was allocated for

Figure 2-23 Schema for Providing Support to Financial Institutions

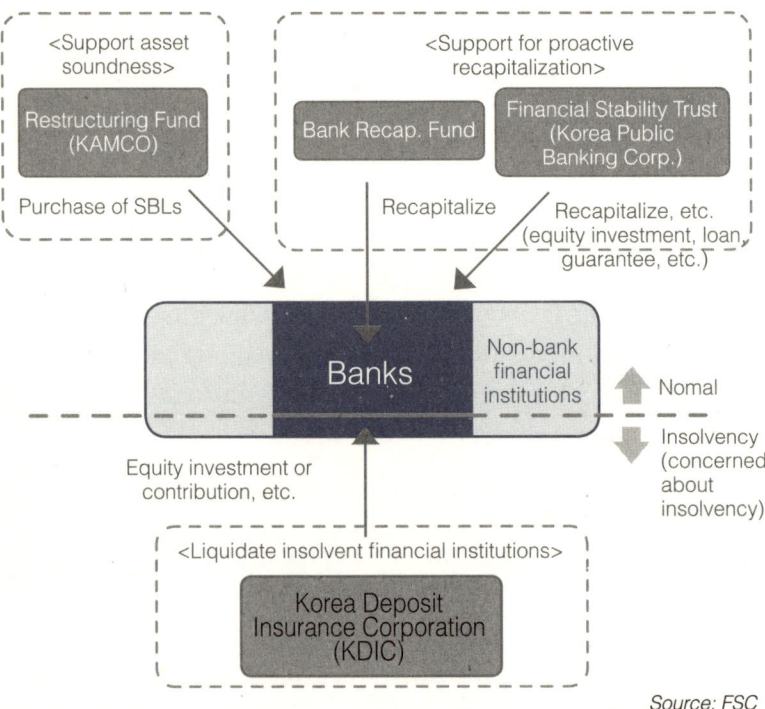

Source: FSC

supporting corporate restructuring. According to the Ministry of Strategy and Finance, KRW462.2 billion in bonds were issued by the fund to purchase substandard or below loans belonging to the financial services industry (project financing loans) up until June.

In the meantime, the Non-Performing Asset Management Fund, which was created during the Asian financial crisis in 1997, was converted into a fund under liquidation. The residual assets of this fund are being distributed to financial institutions and the government according to their percentage of contribution after the fund's purpose of acquiring substandard or below loans had been deemed served on November 22, 2002.

Table 2-15 **Restructuring Fund and Non-Performing Asset Management Fund Comparison**

	Restructuring Fund	Non-Performing Asset Management Fund
Funding Source	- Contributions from financial institutions - Money transferred from KAMCO - Contributions from the government - Capital secured via issuance of bonds - Loans - Fund profits	- Contributions from financial institutions - Money transferred from KAMCO - Contributions from the government - Capital secured via issuance of bonds - Loans - Profits from fund investments
Use	- Purchase of SBLs held by financial institutions - Purchase of non-business purpose assets, assets subject to self-rescue measures by at-risk companies, and assets of companies undergoing restructuring - Bad debt swapped for equity - Equity investment/investment arising in the process of pursuing goals - Lending or payment guarantees to investees or companies on debts that are swapped for equity	- Purchase of SBLs held by financial institutions - Assets subject to self-rescue measures undertaken by companies at risk for default
Period of Operation	- Inception date: 2009 - Deadline for purchase: 12/31/2014 - Deadline for investing: 12/31/2014	- Inception date: 11/13/1997 - Deadline for purchase: 11/22/2002 - Deadline for Investing: 11/22/2012
Residual Assets	- Reverted to national treasury	- On a pro-rata basis according to the percentage of contribution

Source: KAMCO

Financial Stabilization Fund Within Korea Policy Finance Corporation

While operating the Bank Recapitalization Fund, the Korean government submitted a revision to the Financial Industry Restructuring Act to the effect that a Financial Market Stabilization Fund would be established within the Korea Public Banking Corp. as a means to enhance support to the real economy, as well as the soundness of financial institutions.

The primary objective of the revised bill was to expand the scope of support from financial institutions, including banks covered by deposit insurance, to the entire financial services industry, which would include CFCs, financial holding companies, and other institutions. This revision proposed providing support for recapitalization not only to ailing or high-risk financial institutions, but also to sound financial institutions that enjoyed normal operations.

As this revised bill passed the National Assembly on April 29, 2009, the establishment of the Financial Stabilization Fund within the Korea Policy Finance Corporation—which will be created from a split-off of KDB—should be complete in October. The size of the Financial Stabilization Fund is still to be decided.

3. Support for Corporate Funding

Corporations came to face a serious liquidity strain as the global financial crisis gathered momentum. Total funding (bank credit + issuance of stocks and bonds) of Korean corporations, which recorded KRW32 trillion in 2Q 2008, began to decline in the 3rd quarter, registering KRW24.6 trillion in 3Q 2008 before dipping further to KRW14.0 trillion in 4Q 2008.

Accordingly, the Business Survey Index on Corporate Finance (BSI) fell sharply. According to a BOK survey, the FBSI for all industries, which had recorded 90 on average for 2007, dropped to 69 in 4Q 2008. In particular, funding conditions for SMEs had deteriorated to the point that their FBSI fell to 63 in 4Q 2008.

Financial authorities implemented various measures to cope with the liquidity problem faced by these corporations, including

Figure 2-24 **Funding Volume of Domestic Corporations and FBSI (Actuals)**

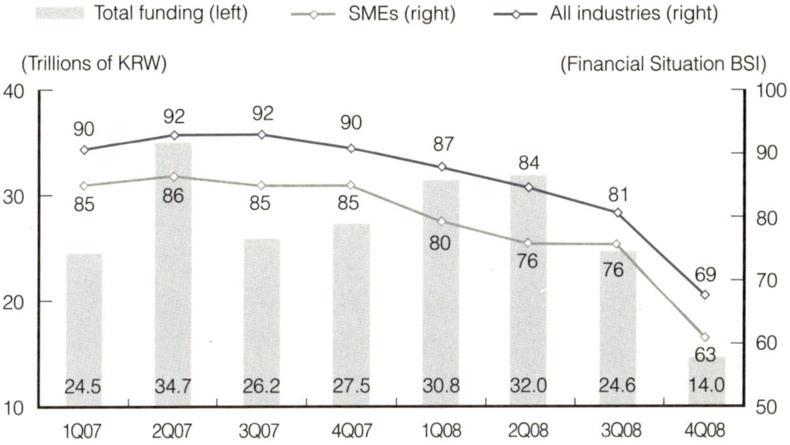

Total funding (left) — SMEs (right) — All industries (right)

(Trillions of KRW)   (Financial Situation BSI)

Note: Funding volume is the sum of bank credit, issuance of stocks and bonds.

Source: FSS, BOK

expanding the role of policy-based financing. The role of banks also broadened to perform such functions as introducing the Fast Track program. Additionally, financial authorities began to explore alternative forms of liquidity such as support for bond issuance, increased funding via the direct financing market, and regulatory changes to alleviate the burden on corporations. The following sections go into more detail on these measures.

EXPANDED ROLE OF POLICY FINANCING

In an effort to mitigate the credit crunch caused by the global financial crisis, the Korean government first expanded the role of policy financing. The government increased the amount of funds supplied by state-run banks such as KDB, IBK, and KEXIM for 2009 by 22.3% compared to the previous year, as a way to

Table 2-16 **Funds Supply by Major State-Run Banks**

(Unit: Trillions of KRW)

	Plans for 2008 (A)	Plans for 2009 (B)	Change (B-A)	%	Details
KDB	27	32	5	18.5%	- Facilities investment: 11 - Liquidity support: 11 - Facilitate direct financing: 10
IBK	27	36	9	33.3%	- Facilities investment: 7.5 - Venture support: 6.8 - Startup support: 6 - Liquidity support: 9
KEXIM	40	47	7	17.5%	- Export financing: 32 - SME support: 8.5 - Offshore resources development: 2
Total	94	115	21	22.3%	

Source: Ministry of Strategy and Finance

encourage facilities investment, promote corporate restructuring and support SMEs. Specifically, among the funds supplied by state-run banks for 2009, KRW32 trillion came from KDB (up KRW5 trillion), KRW36 trillion from IBK (up KRW9 trillion) and KRW47 trillion from KEXIM (up KRW7 trillion).

In addition, the amount of guarantees provided by the KODIT and KIBO Technology (Korea Technology Finance Corporation) Fund was increased by KRW14 trillion to KRW56.5 trillion from KRW42.5 trillion in 2008 to help SMEs secure funding more easily. The Korean government also initiated measures to augment credit guarantees to provide support to SMEs and micro-businesses more effectively, recognizing the limitations on banks offering credit as a result of increased credit risks. These guarantees benefited those corporations that experienced declining sales or diminished creditworthiness because of the difficult economic environment. Support in the amount of KRW34 trillion was extended to 237,000 businesses, and, in principle, the terms of all guarantees provided by the KODIT and KIBO Technology Fund maturing in 2009 were extended in full. Furthermore, some 151,000 businesses enjoyed new guarantees in the amount of KRW18 trillion, marking an increase of KRW9.4 trillion from the original target of KRW8.6 trillion, as the screening criteria and restrictions on guarantee limits were significantly eased.

* Measures to Augment Credit Guarantees for SMEs and Micro-Businesses

• **Measures to augment emergency guarantees until end of 2009**

- Roll over the term of guarantees maturing in 2009 in full.
- Greatly ease the qualifications for obtaining guarantee support, guarantee limits, etc.
- Provide 100% guarantees, up to a certain amount, for micro-businesses and core sectors necessary for laying the foundation for growth, such as exporters, green growth companies, high-tech corporations, and startups.
- Drastically cut the processing time and procedures for providing guarantees and remove accountability at the individual level to ensure that guarantees are provided quickly and aggressively at the windows.

• **Measures to prevent moral hazard to ensure that the expanded guarantee program does not lead to any fiscal loss and delays in corporate restructuring**

- Do not provide support to financially distressed or defaulting companies contained in the list of support recipients, or to those under court receivership.
- Provide support to companies undergoing restructuring programs such as workouts, on the condition that they improve their business management.
- Monitor unintended use of credit provided against guarantees.

Source: FSS

On February 16, these measures to augment credit guarantees took effect, complemented by additional efforts by the government. First, those financially distressed businesses that did not meet the conditions for receiving support were identified so that they would not fall through the cracks and capitalize on the extension of the guarantee program. A cooperative framework between the FSS, guarantor and banks was established to prevent any misuse of the guaranteed loans. Second, a measure was introduced to offer immunity to the officers and employees with respect to their provision of the guarantee. Employees and officers are not accountable for loan decisions, in the absence of personal improprieties such as willful or gross negligence or the pursuit of personal interests.

Figure 2-25 **SME Loans by Domestic Banks**

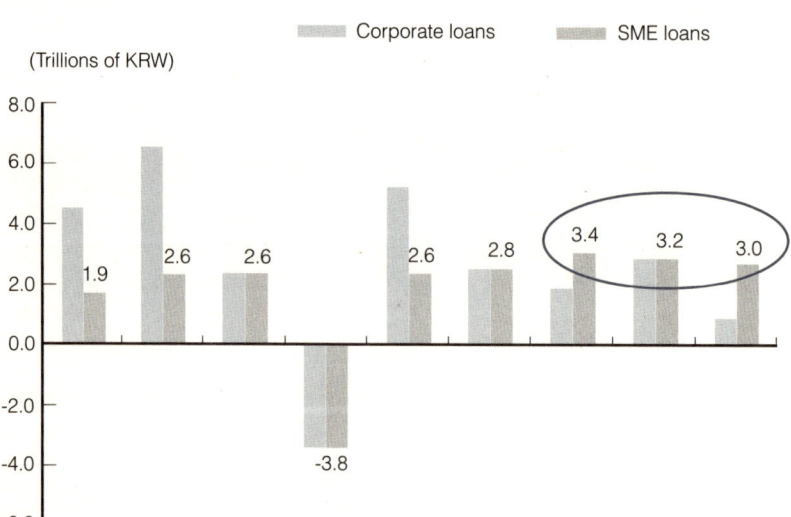

Note: Based on net growth

Source: BOK

These measures taken to augment credit guarantees translated into additional financial support, for SMEs in particular, by alleviating the credit risk of general banks. As shown in Figure 2-25, SME loans had been on a steady increase, marking a monthly net growth of KRW3 trillion since the measures for augmenting credit guarantees were announced in February. The amount of guarantees has also exhibited an upward trend since the measures were implemented.

As shown in Table 2-17, the amount of guarantees over the period of January-May 2009 stood at KRW32.7 trillion, (new guarantees totaled KRW20.5 trillion, and rolled-over guarantees KRW12.2 trillion), up 92.4% (KRW15.7 trillion) from KRW17.0 trillion the year before. Furthermore, KRW13.1 trillion (KRW7.7 trillion from KODIT and KRW5.4 trillion from the KIBO Technology Fund), which accounts for 40.1% of the total KRW32.7 trillion, was provided to core sectors such as exporters, high-tech corporations, green growth companies, and startups, thus setting the stage for an economic resurgence and growth.

The Korean government is aggressively underwriting project finance (PF) loans and other debt via KAMCO to guard against

Table 2-17 **Guarantee Issuances**

(Unit: Trillions of KRW)

	2008		2009					
	2008	Jan-May	Jan-May	Jan	Feb	Mar	Apr	May
New	17.6	5.4	20.5 (17.9)	1.3	3.9	5.9	4.9	4.4
Rollover	29.4	11.6	12.2 (10.6)	0.9	1.6	2.9	3.6	3.2
Total	47.0	17.0	32.7 (28.5)	2.2	5.5	8.8	8.5	7.6

Note: Figures in parentheses indicate actual guarantees provided during the period from February 16 to May 29, 2008, following measures to extend credit guarantees.

Source: FSS

Table 2-18 **Actual Guarantees for Core Sectors in Jan-May 2009**

(Unit: Trillions of KRW)

	Exporters	High-Tech	Green Growth	Startups	Total
KODIT	2.9	0.0	1.1	4.8	7.7
KIBO Tech	0.9	3.8	0.8	2.0	5.4
Total	3.8	3.8	1.9	6.8	13.1

Note: Based on the summation excluding overlaps between categories

Source: FSS

a growth in bad debts held by financial institutions. Through the Korea Housing Finance Corporation, the government is expanding the supply of Bogeumjari loans, supplementing the existing guarantee to cover falling housing prices (January 2009) and aiding in the securitization of the bonds issued by construction companies (December 2008).

In the meantime, the government increased equity investment in state-run financial institutions to strengthen policy financing. Approximately KRW1.4 trillion was invested into KDB, KRW1 trillion into IBK and KRW1.45 trillion into KEXIM Bank in a financial boost to SMEs and trade financing. In particular, government-held Korea Expressway Corporation stocks worth KRW500 billion were invested in kind into KEXIM Bank in March 2009 following an investment in kind amounting to KRW650 billion at the end of 2008 and a cash investment of KRW300 billion in January 2009. Furthermore, an additional contribution worth KRW1.16 trillion (including KRW60 billion to the Korea Federation of Credit Guarantee Foundation) allowed additional room for guarantees by KODIT (KRW900 billion) and the KIBO Technology Fund (KRW200 billion).

An additional in-kind investment worth KRW300 billion was included in the first-round supplementary budget. In addition,

Table 2-19 **Equity Investment as Part of Supplementary Budget**

(Unit: Billions of KRW)

Organization	2009 Budget	Supp. Budget (Draft)	Total
FSC (A)	2,000	700	2,700
(KAMCO)	400	200	600
(KHFC)	200	200	400
(IBK)	500	300	800
(KDB)	900	-	900
SMBA (B)	1,100	1,600	2,700
(KODIT)	900	1,080	1,980
(KIBO Tech. Fund)	200	520	720
Total (A+B)	3,100	2,300	5,400

Note: The aggregate 2009 budget stands at KRW2,186.8 billion (including KRW186.8 billion in labor costs, basic expenditures, working expense, etc.).

Source: FSC

in order to increase the guarantee amount by KRW12.9 trillion compared to the original budget (KRW50.2 → KRW63.1 trillion), the government decided to make an additional contribution of KRW1.6 trillion to KODIT (KRW1,080 billion) and the KIBO Technology Fund (KRW520 billion). For KAMCO, a cash investment worth KRW400 billion was made in January 2009. Furthermore, KRW200 billion in additional investment was made as part of the supplementary budget to expedite the purchases of more substandard or below loans held by banks, mutual savings banks and other similar institutions. As a consequence, an additional purchase worth KRW2.0-4.4 trillion was possible, assuming a 50% purchase rate. Furthermore, a cash investment of KRW200 billion was injected into the Korea Housing Finance Corporation.

EXPANDED ROLE OF BANKS

Raising the Asset Quality of Banks

While providing more funding via state-run banks, guarantee providers, and other institutions, the Korean government also strived to enhance indirect aid with a view to expanding bank credit. Since banks, by their nature, need to take into account asset quality, increased credit risk on the part of borrowers constrained bank credit. As shown in Figure 2-26, domestic banks recognized that SMEs posed a higher credit risk given how relatively vulnerable they are to external shocks in the present financial crisis and economic environment. According to the results of the Survey on Lending Practices of Financial Institutions conducted by the BOK, the credit risk level of SMEs recorded 56

Figure 2-26 **Loan Demand Index, Credit Risk Index and Lending Attitude Index**

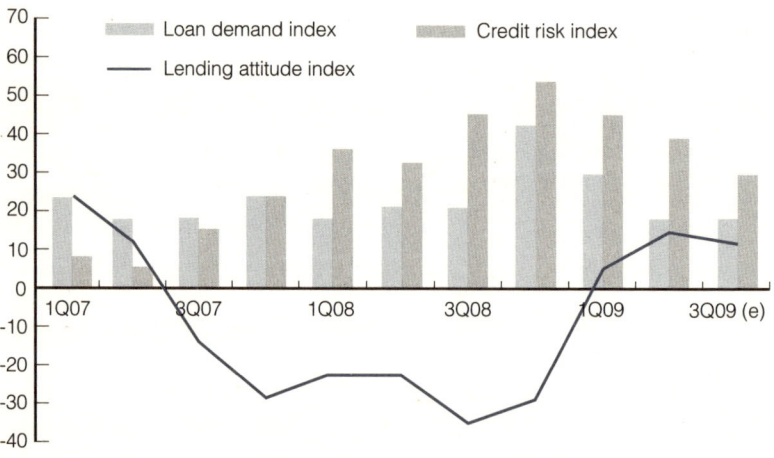

Note: These indices represent assessments of credit demand, credit risk and lending attitude for 16 banks (excluding KDB and KEXIM). Index scores range from -100 to +100, with 0 denoting "neutral." (+) denotes an "increase" in credit demand/ credit risk and "easing" in lending attitude, whereas (-) denotes the opposite.

Source: BOK

in 4Q 2008, marking its highest value in this decade. Interestingly enough, credit demand from SMEs was highest during this same quarter, whereas the Lending Attitude Index for the same period recorded -28, indicating tight credit conditions. The index points to the limited ability of banks to increase the amount of loans to SMEs suffering from a credit crunch, owing to concerns about worsening asset quality.

This being the case, the Korean government took measures to raise asset quality by reducing the risky assets on the debit column of bank balance sheets. Key measures included securitization of potentially bad mortgage loans through the KHFC and purchase of substandard or below loans by KAMCO. The government allocated a total of KRW1 trillion in additional equity investment to these two organizations in two installments, on January

Figure 2-27 **Trends of Growth in Real GDP and Bank Credit**

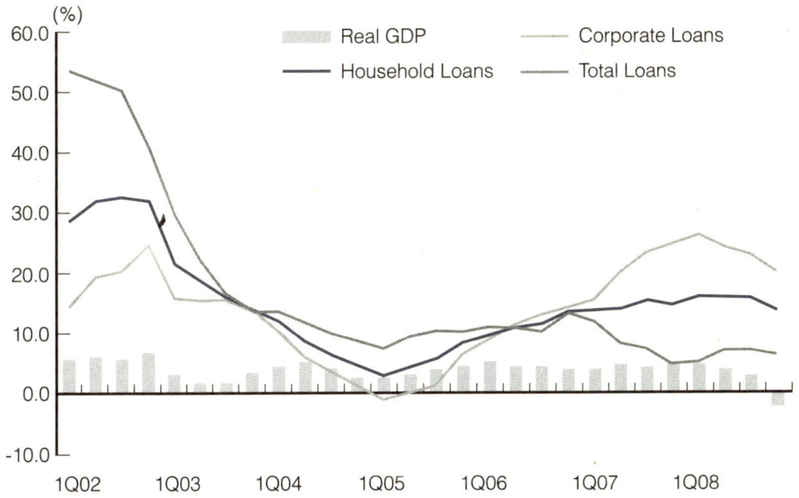

Note: Growth rate is on a year-on-year basis.

Source: BOK

and May 2009. Consequently, the KHFC's maximum cap for purchasing mortgage loans grew from KRW7 trillion to KRW11 trillion. The government also helped to increase equity on the credit column of bank balance sheets by setting up the Bank Recapitalization Fund, which was worth KRW20 trillion. These measures paved the way for an increased lending capacity among general banks by mitigating their fears of credit risk and potential deterioration in asset quality.

One of the reasons that domestic banks have been somewhat reluctant to extend credit, amid concerns over asset quality deterioration with the financial crisis, has to do with the competition among banks for the leadership position in the banking industry. As shown in Figure 2-27, domestic banks had been expanding their credit in excess of the real GDP growth rate.

Autonomous Liquidity Support by Banks

The Korean government developed its "Fast Track Program for the Support of SMEs" [Liquidity Support Measure for SMEs (October 1, 2008)] to aid in the autonomous expansion of liquidity support by banks. This measure was aimed at providing quick funding to those institutions that have been singled out for their strong portfolios but have been experiencing funding difficulties.

As shown in Figure 2-28, this program requires banks to classify companies into four different groups based on the FSS guidelines for continuous credit risk assessment. That is, companies in normal condition are classified as A grade; companies that are potentially ailing, though not ailing now, as B grade; companies regarded as viable but showing symptoms of a possible default as C grade; and companies that show clear signs of default and are regarded as not viable as D grade.

Figure 2-28 **Structure of Fast Track Program**

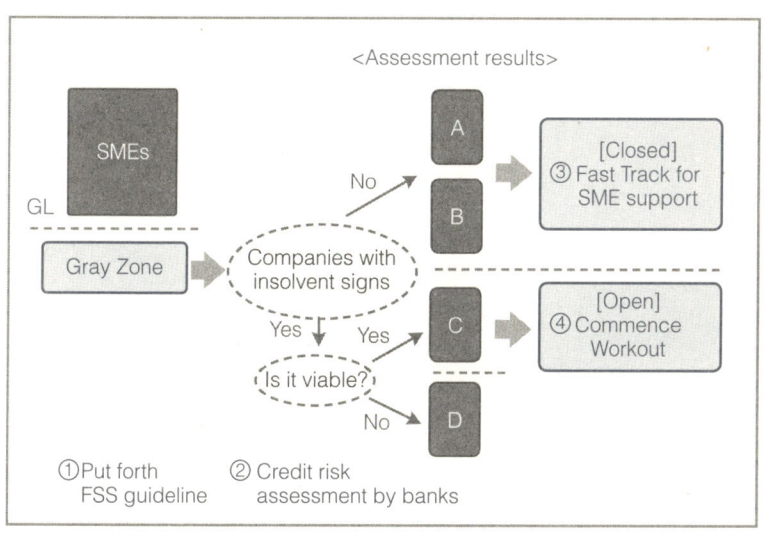

Source: FSS

For those companies classified as A or B grade, a closed Fast Track Program will be formulated to inject new liquidity. This effort will entail the Financial Supervisory Service (FSS) and creditor banks forming a task force team in cooperation with the guarantee providers to produce various benchmarks, which banks will then customize on an individual basis.

Furthermore, policy measures in support of banks were put in place to alleviate potential crisis-driven constraints on the banks' ability to generate liquidity on their own. For example, the weight given to SME liquidity support in the CAMEL rating was increased as an incentive for banks to support SMEs. Also, the government opened the way for more levels of bank staff to approve and grant new liquidity support to SMEs by removing the KPI requirements of the original Fast Track Program. A measure to allow KODIT and the KIBO Technology Fund to issue special payment guarantees was initiated in order to relieve banks of the

Figure 2-29 Liquidity Support for Companies Under KIKO

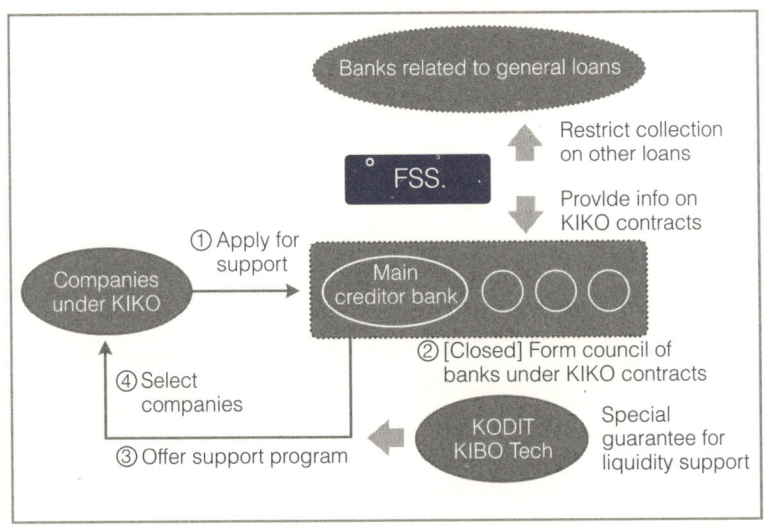

risk arising from the extension of new credit [The Measure to Expand Payment Guarantee for Supporting SMEs and Micro-Businesses (February 12, 2009)].

In addition, a Fast Track Program that specifically accommodates features of the KIKO was initiated to assist those companies under this contract. As shown in Figure 2-29, a closed-to-the-public "KIKO Bank Council" made up of the main creditor banks was formed, with the FSS playing a key role. Upon receiving an application for the Fast Track Program, the council reviews whether or not the company is viable and then offers a choice of various support options, such as company liquidation, repayment in installments, rescheduling, fee waivers and interest rate discounts (in the case of small losses). A blanket liquidation involves granting new credit or conducting a debt-to-equity swap

Figure 2-30 **Actual Fast Track Program Support**

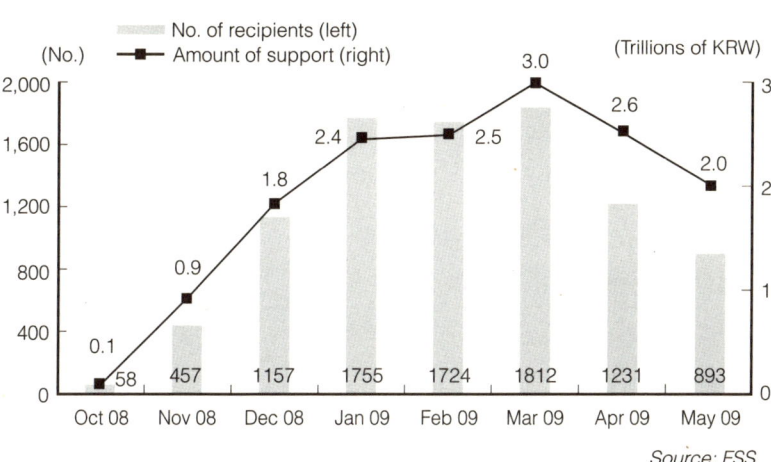

Source: FSS

to cover the amount of loss identified at the time the application for support is received. Repayment in installments is the provision of a product that hedges against FX exposure until maturity, or the supply of new credit every month on the settlement date. Rescheduling refers to temporary relief of settlement obligations by altering the transactional structure of the KIKO contract.

Figure 2-30 presents the amount of actual support granted between the inception of the Fast Track Program and the end of May 2009. Requests for support from this program steadily increased through March 2009 after the government began heavily promoting the program in December 2008. Its popularity witnessed a decline commencing in April, however, as the financial circumstances surrounding SMEs began to improve and the benefits of steady liquidity support came to fruition.

Table 2-20 shows the actual support provided until the end of May 2009 by company type and support option. Over the same period, a total of 15,231 companies applied for the support,

Table 2-20 **Fast Track Program by Company Type and Support Option**

(Unit: No. of Companies, Billions of KRW)

	No. of Companies			Support Amount				
	Application	Assessment Completed	Support Granted	Loan Conversion	New Loans	Maturity Extensions	Other	Total
KIKO firms	754	730	**588**	1,295.9	715.1	2,021.5	0.9	**4,033.4**
General firms	14,477	12,239	**8,499**	11.4	2,838.1	8,368.6	15.3	**11,233.4**
Total	15,231	12,969	**9,087**	1,307.3	3,553.2	10,390.1	16.2	**15,266.8**

Note: "Support granted" is based on the simple summation of companies that applied for the program.

Source: FSS

Figure 2-31 **Financial Situation of SMEs**

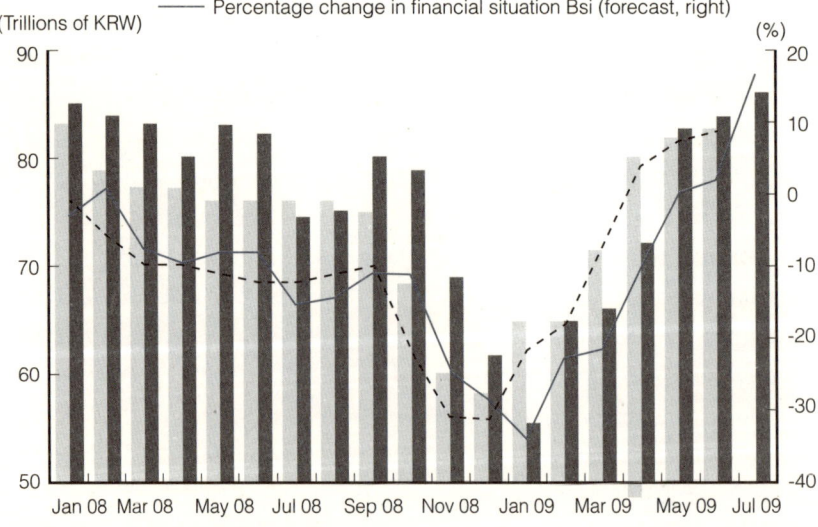

Note: Percentage changes are YOY.

Source: BOK

and 9,087 applicants benefited from liquidity support worth of KRW15.3 trillion in aggregate. Among those recipients, 588 companies under KIKO contracts received a total of KRW4 trillion. Among the support options, maturity extensions accounted for the largest share at 68.1% (KRW10.4 trillion).

The financial situation of SMEs improved considerably thanks to the implementation of the Fast Track Program. According to Figure 2-31, as of June 2009 both the actual and forecasted financial data for SMEs were approaching the levels seen during the first half of 2008. Figures point to some relief in the credit crunch that had confronted SMES at the beginning of 4Q 2008. Given ongoing concerns about the pace of economic recovery and corporate restructuring efforts that are still under way, financial authorities are cautious about this improvement in the liquidity situation of SMEs and have decided to extend the Fast Track Program to the end of 2009 beyond its original expiration date of June 2009.

SUPPORT FOR BOND ISSUANCE AND OTHER ALTERNATIVE LIQUIDITY

Figure 2-32 below shows that the main funding source for SMEs is bank loans. SME lending accounts for more than 80% of Korea's aggregate corporate lending. The share of funding by SMEs in the direct financing market is minimal. The global financial crisis, however, led to a deceleration in the growth of SME lending to the extent that the "BSI on Corporate Finance-Performance" dropped from 83 in January to 68 in October 2008. Recognizing this adverse impact on the financial situation of SMEs, financial authorities announced measures for providing alternative liquidity, including support for bond issuance, by supplementing the guarantee capacity of KODIT (SME Liquidity Support Program,

Figure 2-32 **Financing by Corporate Size and Share of SME Lending**

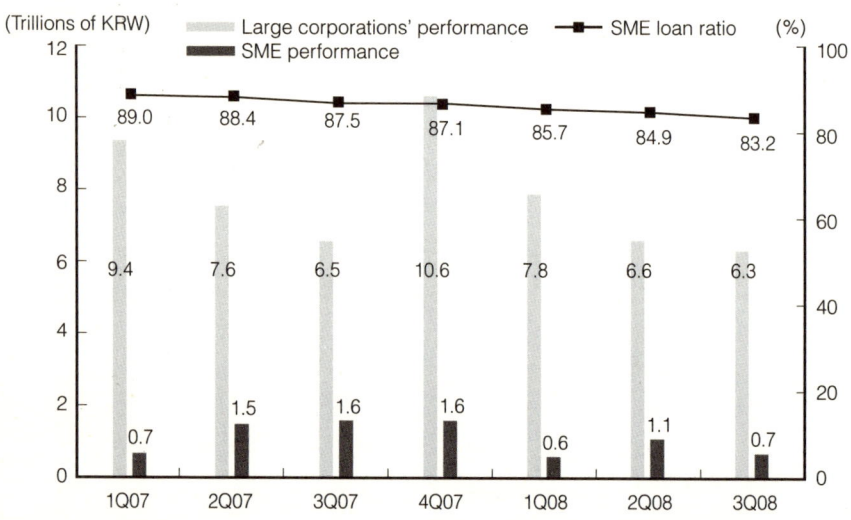

Note: 1) Direct financing is based on the issuance of stocks and corporate bonds.
2) Share of SME lending is relative to total corporate KRW lending by domestic banks.

Source: FSS

October 1, 2008).

The government decided to provide support for the issuance of P-CBOs worth KRW1 trillion via KODIT until the end of 2008. In line with the program, KODIT provided support for the issuance of KRW1.1 trillion in P-CBOs on three occasions from November to the end of December 2008. Furthermore, the creation of the BMSF in December 2008 led to a significant increase in the issuance of P-CBOs guaranteed by KODIT in the first quarter of 2009. Figure 2-33 shows a continuous and sharp growth in P-CBO issuance commencing in 2008.

In addition, a decision was reached to proceed with the introduction of the Special Purpose Company (SPC) Guarantee Program to facilitate bond issuance by SMEs. The purpose of this

Figure 2-33 **Trend of P-CBO Issuance and Percentage Change**

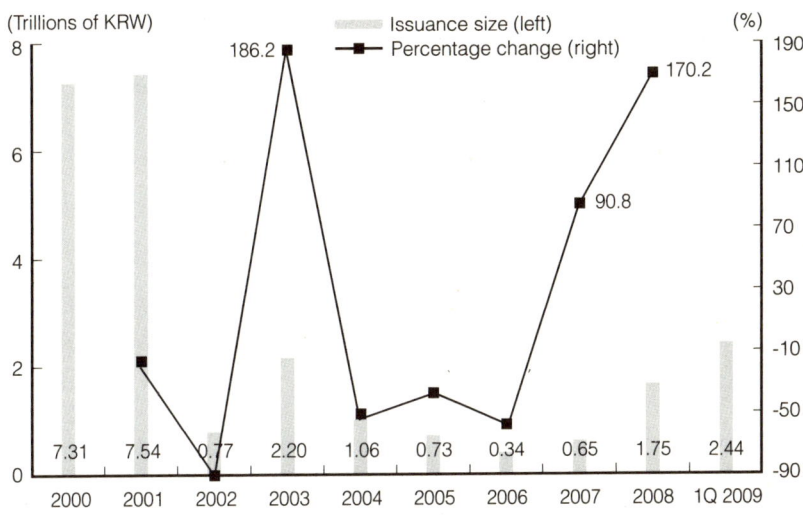

Note: P-CBOs were issued for the first time in August 2000.
None were issued in 1Q 2008.

Source: FSS

Figure 2-34 **Schematics of the SPC Guarantee Program**

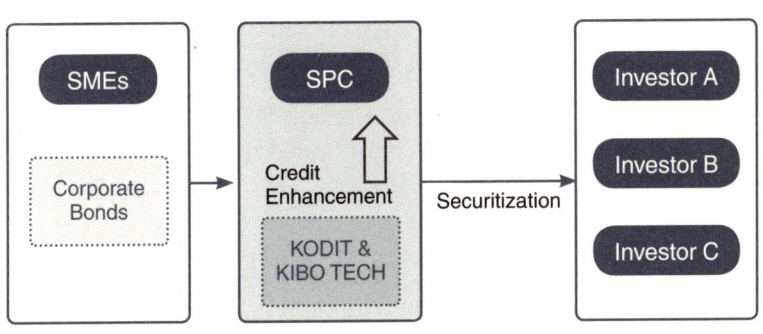

Source: FSC

program is to help SPCs issue asset-backed securities (ABSs) whose underlying asset is bonds issued by SMEs. Since SMEs cannot easily access the bond market, the program would come with a guarantee provided by KODIT or the KIBO Technology Fund, thus facilitating the ability of SPCs to sell the ABSs in the market. A revision to the KODIT Act and KIBO Technology Fund Act intended to allow the adoption of this program went into effect in May 2009.

INCREASE IN FUND SUPPLY THROUGH DIRECT FINANCING

A look at Figure 2-35 reveals that in 2008, the size of capital raised in the stock market sharply declined compared to 2007. By the end of 2008, the amount of capital registered KRW5.1 trillion, down 70.3% from KRW17.2 trillion in 2007. Exchange rate volatility, soaring oil and raw material prices, and falling stock prices stemming from the financial crisis and other economic shocks throughout 2008 made raising capital very difficult. In particular, the decline in funding needs for facilities investment, attributable to the weakened business environment, played a significant role.

The FSC responded with stock-boosting measures ("Ways to Overcome the Financial Crisis," December 18, 2008) to combat this trend of rapidly decreasing capital in the stock market. In November 2008, the government decided to continue the Stock Market Stabilization Fund (SMSF). The size of the SMSF is KRW515 billion, financed by securities-related organizations such as the Korea Financial Investment Association (KRW55 billion), Korea Exchange (KRW250 billion), and Korea Securities Depository (KRW210 billion), in an effort to heighten demand

Figure 2-35 **Capital Raised in Stock Market by Korean Companies**

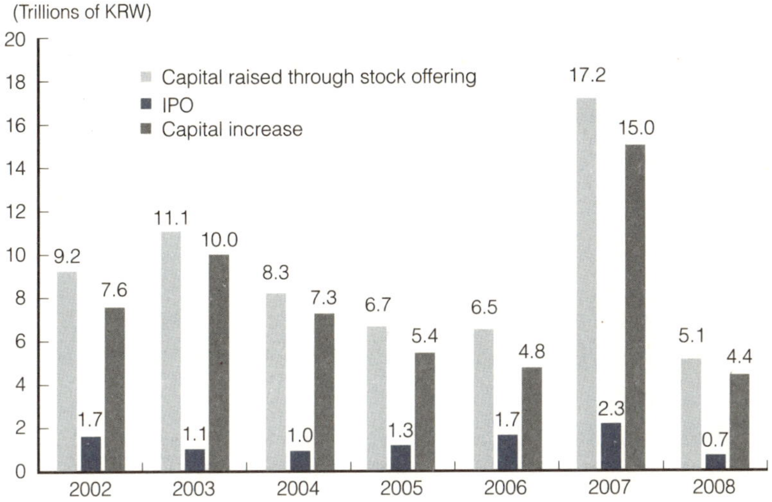

(Trillions of KRW)

Source: FSS

for stocks and boost market confidence. Since its formation, the SMSF has invested KRW103 billion into the stock market on five occasions, for a total injection of KRW515 billion.

Disclosure requirements for securities offerings often translate into delays and a hindrance in capital raising efforts. Even corporations that conducted frequent and numerous offers were required to follow the same lengthy procedures with every market transaction. To facilitate securities offerings, the Korean government introduced the WKSI (Well Known Seasoned Issuers) Program, made up of roughly the top 10% of all listed corporations. Another qualification for this list is a market capitalization of KRW500 billion or more. By permitting these companies to file an automatic self-registration statement when offering securities, financial authorities effectively facilitated securities transactions by easing the disclosure requirements.

The WKSI program went into effect after the revision of the Enforcement Decree of the Financial Investment Services and Capital Market Act.

The FSC announced other measures to boost the bond market, which included adding new products and new policy instruments such as short-term bonds and structured covered bonds. Short-term bonds are electronic commercial paper that is designed to add transparency and efficiency to the money market. The FSC announced that it would support the issuance of structured covered bonds and capitalize on the Asset Securitization Act to aid in the mid- and long-term foreign currency funding efforts of Korean banks.

As shown in Figure 2-36, Assets Under Management (AUM) at money market funds (MMFs) grew sharply over financial market anxieties since the appearance of the global financial crisis. The FSC established a temporary limit (e.g., 30%) on deposits (including CDs) that an MMF can place with financial institutions to ensure that funds flowing into the MMF can be redirected to investment in corporate bonds and commercial paper. As a

---

* WKSI Program Criteria

To qualify for the WKSI Program, a corporation must have met the following conditions:

- Listing on the stock market for at least five years
- Market cap of at least KRW500 billion
- Three years of reporting history submitted in a timely manner (annual-semi-annual-quarterly reports)
- No record of having received any sanctions from the FSC and KRX for a disclosure breach in the last three years
- Approved audit of financial statements for the most recent fiscal year
- No record of fines or more serious penalties incurred as a result of accounting fraud or other violations of the Financial Investment Services and Capital Market Act in the last three years

Source: FSC

Figure 2-36 **AUM and Growth in MMFs**

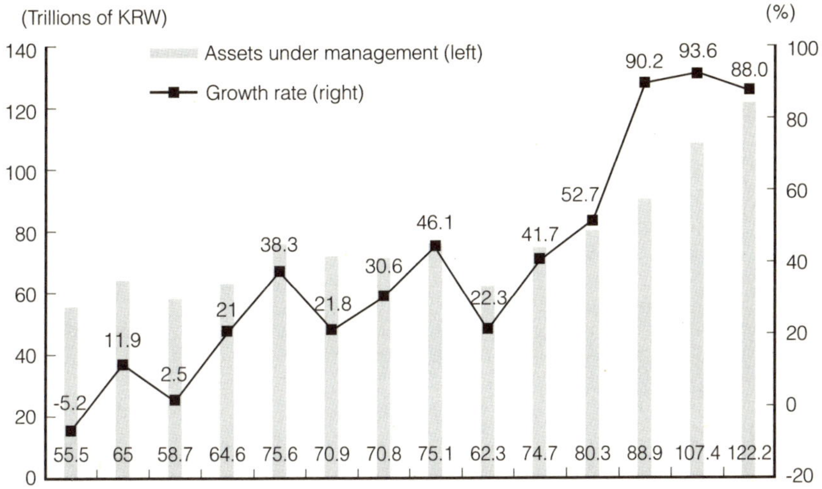

(Trillions of KRW)   (%)

Note: On a YOY basis

Source: KOFIA

follow-up measure, the FSC announced in March 2009 the MMF Asset Management Rationalization Policy, which proposes a minimum investment limit of 40% for corporate bonds, CPs and other products. The FSC also revised the Regulation on Financial Investment Business in July 2009.

POLICY REFURBISHMENT TO ALLEVIATE CORPORATE BURDEN

On the eve of having to submit combined financial statements in 2008, corporations in Korea were faced with significant FX losses as a result of abnormal surges in exchange rates. As shown in Table 2-21, the intraday variation and day-to-day variation (based on daily averages) in the won-dollar rate in 2008 recorded KRW18.3 and KRW12.0, respectively, up sharply from the

Table 2-21 **USD/KRW Exchange Rate Volatility Based on Daily Averages**

(Unit: KRW, %)

	2006	2007	2008	2008			
				1/4	2/4	3/4	4/4
Intraday change	4.6	3.0	18.3	6.0	8.2	13.1	45.2
Percentage change (%)	0.48	0.32	1.50	0.62	0.80	1.20	3.32
Day-on-day change	3.2	2.1	12.0	4.0	4.8	9.3	29.2
Percentage change (%)	0.33	0.22	0.99	0.41	0.47	0.85	2.18

Note: 1) Intraday change (%) = 100 × (intraday highest rate - intraday lowest rate)/
intraday average rate
2) Day-on-day change (%) = 100 × absolute value of (closing rate for the day -
closing rate for the previous day)/closing rate for the previous day

Source: BOK

KRW3.0 and KRW2.1 recorded in the previous year. In the fourth quarter of 2008, marking perhaps the most volatile exchange rate period, the intraday variation and day-to-day variation soared to KRW45.2 and KRW29.2, respectively, recording the highest variation since the first quarter of 1998 (KRW48.3 and KRW31.2).

In addition to exchange rate instability, other factors such as ratings downgrades, pressure for early repayment, and spiraling borrowing costs were likely to make obtaining new loans even more difficult. Furthermore, there were concerns that banks could experience diminishing BIS capital ratios, thus setting off a curtailment of bank credit, which, in turn, would exacerbate effective corporate management and cause delays in economic recovery, among tertiary and quaternary flow-on effects.

The FSC put forward a proposal on December 22, 2008, that effectively improved accounting applications with regard to FX transactions, which would mitigate the risk facing companies vulnerable to extreme fluctuations. Enforcement of the decree began on January 14, 2009, with the amendment of the Corporate

Accounting Standards of the Korea Accounting Standards Board. According to the revised accounting standards, companies can revalue tangible assets, while FX translation gains and losses on financial products (including financial products in foreign currencies) can be placed in the equity column for listed and non-listed large companies. Furthermore, a so-called Functional Currency Rule was introduced for corporations conducting business operations overseas whose primary functional currency is also foreign. This new rule allows corporations to maintain their accounting books in the functional currency throughout the fiscal year and then convert the numbers in their financial statements into KRW at the year end. Non-listed SMEs, which already enjoyed far less rigorous accounting requirements, were also granted special accounting concessions applicable to foreign currency translations. That is, SMEs could close their accounts on December 31, 2008, as well as apply any FX rate during the year instead of the rate on the year-end date.

4. Intensified Corporate Restructuring Efforts

ESTABLISHMENT OF A CORPORATE ESTRUCTURING FRAMEWORK

Background

Following the failure of Lehman Brothers in 4Q 2008, there were fears that financial market uncertainties stemming from a credit strain and potential losses by financial institutions would negatively impact corporate liquidity and drive a slowdown in the real economy. As illustrated in Figure 2-37, the growth rate YOY

Figure 2-37 **SBL Growth Rates and Bad Debt Expense**

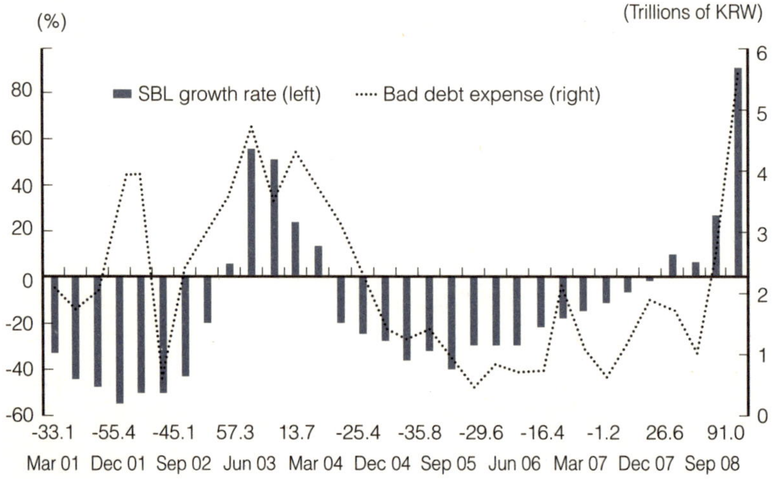

(%)   (Trillions of KRW)

- SBL growth rate (left)   ···· Bad debt expense (right)

-33.1 -55.4 -45.1 57.3 13.7 -25.4 -35.8 -29.6 -16.4 -1.2 26.6 91.0
Mar 01 Dec 01 Sep 02 Jun 03 Mar 04 Dec 04 Sep 05 Jun 06 Mar 07 Dec 07 Sep 08

Note: SBL growth rates are YOY, and bad debt expenses are listed on a quarterly basis.

Source: FSS

of domestic bank SBLs in 4Q 2008 stood at 91.0%, the highest since the financial crisis of 1998 and far exceeding even the 57.3% recorded at the peak of the credit card crisis (2Q 2003).

In the same quarter, domestic banks recorded a quarterly deficit (KRW0.5 trillion) for the first time in eight years (4Q 2000) due to an increase in loan loss provisions brought about by a rise in substandard or below loans. During 4Q 2008, a total of KRW5.4 trillion was newly set aside in loan loss provisions, including KRW1 trillion to cover the 16 construction companies/shipbuilders that were either under a workout program or close to exiting altogether. By the end of 2008, ROA recorded 0.47%, marking its lowest level since the Asian financial crisis in 1998, with the exception of the 0.17% recorded during the credit card crisis in 2003. In particular, the structured income ratio, which was suggested by the BIS in 2002 as an indicator representing a

Table 2-22 **Quarterly Net Income of Domestic Banks in 2008**

(Unit: Trillions of KRW)

	2007	2008				
		1Q	2Q	3Q	4Q	Cumulative
General banks	10.2	2.5	2.5	1.4	-0.3	6.1
Special banks	4.8	0.8	0.9	0.1	-0.2	1.5
Domestic banks	15.0	3.3	3.4	1.5	-0.5	7.6
LLP	4.5	1.6	0.7	2.5	5.4	10.2

Source: FSS

Figure 2-38 **Earnings Power Measurements of Domestic Banks**

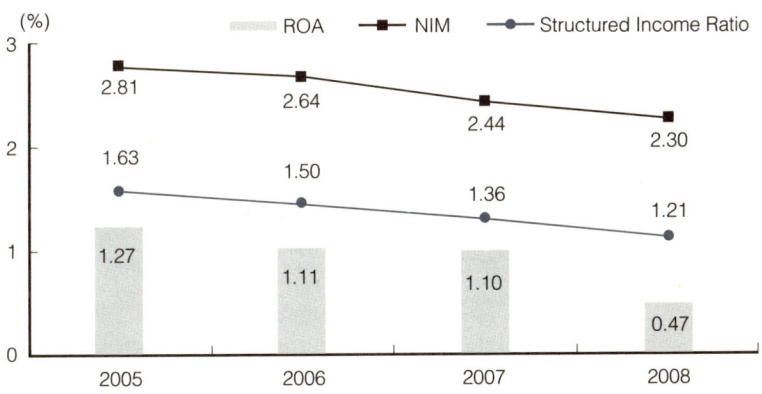

Note: Structured income ratio = (interest income + income from trust + fee income - sales and administration expenses) / total assets

Source: FSS

bank's ability to generate fundamental earnings, declined every year from 1.63% in 2005 to 1.21% in 2008.

Any prolonged economic decline was likely to worsen banks' asset quality and earnings power as growing bad debts continued to fuel uncertainties in the financial market. Hence, there was a need not only to improve banks' asset quality but also to address the anxieties and uncertainties in the market by implementing corporate restructuring promptly and in an organized fashion. The first step involved clearly identifying the appropriate restructuring method and flag-bearers. A concerted effort toward the restructuring of ailing companies ensured a stronger corporate sector that would eventually lead the Korean economy out of the global slowdown and ahead to the growth that would inevitably follow.

Corporate Restructuring Overview and Progress (Jan- April 2009)

On December 9, 2008, the FSC announced its "Direction and Framework of Corporate Restructuring" plan. Basically, the FSC stated that the restructuring process should be focused on reviving viable companies and promptly expelling non-viable companies from the market. Following the Asian financial crisis in 1998, a restructuring program was implemented across the board for all ailing companies. This time, however, the restructuring process was to be more focused and adapted at the individual company or conglomerate group level, or at the industry-wide level if necessary. At the same time, other financial support and restructuring measures initiated in the wake of the Lehman Brothers failure, such as the Fast Track Program and Corporate Restructuring Agreement, were to be simultaneously implemented for those companies experiencing temporary liquidity shortages.

In principle, corporate restructuring was to be autonomously implemented by creditor financial institutions, and a mechanism was put in place identifying specific roles for the Corporate Credit Support Task Force, Council of Creditor Financial Institutions, Creditor Financial Institutions Steering Committee and the government. The Corporate Credit Support Task Force is an organization jointly established by the FSC and FSS to support the efficient implementation of corporate restructuring and had already been launched on November 28, 2008, prior to the announcement of the new corporate restructuring effort initiative.

Figure 2-39 **Corporate Restructuring Procedures** (Announced on Dec 9, 2008)

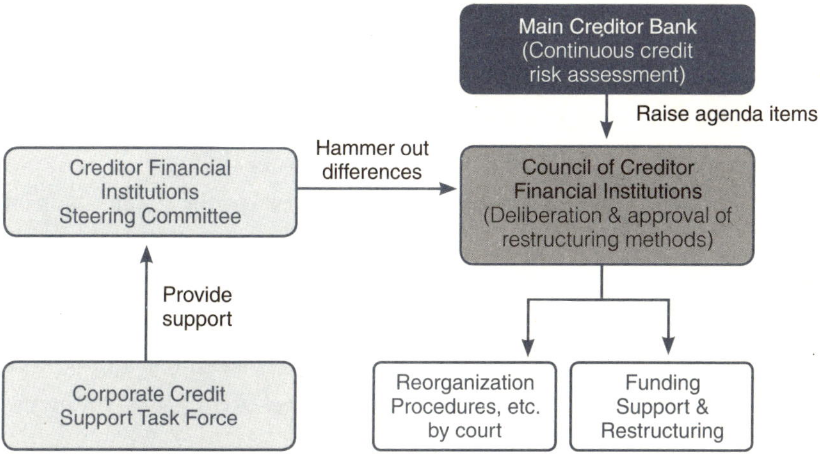

Source: FSS

This one-year temporary support group was established within the FSS and was scheduled to end on November 27, 2009.

Under this arrangement, the main creditor bank convenes a Council of Creditor Financial Institutions to discuss and decide upon the restructuring measures for each company concerned. Creditor banks classify corporate borrowers into "normal" (A), "temporary liquidity shortage" (B), "signs of insolvency" (C) and "insolvent" (D) through continuous credit risk assessments. The main creditor bank then formulates measures of financial support and restructuring, before finalizing them through consultations with the Council of Creditor Financial Institutions. The Creditor Financial Institutions Steering Committee can also provide input regarding companies experiencing temporary liquidity shortages as creditors request financial support.

Finally, the role of the government is to lay a legal and policy foundation to facilitate corporate restructuring and provide policy support.

Even though a broad framework for conducting corporate restructuring was established, it was difficult to implement on a large scale—unlike the mass reorganization that took place during the Asian financial crisis—because the companies in question were not clearly insolvent this time. Another difference was that the global slowdown would linger longer than the Asian financial crisis, limiting the effectiveness of temporary restructuring efforts in alleviating market uncertainties. On February 19, 2009, the government proposed more elaborate principles for corporate restructuring efforts at an "Emergency Economic Committee Meeting" presided over by President Lee Myung-bak following consultations with the relevant ministries.

The first principle involves continuous implementation of restructuring, led chiefly by creditor banks. It was therefore decided that the role of the Creditor Financial Institutions Steering Committee, a civil coordinating body, should be strengthened to ensure consistent and prompt restructuring. Furthermore, as shown in Table 2-23, the laws related to corporate restructuring prescribe that creditor banks should take the lead in the restructuring process of their borrowers. Specifically, the Corporate Restructuring Promotion Act mainly targets large corporations, while the Creditor Banks' Agreement focuses on SMEs. All construction companies faced with a temporary liquidity shortage are subject to the Corporate Restructuring Agreement, and the decision of whether or not to allow maturity extensions or provide new credit is reached after an assessment of the borrowers by the creditor group [Measures for Easing Household Burden and Supporting the Restructuring of and Liquidity Supply to the Construction Industry (October 21, 2008)]. These assessments by the creditor group determined that small- and mid-sized construction companies given A/B grades were subject to the Fast Track Program, and those given the C grade fell under the workout program.

The second principle put forth is that the market-oriented restructuring method, designed to encourage companies to engage in autonomous restructuring, should be undertaken in parallel

Table 2-23 Comparison Between Creditor-Led Corporate Restructuring Procedures

	Corporate Restructuring Promotion Act (June 2001-)	Creditor Bank Agreement (July 2004-)	Creditor Group Agreement (April 2008-Feb 2010)
Target Companies	• Companies showing signs of insolvency with credit of KRW50 bn or more • Large corporations	• Companies showing signs of insolvency with credit of KRW50 bn or less • SMEs	• All construction companies regardless of credit size
Relevant Basis	• Required by law (mandatory)	• Voluntary agreement	• Voluntary agreement
Member Financial Institutions	• All financial institutions; banks, insurance companies, securities firms, CFCs, etc. • KDIC, KAMCO, CRV, etc.	• 23 institutions including domestic banks, etc. • KODIT, KIBO Tech., KEIC, KAMCO, SBC	• 93% of all financial institutions • Banks (100%), savings banks (94.4%), securities firms (91.3%), asset managers (84.6%), CFCs (95.2%), etc. * As of Oct. 8, 2008
Coordinator	• Creditors Coordination Committee	• Creditors Coordination Committee	None
Overview	• Administered by creditors • Debt-to-equity swap, debt restructuring upon approval from 75% of creditors • Implement business normalization plan	• Similar to the CRPA • Automatic stay on creditors' claims on loans • Mandatory joint workout	• Waive creditors' claims on loans for one year • Decision to grant new credit made by each financial institution • Debt-to-equity swap, debt restructuring

Source: FSS, KFB

with creditor-led restructuring. This method includes support via capital market mechanisms such as the creation of funds for the facilitation of asset sales, equity investment, and other activities.

Third, the government should provide support to ensure that corporate restructuring proceeds speedily and smoothly. The roles of the government include the implementation of deregulation and tax incentives necessary for expediting autonomous restructuring. In addition, establishing a legal basis and setting up policy instruments would support such efforts as the recapitalization activities of financial institutions and the purchasing of substandard or below loans. Furthermore, the government decided to revisit the direction of economic restructuring policies and support measures from the perspective of overall industrial policy by lending greater consideration to their impact on industrial competitiveness and the economy as a whole.

Discussions on these aspects of corporate restructuring concluded that in 2009, construction companies and shipbuilders should be prioritized when assessing credit risk. At this time, the financial condition of construction companies was deteriorating due to an increase in unsold housing units caused by the sluggish construction and real estate industries. The business environment for shipbuilders continued to worsen owing to fiercer competition, slumping demand, KIKO losses, and other factors. Creditors conducted credit assessments of the construction companies and shipbuilders in January and March, respectively, and selected a total of 36 companies (16 for the first round and 20 for the second round) for restructuring.

In the meantime, the government formulated its Guidelines for Restructuring the Shipping Industry in March 2009 as business conditions in that sector worsened. Failures among shipping lines were likely to spread throughout the industry on account of rapidly falling shipping charges and other revenue. In accordance with the guidelines, a credit assessment of 38 large shipping lines with credit amounting to KRW50 billion or more was conducted.

Future Plans (As of May 2009)

Although corporate restructuring began in earnest in the second half of 2008, and construction companies, shipbuilders and shipping lines were the first to be subject to the restructuring process, questions were raised about the slow restructuring progress, and the limitations of creditor-led restructuring efforts in particular. For instance, creditors did not pursue the aggressive expulsion of ailing companies, in order to avoid having to sustain the loss. Also, companies that did not truly qualify under the original intent of the restructuring initiative were accepted into court receivership and other similar programs. Hence, conditions for more aggressive implementation of restructuring ripened in 2Q 2009 as the financial market began to stabilize and the laws related to corporate restructuring became increasingly fine-tuned. On April 30, 2009, the government released its Future Plan for Corporate Restructuring, which contained more intensive restructuring measures. The plan reflects the government's strong commitment to restructuring and identifies as its beneficiaries a diverse range of companies, including large corporations under business conglomerates, individual large corporations, SMEs, single office/home office (SOHO) operations, and construction/shipbuilding/shipping companies. Figure 2-40 illustrates in broad terms the corporate restructuring process based on company size and sector type.

① Restructuring by Corporate Size

Going by corporate size, main creditor banks completed the assessment of the financial structure of 45 conglomerate groups (with credit amounting to no less than 0.1% of the total credit extended by the financial services industry) at the end of April.

Figure 2-40 **Corporate Restructuring Framework and Future Plans**

* **Restructuring by Corporate Size**

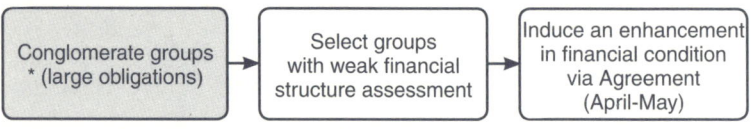

* With credit not less than 0.1% of the total credit by financial institutions

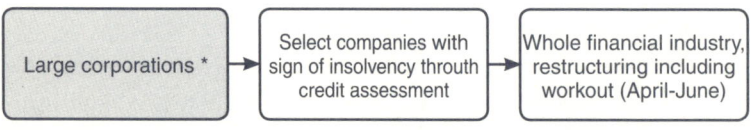

* With credit of KRW50 billion or above

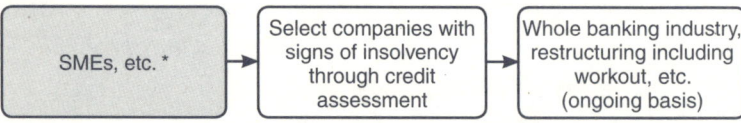

* Companies, SOHOs of less than KRW50 billion

* **Restructuring by Corporate Size**

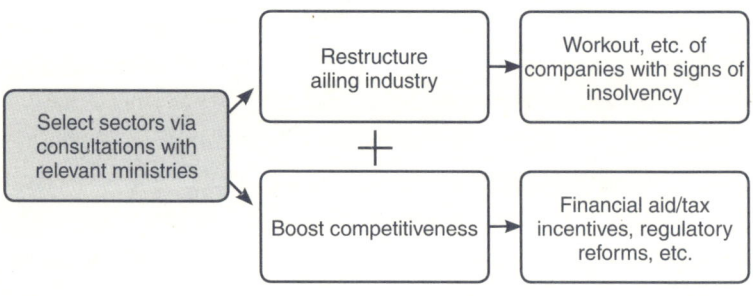

Source: FSS

Four creditors—KDB, KEB, Hana Bank and NACF—concluded the Financial Structure Enhancement Agreement with nine conglomerate groups that received a failing grade. The agreement contains specific target percentage points for debt-to-equity ratio, interest coverage ratio, operating income ratio, and other indicators that should be met by the conglomerate groups on a quarterly basis. It also contained detailed self-rescue measures such as asset sales (sale of subsidiaries/real estate, etc.), funding plans and repayment plans.

According to the Corporate Restructuring Promotion Act, creditor banks assess the creditworthiness of large corporations (with credit of no less than KRW50 billion) in the period of April-June every year, implementing the restructuring process based on their assessment findings. Financial authorities now ensure intensive restructuring efforts by exercising ongoing supervision of the assessment's progress, further encouraging creditors to conduct rigorous assessments. On June 11, eighteen creditor banks released the results of their credit assessments. A total of 33 out of 433 companies that underwent a detailed review were identified as Grades C or D and selected for restructuring. Among them, twenty-two C-graded companies were placed under a workout program led by creditors, and the remaining Grade D firms were to undergo business normalization through such means as applying for reorganization.

Meanwhile, the restructuring of SMEs had been under way based on the Creditor Banks' Agreement. Since the introduction of the Fast Track Program in October 2008 following the financial crisis, application of the SME workout program was extended to companies classified as C grade. Given the large number of SMEs and the limited information available for this group of companies, financial authorities eventually formulated an implementation plan for conducting credit assessments on SMEs in three stages, depending on the size of their credit (June 23, 2009, SMEs Restructuring Plan).

Among 5,214 companies with debt ranging from KRW5 billion to KRW50 billion and subject to an external audit, a total of 861 were confirmed as requiring a more detailed review based on credit assessments conducted by domestic banks. According to the results of the assessment released on July 15, a total of 113 companies (13.1%) were selected for restructuring, with 77 and 36 receiving

* SME Workout Program

There was a sharp increase in the number of SMEs selected for the workout program in the beginning of the second half of 2008. The total number of SMEs that went into the workout program in 2008 was 1,428, up 474 compared to 954 for 2007. This upward trend continued into 2009, and the number of SMEs newly selected for the workout in the first quarter of 2009 stood at 580, up 360.3% from the previous year (126).

Since the inception of the workout program in July 2004, a total of 7,267 companies went into the program through the end of March 2009. Of this number, 5,423 companies (74.6%) completed the workout, and 1,844 companies (25.4%) are still undergoing the program. Among the companies that came out of the program, 3,636 companies (67.1%) were successfully normalized. Though the operations of some of these companies worsened due to the financial crisis, the program allowed banks to manage risks proactively by identifying SMEs that were at risk but viable.

Progress of the SME Workout Program

(Unit: Number, %)

	2H 2004	2005	2006	2007	2008	1Q	2009 1Q	Total
Newly Selected	769	2,120	1,416	954	1,428	126	580	7,267 (100.0)
Graduated	144	322	1,161	1,010	771	154	228	3,636 (50.0)
Suspended	216	259	330	343	448	80	191	1,787 (24.6)
SMEs under Workout	409	1,948	1,873	1,474	1,683	1,366	1,844	1,844 (25.4)

Source: FSS

C and D grades, respectively. Creditor banks agreed to apply the revised Creditor Banks' Agreement to the C-rated companies and support their debt restructuring, assisting in their recovery.

According to the revised (July 3, 2009) Creditor Banks' Agreement, a creditor bank can implement the workout program without consulting the creditor banks. In the past, consultations with creditor banks typically took two or three months. Furthermore, in the event that the workout program is suspended as a result of a disagreement among the other banks regarding maturity extensions, the bank concerned has a priority claim on the new credit granted to the company in the program.

The companies subject to the second-stage assessment are those that have debt ranging from KRW3 billion to KRW5 billion and are subject to an external audit. Target companies will be selected by the end of July, and assessment will proceed until the end of September. In the first-stage assessment, target companies were chosen based on financial ratios such as cash flow from operating activities and interest coverage ratios. For the second-stage assessment, qualitative factors such as delinquency potential, attachments and other factors are incorporated as well.

The third-stage assessment is slated to proceed until the end of November 2009 for companies not subject to an external audit and SOHOs with credit of no less than KRW3 billion, as well as for companies requiring an external audit with credit of KRW1 billion or more. Smaller SMEs that are not subject to any of the credit assessments are immediately chosen for restructuring if something out of the ordinary occurs, such as continued delinquency or attachment.

② **Restructuring at Sector Level**
At the sector level, target sectors subject to restructuring are selected through consultations with the relevant ministries. For the

sectors requiring restructuring, support in terms of financing and tax incentives will be provided to strengthen their competitiveness and facilitate the effort to liquidate insolvent companies.

The focus of the policy is to ensure that construction companies and SME shipbuilders that have completed their credit assessments conclude the workout procedure as promptly as possible. Of the 36 companies (29 with a C grade and 7 with a D grade), five have completed the workout program, while nine are undergoing the program following the execution of the MOU as of July 3, 2009. Debt collection via auction, reorganization or other means is under way with the seven companies that were assigned a D grade. As for the companies that are potentially insolvent even though they were assigned a B grade or higher in the first assessment (based on financial statements as of September 2008), another round of credit assessments will be conducted based on the financial statements as of the end of December 2008.

For the shipping lines chosen for restructuring as a result of the credit assessment conducted at the end of April, restructuring and rescue measures are to be formulated in July 2009. In addition, a credit assessment will be conducted on the smaller shipping lines (roughly 140 companies) that are considered vulnerable to a liquidity crunch.

Table 2-24 **Progress of Workout Program for Construction and Shipbuilding Companies as of July 3, 2009**

(Unit: Number)

Due Diligence and Reorganization	Business Normalization Plan Finalized	MOU Executed	Workout Underway	Graduated	Total
9	3	3	9	5	29

Note: Based on 29 companies that were assigned a C grade. For companies under reorganization, workout procedures have been suspended.

Source: FSS

PROACTIVE RESPONSE TO POTENTIALLY PROBLEMATIC SEGMENTS: PROJECT FINANCE

Since 2005, financial authorities have been tightening supervision by adopting the 30% rule (PF loans should be limited to 30% of total loans), the Project Finance Loan Autonomous Workout Program (June 2007), and other measures to proactively address potential risks arising from a steady increase in real estate project financing. However, with the construction economy suffering from the financial crisis, project financing extended to construction companies by financial institutions is at greater and greater risk of turning into bad debt.

Accordingly, financial authorities conducted a complete review of 899 sites that were regarded as potentially problematic, backed by project financing extended by mutual savings banks from September to November 2008. The results of the review indicated that development projects likely to worsen account for 12% (KRW1.5 trillion) in terms of debt amount and 21% (189) in terms of number of projects. Countermeasures such as close monitoring, continued implementation of autonomous restructuring, and support for a normalization plan tailored to each site were put into operation. In connection with this, KAMCO purchased bad debt worth KRW1.7 trillion in two installments beginning in December 2008. As shown in Figure 2-41, the delinquency ratio of mutual savings banks, which stood at 16.9% at the end of September 2008, plunged to 13.0% at the end of 2008 thanks to the government's proactive measures aimed at ushering in a soft landing for project financing activities, such as the sale of potentially defaulting project financing deals.

The period of November 2008-January 2009 also saw financial authorities complete a review of 1,667 development projects backed by project financing from other financial sub-

Figure 2-41 **Real Estate Project Financing by Mutual Savings Banks**

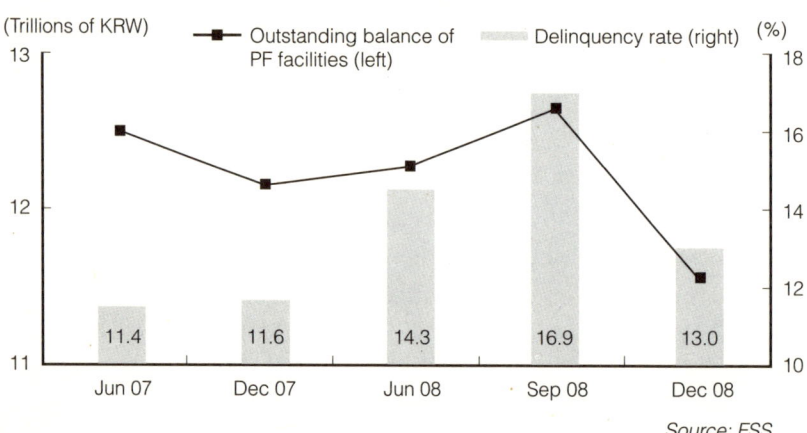

Source: FSS

sectors such as banks and insurance companies, excluding mutual savings banks. The results showed that the entire financial services industry, including mutual savings banks, had extended real estate project financing to a total of 2,443 projects in the amount of KRW81.7 trillion as of September 2008. By sub-sector, a total of 1,263 loans (KRW50.5 trillion) belonged to banks, 899 (KRW12.2 trillion, as of the end of June 2008) to mutual savings banks, 158 (KRW5.3 trillion) to insurance companies, 270 (KRW4.3 trillion) to CFCs, and 157 (KRW2.8 trillion) to securities firms.

A total of 1,667 development projects worth KRW69.5 trillion were placed under review and classified into three grades. About 60% (996) of the projects were classified as "robust," 30% (506) as "mediocre" and 10% (165) as "potentially ailing." In terms of the project financing amount, "robust" accounted for 59% (41.3 trillion won), "mediocre" for 34% (23.5 trillion won), and "potentially ailing" for 7% (KRW4.7 trillion). Robust projects refer to those that have a strong earnings capacity and are progressing smoothly despite recessionary economic conditions.

Table 2-25 **Development Projects as of End of September 2008 and Earnings Capacity Study Results**

(Unit: Number, Trillions of KRW)

Category	Robust	Mediocre	Potentially Ailing	Total
No. of Sites	996 (60%)	506 (30%)	165 (10%)	1,667 (100%)
Amount	41.3 (59%)	23.5 (34%)	4.7 (7%)	69.5 (100%)

Note: 1) KRW81.7 trillion (2,443 sites) when including projects backed by mutual savings banks (KRW12.2 trillion, 899 projects as of the end of June 2008).
2) Based on the loan amount of each financial institution. Figures in parentheses indicate share percentage for each classification category.

Source: FSS

"Mediocre" projects have a robust earnings capacity but have been clearly affected by the troubled market environment. "Potentially ailing" projects are those that have a weak earnings capacity and are experiencing severe economic setbacks.

Financial authorities responded to the results of these reviews by announcing countermeasures to prevent the further deterioration of bad project financing debt by inducing financial institutions to liquidate or normalize the projects involved (Results of the Development Project Reviews and Countermeasures, March 30, 2009). Also, KAMCO is to purchase project financing extended to those development projects considered at greater risk of default. It was also decided that projects classified as "mediocre" projects would undergo normalization through such efforts as the "Agreement on the Autonomous Workout of Development Projects."

5. Greater Support to Low- and Middle-Income Population

MEASURES TO EASE HOUSEHOLD BURDENS

The government announced measures to ease the burden on households as economic declines and other symptoms of the financial crisis began to compromise the repayment capacity of households. These measures allowed borrowers to extend the maturity and grace period of bank residential mortgage loans. Borrowers could switch over from a floating-rate loan to a fixed-rate loan without incurring a prepayment fee, alleviating their interest expenses. Furthermore, as a way to make up for the fall in the collateral value of residential homes, "collateral top-up" guarantees were initiated to provide a supplemental guarantee of up to KRW100 million for ordinary and middle-income households. Beginning in January 2009, the KHFC provided supplemental guarantees of up to KRW500 billion.

Conversion loans (transfer loans) allow the conversion of a loan with a high lending rate of 30% or more into a loan with a lending rate of around 20% backed by the Credit Recovery Fund. In December 2008, coverage of these conversion loans was expanded from loans valued at no more than KRW10 million to

---

* Extended Application of Conversion Loans Since June 2009

- Higher guarantee coverage: 50-90% → 100%
- Increased coverage of loans: Loans of 30% lending rate or higher → Loans of 20% lending rate or higher
- Loosened requirements: Must be delinquent for 25 days or more in the last six months → delinquent for 30 days or more in the last three months
- Extended repayment terms: Up to three years → Up to five years

Source: FSC

those of up to KRW30 million won. Six banks had joined this conversion loan program as of May 2009, and a total of 5,600 people were able to convert their loans from a sub-prime lender, mutual savings bank, or installment financing company to a loan from a bank backed by a Credit Recovery Fund guarantee. Since June, the benefits of the conversion loans have been expanded to include higher guarantee coverage, increased coverage of loans, and extended repayment terms. This extended application of the conversion loan program is expected to support financially strapped households with low credit lines by curtailing their interest rates to the 9.5-13.5% range.

SUPPORT FOR THE UNDERPRIVILEGED AND OTHER MEASURES

The FSC formulated comprehensive measures to support the financially underprivileged in July 2008, prior to the financial crisis. As shown in Figure 2-42 below, measures included support for credit restoration, relief from high lending rates, facilitation of self-support, relief from illegal debt collection activities, and financial education.

In the meantime, the government also reinforced existing comprehensive measures amidst concerns that the financially underprivileged would face greater difficulties owing to the financial crisis. The Microfinance Foundation budgeted KRW44 billion for the social welfare industry for 2009, up 63% over the previous year's KRW27 billion. This foundation is designed to assist the low-income bracket by granting unsecured loans for microcredit, which can be used to start a new business or obtain a job. Those with poor credit histories also benefit from the fund, as do CSR-minded companies that create jobs and assist low-income individuals in purchasing and retaining insurance. This foundation

Figure 2-42 Overview of Comprehensive Measures for the Underprivileged

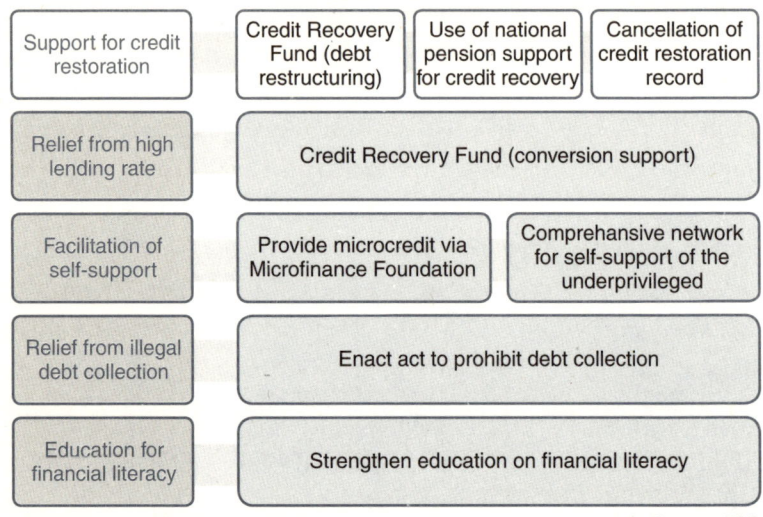

Support for credit restoration	Credit Recovery Fund (debt restructuring)	Use of national pension support for credit recovery	Cancellation of credit restoration record
Relief from high lending rate	Credit Recovery Fund (conversion support)		
Facilitation of self-support	Provide microcredit via Microfinance Foundation	Comprehansive network for self-support of the underprivileged	
Relief from illegal debt collection	Enact act to prohibit debt collection		
Education for financial literacy	Strengthen education on financial literacy		

Source: FSC

was launched on March 27, 2008, and was financed with deposits in dormant accounts contributed by financial institutions in the aggregate amount of KRW27 billion in 2008. Of this amount, KRW18 billion was set aside for the credit restoration of credit defaulters, KRW3.1 billion for startups, KRW2 billion for CSR-minded companies, KRW1 billion for vendors in conventional markets, and KRW3 billion for micro-insurance businesses.

Furthermore, the government expanded the business scope of the Credit Recovery Fund to ratchet up support for the financially underprivileged. This fund was established within KAMCO pursuant to the government's overall policy of supporting the financially underprivileged and went into operation on December 19, 2008. It engages in activities such as debt restructuring through the purchase of delinquent loans granted to the underprivileged, payment guarantees for conversion loans (conversion of high-rate loans into low-rate loans), and the provision of financial education and information to the public. Debt restructuring was initially carried out under a pilot program applying only to borrowers of KRW10 million or less, but it was eventually expanded to cover borrowers of up to KRW30 million in 2009. Complementing this measure were the extension of conversion loan guarantee coverage, as well as more target loans, fewer application requirements, and improved repayment terms starting in June 2009.

The government also revised the Registration of Sub-Prime Lending and Protection of Credit Users Act (Sub-Prime Lending Act) and enacted the Fair Debt Collection Practices Act (Debt Collection Act) to strengthen legal protection for microcredit recipients. The revised Sub-Prime Lending Act (which went into effect on April 22) required that lending brokers as well as debt collectors register with the government as sub-prime lending businesses. Educating sub-prime lenders and lending brokers also became mandatory. The revised act prescribes stronger protection

Figure 2-43 **Operational Structure of Credit Recovery Fund**

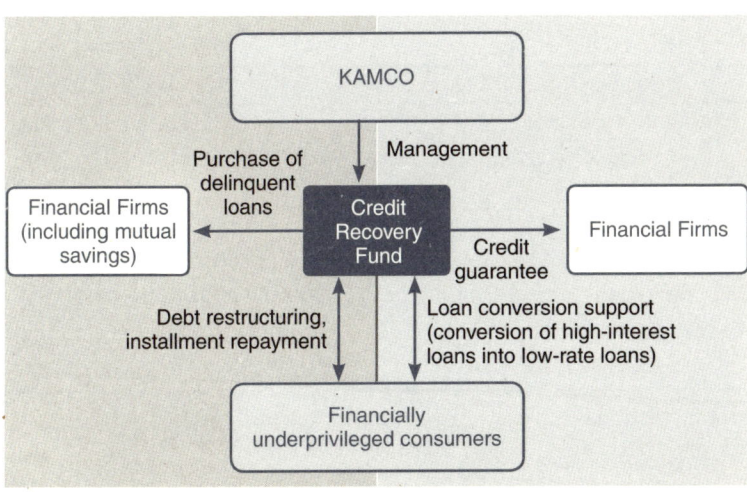

Source: FSC

for credit users and stipulates that any unregistered sub-prime lender that charges an interest rate exceeding the limit set forth in the Interest Rate Ceiling Act (30% per annum) will be subject to criminal charges. Apart from this, the sunset period for the maximum legal interest rate (60%) as set forth in Section 8 of the Sub-Prime Lending Act has been extended for 5 years from December 31, 2008, to December 31, 2013. The extension went into effect on January 21.

The government also enacted the Debt Collection Act, slated to take effect in August, to protect low income families and those with poor credit histories. Different provisions of the laws related to debt collection had been dispersed among several regulations, such as the Use and Protection of Credit Information Act (Credit Information Act) and Sub-Prime Lending Act, which had the inevitable effect of creating gaps in legal debt protection. The Debt Collection Act specifies illegal collection activities that are subject to punishment and prescribes the kinds of punishment imposed for such violations. Table 2-26 illustrates that among the

Table 2-26 Predatory Lending Counseling Center Inquiries by Year and Type

(Unit: Number)

Type	2004	2005	2006	2007	2008	Total[1]
High Interest Rate	872	479	387	576	605 (15%)	5,883 (22%)
Illegal Collection	551	374	295	450	679 (16%)	3,785 (14%)
Registration Advertising	7	483	254	244	360 (9%)	2,218 (8%)
Brokerage Fee	9	73	69	156	272 (7%)	775 (3%)
Other Improprieties[2]	410	484	510	348	313 (8%)	3,060 (12%)
Simple Counseling[3]	1,049	1,334	1,551	1,647	1,846 (45%)	11,037 (41%)
Total	2,898	3,227	3,066	3,421	4,075 (100%)	26,758 (100%)

Note: 1) Total indicates the summation of counseling sessions in 2001-2008.
    2) Lending fraud, unregistered/illegal operations, unfair contracts, etc.
    3) Provisional attachment, foreclosure, payroll garnishment, lending rate limit, etc.

Source: FSS

1,284 complaints addressed by the Predatory Lending Counseling Center, those related to high interest rates and illegal debt collection activities accounted for 31%.

The government also proposed boosting financial support for job creation. More specifically, the government is planning to provide financing and guarantees worth KRW12-13 trillion to those industries with the largest job creation effect via state-run institutions such as KDB, IBK, KODIT and the KIBO Technology Fund. The government is also encouraging job creation by encouraging financial institutions to offer internship opportunities to young adults.

6. BOK Monetary Policy in Response to Global Financial Crisis

Since the bankruptcy of Lehman Brothers, the BOK has responded to declines in the real economy stemming from the global financial crisis through various market stabilization measures aimed at easing anxieties in the domestic financial market.

LOWERING BENCHMARK RATE

To slow the decline in the real economy, the BOK lowered the benchmark rate on six occasions since October 2008, for a total reduction of 325bp (5.25% → 2.00%).

Table 2-27 **BOK Benchmark Rates**

(Unit: %)

Jul 10, 08	Aug 7	Sep 11	Oct 9	Oct 27	Nov 7	Dec 11	Jan 9, 09	Feb 12
5.00	5.25	5.25	5.00	4.25	4.00	3.00	2.50	2.00

Source: BOK

WON-CURRENCY LIQUIDITY SUPPORT

Increase in C2 Loan Limit and Changes to Target Recipients

As the financial situation for SMEs worsened due to falling domestic demand and tightened risk management by financial institutions—conditions expected to drag on for some time—one of the actions taken was to increase the C2 loan limit. The limit was raised from KRW6.5 trillion to KRW9.0 trillion in October 2008, and then again to KRW10.0 trillion in March 2009. Of the KRW3.5 trillion increase, KRW1.5 trillion was allocated based on actual support given to existing C2 loan recipients, while KRW2.0 trillion is to be applied toward supporting the SME Fast Track Program, which is aimed at helping companies mitigate exchange rate losses (losses from KIKO transactions) and other challenges. In addition, a basis for flexible adjustment of the C2 limit depending on financial and economic conditions has been established through a new provision to the effect that C2 loans can be provided according to the "actual support given by financial institutions" as determined by the BOK Governor with reference to target recipients.

Expanded List of Securities/Organizations Subject to Open Market Operation and Liquidity Support

Since Lehman Brothers filed for bankruptcy protection, domestic and foreign financial markets have exercised heightened caution, which has led to rises in short-term and long-term interest rates and a disturbance in fund flows due to relatively constrained credit markets, including that of bank debentures. As such, the open market operation policy was altered to bring stability to the financial market.

In addition to treasury bonds, government-guaranteed bonds and MSBs, the types of securities subject to open market operation were expanded to include bank debentures and some special bonds. A total of 12 securities firms were added to the list of institutions subject to repo transactions to help revitalize the bond and money markets. Furthermore, the purchase of long-term and non-regular repos (KRW16.8 trillion) and KTBs (KRW1.0 trillion) and the early redemption of MSBs (KRW0.7 trillion) were effectuated to expand the liquidity supply.

Fund Support to BMSF (November 24, 2008)
In addition to efforts to lower market rates through substantial reduction of the benchmark rate and various other measures to provide liquidity, a decision was reached to provide liquidity support of up to KRW5 trillion (within 50% of the equity investment made by financial institutions) to the financial institutions that financed the BMSF. The decision was intended to facilitate fund flow directly to the financial market. A total of KRW2.1 trillion in liquidity has already been provided.

Payment of Interest on Bank Reserves (December 3, 2008)
Interest on bank reserves amounting to KRW500.2 billion was paid to boost the financial strength of banks, thus enabling them to increase their capacity for greater credit supply.

Modifications to Collateral Policy and Lending/Deposit-Taking Scheme for Funds Adjustment (January 22, 2009)
Financial institutions can now provide credit papers such as promissory notes and exchange bills as collateral in addition to government and public bonds when borrowing from the BOK. Also, in an effort to alleviate some of the pressure in supplying collateral, the BOK extended the terms of loans intended for funds adjustment and loosened the requirements for adjusting interest rates on lending and deposit-taking. The BOK's lending/deposit-

taking scheme for funds adjustment is an extremely short-term lending and deposit-taking medium benefiting financial institutions and can now be used flexibly toward stabilizing the financial market.

Decision to Provide Recapitalization Fund Support and Grant Loans (Feb 25, March 26, 2009)

The Bank Recapitalization Fund will receive an infusion of up to KRW10 trillion in financial support to strengthen the capital of banks, providing them the ability to lend support to the real economy and corporate restructuring. The BOK will supply KRW3 trillion to this end. In addition, KRW296.6 billion will go to KDB, and the BOK will grant KODIT up to KRW430 billion to ensure that it is able to provide guarantees for payment of the principal and interest on loans already made or to be made by the Fund.

FOREIGN CURRENCY LIQUIDITY SUPPORT

Supply of Foreign Currency Financing Through Competitive Bid Swap Transactions (October 21, 2008)

The purpose of this program was to enhance the consistency and efficiency of the supply of foreign currency financing and to stabilize the foreign currency funding market. The program helped bring stability to the foreign currency financing market by efficiently supplying foreign currency funds in the form of bid swap transactions. Domestic foreign exchange banks were experiencing difficulties in securing foreign currency financing owing to the severe tightening of the global credit market. Through this program, competitive bid swap transactions resulted in a total of USD15.57 billion in foreign currency funds being supplied to domestic foreign exchange banks (Oct. 21, 2008–Feb. 17, 2009).

Lending Secured by Export Bills (Nov. 17, 2008)

In order to facilitate the supply of trade financing to SMEs, the BOK granted loans in foreign currency to foreign exchange banks, secured by foreign currency-denominated export bills. At the outset, the loan amount was determined based on the net growth in the amount at which the export bills were negotiated. As of December 1, 2008, however, loans were granted according to the amount of the newly negotiated export bills. The BOK lowered the lending rates by 20-30bp to give banks the incentive to negotiate export bills more and ease the burden on SMEs.

Execution of Currency Swap Agreements with Foreign Central Banks and Expansion of Currency Swap Volume

The BOK signed a swap agreement worth USD30 billion with the U.S. Federal Reserve (October 30, 2008) and extended loans to domestic foreign exchange banks totaling USD26.35 billion through a competitive bid (December 1, 2008-March 17, 2009). This currency swap arrangement was implemented as part of a global cooperative effort to ease the liquidity shortage in global financial markets and check the spread of U.S. dollar funding difficulties into economies with otherwise robust fundamentals. On February 4, 2009, the period of this currency swap line of credit was extended by six months from April 30 to October 30, 2009.

The size of the won-yen swap arrangement with the Japanese Central Bank was increased from USD3 billion to USD20 billion (December 12, 2008). This step was taken to mitigate the potential negative impact of anxieties in the global financial market on the two robust and well-managed economies, as well as to maintain stability in the regional financial market. The won-yen swap arrangement was also extended until October 30, 2009.

Finally, a won-yuan currency swap arrangement worth

Table 2-28 **Currency Swap Arrangements with U.S., China and Japan**

Counterpart	Limit	Support Type
U.S. Federal Reserve	USD30 billion	Unilateral support (won-dollar)
Bank of Japan	Equivalent of USD20 billion[1] USD10 billion[2][3]	Bilateral support (won-yen) Bilateral support (requesting nation's currency-dollar)
Bank of China	RMB180 billion Equivalent of USD4 billion[2]	Bilateral support (won-dollar) Bilateral support (won-dollar)

Note: 1) The swap line was originally equivalent to USD3 billion and has since been temporarily increased to USD20 billion until October 30, 2009.
2) Currency swap for crisis use under the CMI
3) Korea → Japan: USD5 billion, Japan → Korea: USD10 billion

Source: BOK

RMB180 billion (KRW38 trillion) was also signed with the Chinese Central Bank (December 12, 2008). This swap arrangement is separate from the bilateral currency swap currently in place, which had been signed following the Chiang Mai Initiative (CMI). Under the CMI, both countries agreed to provide support to the other in the amount of USD4 billion, or its RMB equivalent, if faced with a crisis.

Easing of Restrictions on the Use of Foreign Currency Loans and Repealing of Deadline Restrictions

On account of surges in the won-dollar and won-yen exchange rates in the second half of 2008, domestic SME exporters that had signed currency option contracts such as KIKO contracts and borrowers of working capital loans denominated in foreign currency faced severe difficulties. To put it simply, SME exporters that signed currency option contracts faced tremendous transaction or valuation losses, sparking concerns of more bankruptcies and, inexorably, triggering declines in the real economy.

Accordingly, the BOK allowed domestic exporters to take out foreign currency loans to pay for currency option products such as KIKO transactions (October 27, 2008). In addition, the BOK removed restrictions on the due date for repaying working capital loans in foreign currency (December 1, 2008). Two previous extensions of the repayment terms had failed to sufficiently alleviate the burden on borrowers who used won currency funds to pay the principal and interest on working capital loans—especially those who took out the loans in yen.

7. Government Fiscal and Economic Policy Response to Global Financial Crisis

The government's fiscal policy had been conducted in the larger context of effectuating market stabilization since Lehman Brothers filed for bankruptcy protection. Stabilization measures for the financial and FX markets were mostly conducted by the FSC and BOK. The government therefore undertook the overarching fiscal and economic policy challenges of preventing disturbances in the domestic financial market stemming from the global financial crisis and the decline in the real economy.

STRENGTHENING RESPONSIVENESS OF FISCAL POLICY TO ECONOMIC CYCLES

Government fiscal policy focused on addressing the drastic decline in economic growth and continued worsening of the labor market as the global financial crisis triggered a rapid slump in domestic demand. Naturally, reinforcing the function of fiscal policy in responding to economic cycles in order to reinvigorate the real economy became an important task for the government. Two broad approaches were the expansion of fiscal expenditures aimed at lending support to low-income groups and maintaining jobs, and greater tax incentives to induce greater private investment.

In this context, expansionary fiscal policy, in the form of tax cuts and increased fiscal expenditure, was initiated to maintain jobs and boost the economy. Oil reimbursements and oil price-indexed subsidies were provided to alleviate the pressure of high oil prices on the livelihoods of the most affected lower-income groups. The government passed a 2% reduction in income tax, reduced corporate taxes and implemented other tax cuts to maintain a positive ripple effect via job creation. Tax benefits were also increased to expand private investment in facilities. Temporary tax deductions for investment were extended by one year, and new investment in overpopulation control zones in the Seoul metropolitan area was included among the investments benefiting from such deductions. However, the tax deduction rate (standard level of 7%) differs between metropolitan areas (5%) and provinces (10%).

In 2009, a large-scale supplementary budget (KRW28.4 trillion) was formulated (April 2009) in the hope of giving the economy a much-needed economic boost. In particular, considering the expected "low first-half and high second-half" economic cycle, the goal of completing 60% of fiscal expenditures in the first half was set, and as of the end of May, KRW132.9 trillion out of the KRW257.7 trillion budgeted for major investment projects was actually spent (progress rate: 51.6%).

In addition, the government initiated efforts to expand the treasuries of the individual provinces and revise provincial tax laws to induce an increase in provincial government spending. It encouraged provincial governments to strengthen their self-funding efforts by, for example, linking intergovernmental transfers with the issuance of provincial bonds. In a bid to expand the coffers of the provincial governments, the central government provided support in consideration of changes in tax regulations such as the reduction of shared taxes for real estate, which resulted from the revision of the global real estate tax scheme. The government also encouraged autonomous expenditures from provincial coffers by adopting an across-the-board subsidy, as well as increasing support for the Special Account for Balanced National Development. As for provincial tax reform, provincial governments continued to enjoy autonomy in tax creation and the tax rates in their ordinances, depending on the size of their coffers and tax revenue sources.

In addition to the expansion of fiscal expenditure and tax reductions, other measures were implemented to revive the real estate and construction economies and the overall economy. The government revised policies—such as a reduction in the capital gains tax—that were mainly aimed at mitigating the problem of an excess supply of unsold housing units in the provinces. Overly stringent regulations that had been enforced to restrict speculation in land redevelopment, reconstruction and real estate were eased. Furthermore, measures were taken for KODIT to provide construction companies with guarantees of up to KRW30 billion on top of the company's payables for public construction work. This act was intended to provide liquidity support to the construction companies (November 2008) and give some relief to hard-pressed home developers who were delinquent in payment for land lots purchased from the Korea Land Corporation and forced to pay a default interest rate.

In an effort to induce greater investment through regulatory reform, the Korean government ensured that easing of the core regulations that had served as a bottleneck to corporate investment would lead to a noticeable expansion in corporate investment, FDI and job creation. Land use restrictions were rationalized to improve the efficiency of national land use, while the development of well-established living areas in rural, fishing, mountainous regions and small and medium-sized cities was pursued, with the aim of improving their residents' quality of life. Additionally, environmental regulations considered far more rigorous than those in other advanced nations were adjusted, and increased flexibility of the labor market was balanced against improvements in policies related to the employment of temporary agency workers and fixed-term workers in order to facilitate, for example, job stability among non-regular workers. Regulations in the services industry were also relaxed, with a reduction in entry barriers.

GREATER EFFORTS TO CREATE JOBS AND STABILIZE SMES AND LIVELIHOODS

As low-income families faced increasing difficulties amid the worsening employment conditions caused by the accelerated economic slowdown, the government implemented job sharing, internship programs for young adults, "Hope Work" projects and other such programs chiefly for Korea's less privileged population in order to promote job stability and alternatives to job creation.

To promote job sharing practices, the government increased labor cost subsidies to cover job sharing-related expenses such as training during paid leave and shorter working hours. Subsidies for training employees on paid leave alleviated the burden on SMEs of paying not only employees who are being trained but also those temporarily taking their place during the training period.

A total of 1,000 people benefited from this subsidy in 2009. As for shorter working hours, the government expanded support for those SMEs that increased their staff size with the early adoption of the 40-hour-a-week policy (KRW1.8 million per capita per quarter → KRW2.4 million; up to 10% of the employees prior to the shortening of working hours subsidized → up to 30%).

In order to encourage adoption of the internship program for young adults, the government provided a subsidy equivalent to 50% of the salary per capita to the SMEs that hired these workers as interns (original budget for 2009: 5,000 young adults → amended budget: 20,000 → figure finalized in the National Assembly: 25,000) and initiated a public sector internship program to provide jobs and career-building opportunities to unemployed college graduates (originally 10,000 → increased to 23,000). Furthermore, the government extended implementation of the hiring package program, whereby the unemployed are provided customized education and on-the-job training prior to being hired by a participating SME.

Furthermore, the government encouraged the adoption of shorter working hours to promote job retention by easing restrictions on the employment of part-time staff, as well as facilitating the adoption of shorter working hours for workers with young children. An employment support service was phased in whereby a job seeker would be given an assessment to determine a career path, followed by an evaluation of that person's skills and level of motivation before commencing intensive job placement efforts. In particular, the government focused on job creation in key social services such as child care, care and nursing for the elderly, and the care of the disabled.

In response to the funding difficulties experienced by SMEs, the government focused on the expansion of payment guarantees, the rolling-over of loans, and other supportive measures. The expansion of payment guarantees was made possible through entities like KODIT and the KIBO Technology Fund. The capacity for payment guarantees was expanded (KRW6 trillion) thanks to an extra contribution (KRW500 billion) to KODIT and the KIBO Technology Fund, allowing KODIT to increase payment guarantees (KRW1.5 trillion) in local areas. As for the extension of lending terms, the government aggressively induced banks to extend the maturities of the loans granted to SMEs in good credit standing with the execution of an MOU offering government payment guarantees for banks' liabilities in foreign currencies.

Support for micro-business owners, farmers and fishermen was reinforced through the provision of financial and social assistance from the government. Specifically, the Emergency Management Stabilization Fund was expanded significantly to offer relief to micro-businesses and farmers from temporary liquidity shortages. The number of beneficiaries increased from 14,000 to 29,000 businesses. Policy funding was also expanded to help farmers and fishermen (combined agricultural fund KRW1.3 → KRW1.8 trillion, farmers KRW2.9 → KRW3.6 trillion, and fisheries KRW1.6 → 1.9 trillion).

The government also strengthened support for low-income families and the homeless in the form of a supplementary budget (April 2009). Specifically, the government boosted unemployment benefits, provided job training assistance, and increased loans for low-income earners. Unemployment benefit recipients increased from 1.032 million to 1.126 million people, amounting to a net increase of 9,000 beneficiaries. The government broadened the qualifications for receiving welfare benefits and expanded support to include food, medical, and emergency welfare to low-income families. The number of beneficiaries receiving welfare benefits increased from 1.576 million to 1.586 million. Educational welfare was also expanded, in the form of more scholarships to college students and increased subsidization of interest payments on school loans. The number of people who qualified for welfare benefits and scholarships increased from 32,000 to 181,000. Interest subsidies increased from 3.15% to 4.00% for those with an income falling within the 30th to 50th percentiles, and 1.15% to 1.50% for those within the 60th to 70th percentiles. In terms of housing support, the government resumed the permanent rental home guarantee program (5,000 units in 2009), offering low-income tenant housing at 30% of the prevailing rental fee, as well as low-rate financing to support the purchase or rental of these homes.

EFFORTS TO IMPROVE ECONOMIC CONSTITUTION

The government implemented not only immediate policies to cope with these economic crises but also several mid- and long-term policies to prepare for the future amid the global economic crisis. A prime example of this foresight is ongoing corporate restructuring. The cardinal principle of this has been to boost the level of liquidity support to viable companies while inducing non-viable companies to exit the market as promptly as possible. A corporate restructuring plan was prepared with creditors—not the government—taking the initiative (February 2009), and the restructuring of ailing industries such as construction, shipbuilding, and shipping, as well as affiliates of large conglomerate groups, has been under way. Laws and policies related to corporate restructuring, such as the KAMCO Act, were revised in anticipation of a prolonged economic downturn, and the Restructuring Fund (KRW40 trillion) was established with the aim of purchasing substandard or below loans.

Measures to reinforce the competitiveness of the services industry were put in place (May 2009) for nine designated areas: education, digital content development, IT service, design, consulting, medicine, employment support, logistics, and broadcasting and telecommunications. The basic approach was to take the form of market openings, the promotion of competition via the rationalization of entry barriers and regulations, and the development of core competencies for large corporations. In addition, the government tightened disclosure requirements on management information, reinforcing performance evaluations and improving the compensation framework as a way to raise the level of competitiveness and accountability throughout the industry.

8. International Cooperation During Global Financial Crisis

Unlike the financial crisis that occurred across Asia in 1997-1998, the global financial crisis that occurred in 2008 was nothing less than planetary in terms of its magnitude and implications. It led the governments of many nations to recognize the need for international cooperation to overcome the crisis—Korea being no exception.

GREATER ROLE FOR G-20

In 1974, nations came together and formed the economic policy coordination group G-5. Variations of this group have since been created in support of the same principle of global economic policy cooperation for the welfare and advancement of all nations. The G-20, also made up of finance ministers, was established in the wake of the Asian financial crisis in 1997 to promote stability in the global financial markets and promote sustainable growth throughout the globe through intergovernmental cooperation. The importance of close cooperation between developed countries and emerging countries was highlighted again as the financial crisis in 2008 spread all over the world, and the ministerial-level talks were elevated to summit talks. The G-20 meeting has been held three times, laying a visible framework for international cooperation to overcome the crisis. As a member of the Chair Group (Korea chairs the G-20 in 2010), Korea is also making efforts to ensure that the G-20 summit talks establish a primary cooperative framework through which developed countries and emerging countries work together. The following section lays out the findings of the last two G-20 summit talks.

Washington Summit

The first meeting of G-20 leaders was held in Washington, D.C., on November 15, 2008, as global leaders discussed and reached a common understanding on the root causes of the global financial crisis, assessed the action steps taken, and discussed how to cooperate to overcome the crisis at hand. The leaders explored common principles for reforming the international financial system and set a future direction for that system, reinforcing the importance of the basic principles of free trade and market economy.

The G-20 reached several core agreements. First, recognizing the severity of the financial crisis, the heads of the participant nations agreed—in a rare occurrence—that they should employ macroeconomic policies such as intensive fiscal and financial measures to bring stability to the financial markets and inject life into the real economy.

Second, the group agreed on five common principles on the basis of which the world should work together to strengthen

Table 2-29 **Summary of 5 Common Principles**

Common Principles	Summary
Higher Standards of Transparency and Accountability	Tighten the rules for disclosing complex financial products and the financial condition of financial institutions; and improve incentive schemes to prevent immoderate risk-taking behavior
Enhanced Financial Supervision and Regulation	Subject all financial markets, financial products and financial institutions to regulations, and enhance asset quality and risk management functions of the financial services industry
Improved Integrity in Financial Markets	Protect investors and consumers, prevent conflict of interest among market participants and market manipulation by market participants, reinforce information exchange
Greater International Cooperation	Reinforce international cooperation between financial authorities and in cross-border capital transactions
Reform of the Global Financial Institutional Regime	Need to tailor the governance of international financial institutional regimes such as the IMF and WB to new developments in the economic status of emerging countries

Source: Ministry of Strategy and Finance

financial markets, and it discussed and saw eye to eye on 47 specific mid- and short-term steps to be taken based on these principles. The five principles are higher standards of transparency and accountability, enhanced financial supervision and regulation, improved integrity in the financial markets, greater international cooperation, and reformation of the global financial institutional regime. This consensus among the heads of participating nations led to a united effort to implement the Financial Reform Bill around the world. Specific procedures and the timeline for implementing these steps were to be decided by the G-20 finance ministers under the initiative of the 2009 G-20 Chair Group (Brazil, U.K. and Korea).

Third, strengthening crisis response capabilities by securing more funding and implementing an early warning system overseen by the IMF was discussed as a way to cope effectively with the financial crisis. The importance of funding was particularly emphasized to ensure a consistent effort to overcome the crisis.

Fourth, the need to caution against the spread of protectionism and adhere to basic market economy principles was emphasized. In this regard, participants reached an agreement to refrain from creating new barriers to trade and investment, undertaking new steps to curb exports, or implementing export promotion policies that are contrary to WTO principles.

The Washington meeting, the first-ever summit talks of the G-20 nations, was meaningful in that the developed nations and emerging economies gathered together to seek solutions for important and urgent issues affecting the world economy. Despite its short preparation period, the meeting culminated in agreement on many matters of significance, unlike previous summit-level talks.

Second London Summit Talks

The second meeting was held in London on April 2, 2009. Once again, noteworthy agreements were reached, and continuous progress was made on the issues raised in the first summit meeting. This meeting paved the way toward tiding over the global financial crisis as the leaders in attendance adopted a summit declaration composed of 29 points and three supplements ("Enhanced Financial System," "Financial Support Through Global Financial Institutional Regime," and "Action Plan Progress Report"). Four working-level groups put together a report on the implementation of the Action Plans as set out at the Washington summit. Major points of the agreement are as follows.

First, it was agreed that the member nations would actively pursue expansionary fiscal policies in close coordination with each other to expedite recovery of the world economy and employment. Although they did not agree on the actual size of the additional fiscal expenditures for boosting the economy, they did agree on a target of 4% growth of the world economy. It was decided that the size and timing of fiscal spending would be left to each nation's government, and an estimated USD2 trillion in fiscal expenditures would be spent around the world to prevent global economic declines. In addition, the IMF was officially tapped to regularly monitor the progress of fiscal policy implementations and identify actions as needed.

Second, there were several visible achievements in terms of financial regulation and supervision, primarily in the form of the establishment of a supervisory system through the expansion of the Financial Stability Forum into the Financial Stability Board, stronger regulation of hedge funds and credit rating agencies,

Table 2-30 Agreements on Issues Related to Financial Regulations

Issues	Agreements
Establishment of supervisory system	- FSF membership by all G-20 nations - Stronger authority of the IMF and FSB - Creation of the Joint Watch Group - Establishment of Early Warning System operated by the IMF and FSB
Regulation of hedge funds and credit rating agencies	- Disclosure of risk information regarding hedge funds - Mandatory registration of hedge funds and their fund managers - Mandatory registration of credit rating agencies - Standardization of credit derivatives - Establishment of sound compensation schemes
Regulation of tax havens	- Consensus on stricter regulations - Designation of tax havens
BIS Regulation	- Maintain the current level of BIS regulation - Tighten regulation in the expansionary phase

Source: Ministry of Strategy and Finance

regulation of tax havens, and stricter BIS requirements. In addition, it was agreed that an effort would be undertaken to stabilize the financial market by resolving uncertainties through quick handling of substandard or below loans. This agreement culminated in the adoption of the Common Principles for Coping with SBLs, in which Korea actively took part based on its experience during the Asian financial crisis.

Third, an effective system for checking the spread of protectionism was put in place. The number of protectionist measures adopted by the G-20 nations had actually been on the rise, and discussions regarding protectionism hit an impasse at the first G-20 meeting. Specifically, seventeen of the G-20 nations had adopted a total of 47 protectionist measures since the first meeting. Accordingly, at the second meeting, it was decided that the "name and shame" policy, as proposed by Korea, was to be implemented under the oversight of the WTO. Furthermore, in response to the emergence of this new issue, the consensus was reached that member nations should reject financial protectionism in the process of formulating and implementing fiscal and financial measures.

Fourth, it was agreed that financial support in the aggregate amount of USD1.1 trillion would be provided to crisis-stricken emerging markets. Trade financing would be expanded, and assistance would be provided to impoverished nations. A fund of USD750 billion, supplied to the IMF at the initiative of the U.S. and U.K., would be allocated and implemented for support to emerging markets. Of this amount, USD500 billion would come from contributions by developed countries, and USD250 billion by way of the issuance of special drawing rights (SDRs) by the IMF. Furthermore, the member nations decided to contribute USD250 billion for the Export Insurance Corporation of each country, World Bank and Multilateral Development Bank (MDB). These funds would go toward preventing a drastic decline in world trade with trade financing constrained by credit shortages. A total of USD10 billion, including Official Development Aid (ODA) funds, was set aside to support impoverished nations.

Fifth, the G-20 member countries agreed on the need to strengthen the functions of the global financial institutional regimes and reform their governance in line with changes in the world economic environment. It was also agreed that the IMF should reinforce its member country surveillance functions and early warning activities. In terms of the governance structure, the leaders agreed to adjust voting rights by 2011. If the IMF's governance structure is adjusted, the level of influence exerted by the U.S. is likely to shrink, while that of emerging economies like China will gradually increase.

The second London summit was meaningful in that it paved the way toward overcoming the global financial crisis by bringing to the forefront substantive results—instead of rhetoric—for resolving the economic crisis and improving the global financial system. Changes in global governance began to take shape as participation by the emerging economies became increasingly important with the crisis so widespread. Also, given that the crisis actually originated in the developed countries, overcoming it was beyond the capabilities of the advanced economies alone and required the cooperation of emerging countries. At this stage, Korea also demonstrated its expanding role through active participation in the formulation of the agenda with the U.K., which chaired the G-20 meeting in 2009.

STRONGER REGIONAL FINANCIAL COOPERATION

The need arose for coordinated policy implementation to restore financial stability in the East Asian region, which had been experiencing a decline in trade and investment across all nations due to the protracted economic and financial downturn. Accordingly, the CMIM (Chiang Mai Initiative Multilateralization) was agreed upon at the ASEAN+3 finance ministers' meeting held in Bali, Indonesia, on May 3, 2009. The CMIM is a multilateral extension of the existing CMI, which was launched in 2000 to prevent the recurrence of situations like the Asian financial crisis. The initiative sets out a bilateral currency swap arrangement between ASEAN and three Asian nations: Korea, China and Japan. The fact that the global financial crisis was caused by the U.S. sub-prime mortgage problem underscored the importance of regional cooperation and acted as a catalyst for bringing forth an agreement by ASEAN+3 for the new CMIM scheme.

Unlike the Chiang Mai Initiative, which was a bilateral currency swap between the central banks of two countries for a certain previously agreed-upon amount, the CMIM is regarded as a more developed international collaborative mechanism under which a joint fund with a certain amount is set up based on contributions agreed upon among the East Asian countries.

Since becoming the co-chair nation for the ASEAN+3 meeting, Korea has been striving to take the lead in discussions toward stronger regional financial cooperation. In this respect, Korea is

Table 2-31 **Shares of Key Economic Indicators Between Korea, China and Japan**

Counterpart	GDP	FX Reserve	Export/Import Volumes
Korea	9	7	18
China	43	61	55
Japan	48	32	27
Total	100	100	100

Note: GDP and export/import volumes are as of the end of 2008.
Foreign exchange reserve is as of March 2009.

Source: KIEP

also playing an active role in the CMIM. The biggest obstacle to the process of launching the CMIM was how to divvy up the burden of USD120 billion among the member countries. Allocations were made on the basis of GDP, foreign exchange reserves, export and import volumes, and other factors.

According to the final agreement, Korea, China and Japan were to contribute USD96 billion, or 80% of the total, while the remaining 20% was to be covered by ASEAN. The ratio of allocations between the three nations of Korea, China and Japan was 1:2:2; that is, Korea was to contribute USD19.2 billion while China and Japan each pledged USD38.4 billion. Korea played a major role in creating the crisis response mechanism by making the third largest contribution following China and Japan. Thus, it was able to exercise its influence in formulating regional financial policies.

Agreement on the CMIM amid continued global financial uncertainties and declines in the real economy was regarded as a significant symbol of Asia's improved ability to cope with financial

Figure 2-44 **CMIM Proportion to Total Contribution**

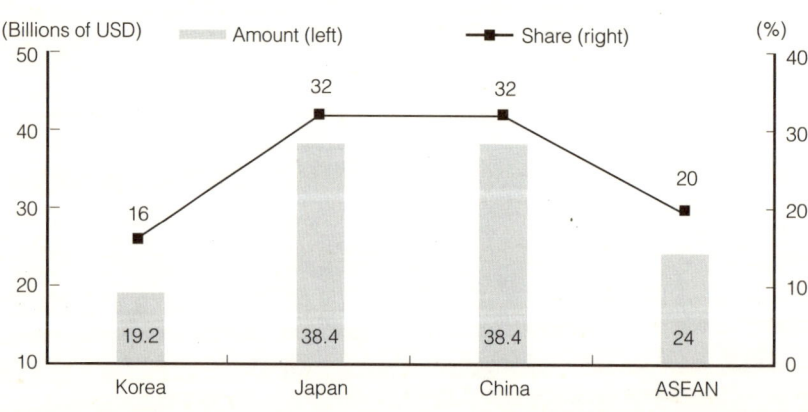

Source: Ministry of Strategy and Finance

crisis. In addition, the CMIM carries significant meaning in that it testifies to how regionalization of financial cooperation is taking place simultaneously with globalization of financial cooperation. The CMIM represents regional financial cooperation, whereas the G-20 discusses alternative solutions and implements policy actions at the global level.

Apart from the CMIM, ways to establish the CGIM (Credit Guarantee Investment Mechanism) for Asian bond markets were discussed in the meeting as well. The creation of the CGIM would in essence establish a mechanism for managing intra-regional capital flows and aggrandizing the size of capital flows within Asia. Asian nations have used income earned from their booming exports to purchase bonds issued in the U.S. and the Eurozone instead of bonds issued in Asia, thus not benefiting the regional economy as much as they could. However, the launching of the CGIM is expected to activate intra-regional investments by Asian funds, rendering the Asian region less affected by financial conditions in the U.S. and Eurozone.

Chapter III

LESSONS FOR CRISIS MANAGEMENT

1. Critical Importance of Preemptive and Decisive Stimulus Packages in Early Phase

DECISIVE STIMULUS PACKAGES

As discussed in Chapter II, Korean policymakers implemented large-scale fiscal stimulus packages in response to the global financial crisis, which are still being applied as crisis conditions persist. Implementing such packages was not unique to Korea; many nations with the fiscal capacity to implement similar policies did so as the crisis loomed. The following sections analyze the nature of the stimulus packages adopted around the world in an effort to extract what lessons can be drawn so as to better manage and break through crises when they occur.

A stimulus package should have certain characteristics (Spilimbergo et al., 2009). To begin with, fiscal spending should be carried out promptly and on a large scale. As mentioned in Chapter II, the Korean government set the goal of spending 60% or more of the 2009 fiscal budget in the first half and actually exceeded this goal in April 2009. Research has shown that budget execution at an earlier stage of the year has an even more potent effect in boosting the economy than execution of the budget throughout a year. According to a study conducted by the KIPF using a short-term macro-financial model, earlier budget execution would bring about an approximately 0.7% higher GDP, as well as greater employment by 48,000 workers compared to even budget execution. Considering the results of this study and the current pace of Korea's economic recovery—though it is not yet completely out of the woods—it seems prudent to implement a stimulus package promptly, in the early stages, and on a massive scale.

The importance of longevity in a stimulus package correlates with the long-term nature of the current global financial crisis. That is, this crisis will be vastly different from previous crises in terms of its severity and breadth, as well as the time needed for recovery. Many studies in macroeconomics have focused on the time lag between policy implementation and realization of its effects, or the "implementation lag." With the current crisis forecast to continue through the next several quarters, it seems the "time lag" issue will be of little importance. In this policy context, Korean policymakers are not letting up on their stimulus package efforts despite the frequent discussion of an exit strategy.

In addition, policy diversification is another factor that should be taken into account in the event of a future crisis. By definition, a crisis is a series of unprecedented incidents and conditions, as has been evident in the unfolding of the current financial crisis. Consequently, it is highly likely that the financial ratios of the past will not provide much information to policymakers as to which policies would be more effective in boosting demand. Therefore, more diversified policies should be developed to correspond with different possible courses that a crisis might take. In the end, a crisis situation compels us to think up ingenious policies that go beyond the existing theoretical frameworks. It is precisely this ingenuity that should be taken away as a crisis lesson.

＊Features of an Optimal Fiscal Stimulus Package

1. Timely: There is an urgent need for action.
2. Large: The drop in demand is large.
3. Lasting: The recession will likely last for some time.
4. Diversified: There is uncertainty regarding which measures will be most effective.
5. Contingent: Further action will be taken if needed.
6. Collective: All countries should use it, given the global nature of the downturn.

Source: Spilimbergo, A., S. Symansky, O. Blanchard, and C. Cottarelli, "Fiscal Policy for the Crisis," VOX, 2009.

In conjunction with these lessons, the following matters should be taken into account for future reference. To wit, preparation is key in guarding against a crisis—particularly in terms of financials. One of the prevailing characteristics of the current crisis has been the resilience of emerging economies—including Korea—compared to their advanced country counterparts in their ability to cope with the crisis. The painful experience of the Asian financial crisis allowed emerging economies to be relatively better prepared, for example with the stronger fiscal capacity that had been secured up until the recent crisis. In the end, these preparations translate into maneuvering room for applying policy tools such as a counter-cyclical fiscal policy that could minimize the adverse economic impact during a crisis outbreak. From this standpoint, the question of better defining such a sustainable level of fiscal reserves deserves further discussion.

MONETARY POLICY AND LIQUIDITY SUPPLY TO COPE WITH DOWNTURN

The recent global financial crisis caused an unprecedented global downturn and credit crunch. Accordingly, the monetary policy that various nations implemented in response to the crisis was on many levels groundbreaking. Particularly noteworthy was the prevalence of zero rates and other quantitative easing measures around the world. The adoption of zero percent interest rates was unprecedented at that point and was perceived as symbolic of the severity of the global financial crisis. The central banks of many nations, including Korea, lowered their benchmark interest rates sharply to fight off the downswing, though not to the zero level. As of November 2009, no OECD nation had made any upward adjustment of its policy rates, owing to continuous uncertainties surrounding the future of the crisis.

While the implementation of these quantitative measures as a way to supply domestic liquidity and their innovative implications attest to the exceptionally drastic measures undertaken amid the crisis, an assessment of the motivators behind policies in EMEs reveal less sweeping conclusions. For example, other than the U.S., U.K., Japan and the Eurozone countries, many nations did not take the quantitative easing approach in providing more liquidity. This diversity in approaches speaks to the need for a more cautious assessment of economic policy-making during times of economic crisis: despite the common goal, each country needs to undertake police appropriate to its unique circumstances.

Korea took an indirect approach by considering various policy objectives in the effort to provide liquidity at home. For instance, the Korean government tried to enhance the loan supply to SMEs by way of increasing the C2 fund and adjusting its target recipients. Measures taken with the banking sector included paying interest on BOK reserves and improving policy instruments related to collateral and the like. These policies demonstrate how Korea strived to tailor its strategies so that they suited its own economic situation when the liquidity supply was raised as a major policy agenda for responding to the credit crunch that had engulfed the Korean financial market.

One insight that can be drawn from the effort of the EMEs to cope with the crisis in connection with the securing of foreign-currency liquidity is the importance of establishing currency swap lines. The Asian region is particularly vulnerable to drastic changes in foreign-currency liquidity, a fact that became painfully evident during this crisis. The root causes of the crisis that erupted in this region shortly after the global outbreak can be summarized into two occurrences: a credit crunch stemming from demand for the redemption of short-term external debts, and a shrinkage in trading volume owing to plunging global demand. As it became clear that the crisis was pandemic, foreign institutions predicted that Korea would be faced with difficulty in paying back its short-term debts and, as a result, experience a massive credit crunch. Hence, for the future, diverse currency swap lines should be put in place in the early stages so as to alleviate the impact of a credit crunch related to external debts. This decision alone could address the issue of excessive accumulation of foreign reserves, which contributes greatly to global imbalances, and having currency swap lines in place would go a long way in ensuring stability in market sentiment as well.

Chapter IV will discuss how establishing currency swap lines with major countries as an alternative to a proper currency and exchange rate cooperative mechanism, which currently does not exist, should be a priority task in guarding against future global crises. In addition, EMEs should make efforts to build up their trade financing activities for the sake of providing liquidity in the event of drastic declines in global demand. This effort holds even more meaning against the current backdrop of a protectionist trend that seems to be intensifying.

Trade financing is especially crucial from the perspective of the traditionally export-dependent EMEs in Asia. Policymakers should support trade financing as a driver of global economic revival, which will also enhance the interests of their own nation in turn. As mentioned in Chapter II, Korea's Central Bank supported trade financing in terms of the provision of foreign currency liquidity and, by doing so, played a role in accelerating the recovery of the global and Korean economies. In particular, this policy pulled off a quick recovery of the Korean economy based on exports and provided policymakers in EMEs with much insight into the global crisis.

FINANCIAL POLICY TO CONTAIN SPILLOFF INTO REAL ECONOMY

One important issue that emerged in the wake of the U.S.-sparked financial crisis was the inevitability of a slowdown of the real economy, thereby leading to the higher possibility of a long-run global economic recession. In this event, the Korean economy would have taken a significant hit, given that it was a partially open market. A proactive response was needed to prevent market anxieties from developing into a long-term economic recession.

Thus, along with the implementation of a proper mix of fiscal and monetary policies in anticipation of a possible downswing, as well as diverse financial measures taken promptly by the FSC, the Korean government put a lot of effort into short-cutting disturbances in the foreign exchange and financial markets and the spread of the financial crisis, that is, the outbreak of systemic risk. As the foreign currency liquidity situation of Korean banks became increasingly serious on account of the global credit crunch triggered by the Chapter 11 filing by Lehman Brothers, the Korean government took such measures as offering a payment guarantee for banks' external liabilities, supplying foreign currency liquidity, and concluding a currency swap agreement with the U.S. As the financial crisis progressed further, causing an increase in credit risk, and the issue of Korean won liquidity in the real economy became more noticeable, countermeasures such as the supply of liquidity and interest rate cuts by the BOK and the establishment of the Bond Market Stabilization Fund were taken. Furthermore, in order to guard against a possible long-term economic recession,

Figure 3-1 **Phases of Korea's Policy Response to Financial Crisis**

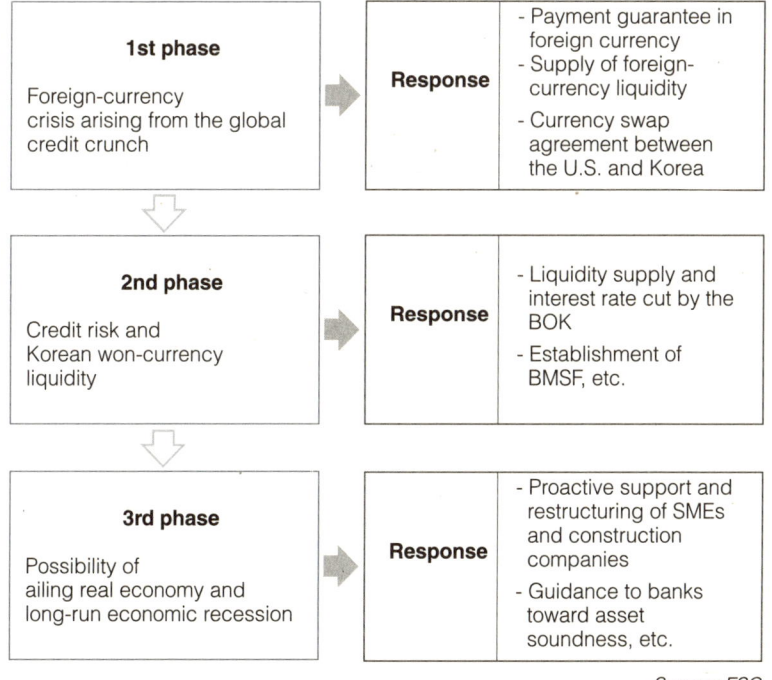

Source: FSC

the Korean government heavily promoted corporate restructuring and proactive financial support (e.g., the Fast Track Program) to address the potential eruption of insolvencies by SMEs, construction companies, and other vulnerable enterprises, along with measures to enhance the asset soundness of the banking sector.

One of the important features of the phased-in proactive measures taken by the Korean government to contain the spread of the financial crisis was the strengthened role of public financing in areas where market mechanisms risked failure (e.g., support for SMEs). To begin with, Korea expanded the supply of funds for 2009 from state-run banks such as KDB, IBK and KEXIM by KRW21 trillion (22.3%). In addition, the Korean government increased its equity investment in public financial companies such as KIBO Technology, KODIT, IBK and KDB in a bid to bring about an increase in credit supply. Based on these proactive

Figure 3-2 **Actual Funding by Korean Companies During Financial Crisis**

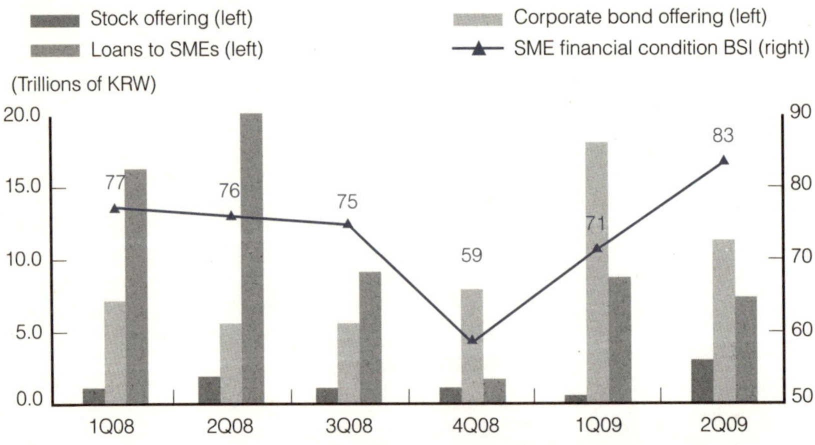

Note: BSI for SMEs is as of end of quarter.
Source: BOK, FSS

measures, the availability of debt payment guarantees for SMEs and micro-businesses faced with serious liquidity problems was expanded as well. By nation, Korea ranked second only to Japan in terms of expansion in the guarantee amount. According to IMF data, payment guarantees were increased by 1.8% of GDP, which was lower than the figure for Japan (5.9%) but higher than those of the U.K. (0.8%) and Mexico (0.4%).

Thanks to the government's timely and appropriate policy responses at the initial stage of the financial crisis, Korea's financial system is stabilizing rapidly, as evidenced by easing anxieties in the financial market, recovery of investor confidence, and other positive indicators. Default risk related to the external liabilities of Korean banks has been neutralized, and mid- and long-term borrowings in the first half of 2009 (USD14.02 billion) exceeded their level for the first half of the previous year (USD10.78 billion). In addition, funding conditions for the won currency,

Figure 3-3 **GDP Growth of OECD Countries in 2Q 2009**

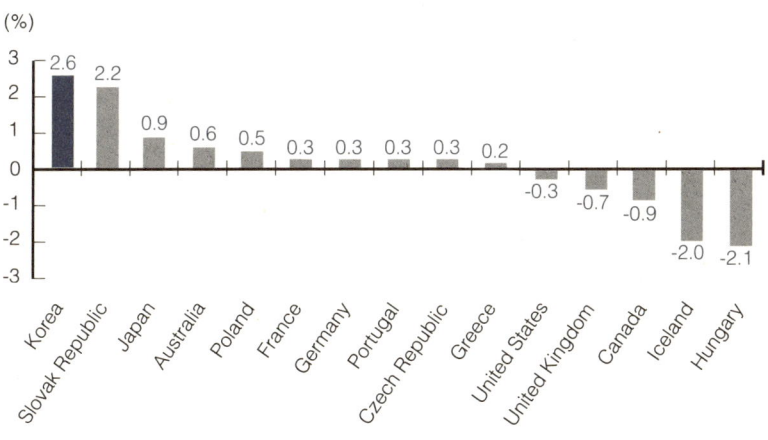

Note: Excluding countries without data for 2Q 2009, on quarter-to-quarter basis
Source: OECD

which worsened rapidly following the financial crisis, have greatly improved, as can be seen in Figure 3-2. In the case of SMEs, which experienced some of the harshest fallout of the credit crunch, financial conditions have nearly returned to pre-crisis levels.

Bolstered by the restored stability of the financial system, the economy is recovering quickly. Korea's GDP growth, which stood at -5.1% in 4Q 2008 quarter-to-quarter, turned over into positive territory at 0.1% in 1Q 2009. In 2Q 2009, Korea registered growth of 2.6%, the highest level among OECD nations.

2. Adhering to Principles and Discipline amid Crisis

GOVERNMENT'S CIRCUMSPECT CRISIS RESPONSE AND MINIMAL INTERVENTION

One of the important factors underlying the positive appraisal of Korea as a country that overcame the crisis successfully and achieved the highest economic growth rate among OECD countries for 2Q 2009 is the government's prudent crisis response and minimal intervention. Countries around the world formulated and implemented unconventional, intensive policies as the financial crisis showed signs of spreading. Against this backdrop, many voiced the opinion that Korea should implement measures that were either identical or similar to those undertaken by countries like the U.S. and U.K. For example, some argued that public funds should be funneled into Korean banks, and that there should be no cap on deposit guarantees. Armed with the belief that circumstances differed among nations, however, the Korean government maintained a tailor-made approach based on market principles and policy discipline instead of unconditionally adopting certain popular measures. Three prime examples involve the recapitalization of banks, the expansion of deposit insurance, and policies regarding mutual savings banks.

Banks are the primary players in providing credit to the market. Immediately following the financial crisis, banks experienced tremendous lending difficulties as they increasingly exposed themselves to credit risk within the aggravated financial environment. Their risk-averse positions, aimed at preventing further deterioration in creditworthiness, led to a shrinking domestic funding market. Furthermore, the BIS capital ratio of Korean banks, though exceeding the regulatory minimum of 8%, had been steadily declining since 2006 before dipping to 10.86% at the end of September 2008.

These trends gave rise to increasingly vociferous claims that public funds should be funneled into banks to increase their lending capacity and relieve the credit crunch. Given that the level of asset soundness and capital adequacy of Korean banks was not serious enough to warrant the transfusion of public funds, the Korean government approached this bank capital adequacy issue in three phases. First and foremost, the government induced Korean banks to adopt self-rescue measures in order to enhance their ability to provide support to the real economy and absorb or cushion against losses. In order to help banks accumulate capital on their own, the Korean government provided institutional support by, for example, expanding the portion of hybrid securities that could be recognized as Tier 1 capital.

However, Korean banks were not charged with undertaking this transformation without support; alongside this effort to encourage banks to adopt self-rescue measures, the Korean government created a bank recapitalization fund worth KRW20 trillion (KRW4 trillion was executed in 1Q 2009). Lastly, a legal basis was established for channeling funds even into healthy financial institutions through the formulation of contingency plans (e.g., the Financial Market Stabilization Fund) to provide against further asset deterioration.

The amount of recapitalization implemented by the banks between 4Q 2008 and 2Q 2009 based on these phased measures was tallied at KRW29 trillion in aggregate (banks' recapitalization: KRW25 trillion; purchases by the Recapitalization Fund: KRW4.0 trillion). The BIS ratios of Korean banks as of the end of June 2009 recorded 13.74%, marking 2.88%p more than the 10.86% recorded at the end of September 2008. In addition, the Tier 1 ratios of Korean banks rose 1.97%p to 10.30%, attesting to the significant improvement of their capital structure in qualitative terms. This figure put Korea well above the level equivalent to first grade Bank CAMEL ratings (BIS capital ratio 10%, Tier 1 ratio 7%). This level of capital adequacy shown by Korean banks is considered sufficient to absorb downward pressure on BIS capital ratios stemming from economic recessionary factors and corporate restructuring.

Table 3-1 **BIS Capital Ratio and Tier 1 Ratios of Korean Banks**

(Unit: %)

	2006	2007	2008				2009	
			Mar	Jun	Sep	Dec	Mar	Jun
BIS Capital Ratio	12.75 (12.31)	12.31 (11.95)	11.20 (10.97)	11.36 (11.16)	10.86 (10.66)	12.31 (12.72)	12.94 (13.40)	13.74 (14.25)
Tier 1 Ratio	9.15 (8.52)	8.97 (8.45)	8.22 (7.89)	8.54 (8.24)	8.33 (8.24)	8.84 (9.01)	9.51 (9.72)	10.30 (10.50)

Note: 1) Based on Basel I for 2006 and 2007, and Basel II for 2008 and 2009
 2) Figures in parentheses based on general banks
 (commercial banks + local banks)

Source: FSS

The second example pertains to the expansion of deposit insurance. In the wake of the Chapter 11 filing by Lehman Brothers, the U.S. and EU countries, in addition to nationalizing certain banks, expanded deposit insurance by the government in a bid to contain the spread of the global financial crisis. The U.S. raised the cap for deposit insurance from USD100,000 to USD250,000, effective until the end of 2009. The EU followed suit by raising its deposit insurance limit from EUR20,000 to EUR50,000. Germany, Iceland and Hungary went so far as to eliminate the cap on deposit insurance altogether. Among the Asian nations, Taiwan announced that it would guarantee all bank deposits in an effort to prevent a run on banks. Such fears of a mass exodus of deposits from banks as possible fallout from the financial crisis existed among Korean policymakers as well. Many believed that the Korean government should either increase the protection limit or remove the limit altogether.

Instead, the Korean government took slightly different measures. First of all, under the broad principle of international collaboration, it started to provide guarantees for the payment of external liabilities incurred by Korean banks. The Korean government chose the path of encouraging self-rescue measures as opposed to implementing nationalization efforts or increasing the deposit protection limit. A transfusion of public funds would have been premature given the relatively sound state of Korean bank assets. Nor were there any signs that a bank run was imminent. The possibility of a so-called ballooning effect, referring to market disturbances caused by a drastic shift of money from non-banking financial institutions to the banking sector, compelled the government to refrain from expanding the protection limit. In retrospect, the decisions made by the Korean government one year on from the outbreak of the financial crisis were appropriate.

The third example has to do with the way the Korean

government persuaded mutual savings banks to conduct autonomous restructuring amid increasing concerns regarding the asset quality of project financing. The revision of the Enforcement Decree of the Mutual Savings Banks Act was announced on September 26, 2008, and put into effect on September 30. This revision was aimed at improving the institutional instruments to facilitate autonomous restructuring so as to avoid having to intervene directly—particularly in the management of these banks. According to the policy measure, if an ailing or potentially ailing mutual savings bank is picked up by a qualified acquirer and becomes normalized, the acquirer is allowed to establish up to five branches outside of its usual business scope, depending on the amount of funds invested toward normalization. In addition, the government approved a special exemption that allowed these funds to be recognized as capital, assisting in the normalization efforts of the acquired mutual savings banks and extending the

Table 3-2 **Approved Stock Acquisitions of 4 Mutual Savings Banks**

(Unit: Billions of KRW , %)

| Applicant for Approval | Status of Acquired Mutual Savings Banks | | | | | | |
| | Bank Name | Stake Sold | Total Assets | Own Capital | | BIS Ratio | |
				Before Approval	After Approval	Before Approval	After Approval
A Mutual Savings Bank, etc.+B PEF	AAA	99.9	792.3	-80.9	31.1	-13.42	8.08
A Mutual Savings Bank, etc.	BBB	100	215.8	-22.4	12.6	-13.95	9.60
C Mutual Savings Bank	CCC	72.9	130.2	-28.5	7.5	-27.28	8.88
Five Affiliates of D Group	DDD	90.0	382.4	-94.1	3.9	-20.30	8.84

Source: FSS

business scope of the depository and lending institution. The receipt of public dues and bills would also be allowed. Meanwhile, the FSC approved the purchase of stocks in four savings banks in November 2008, marking the first case of autonomous restructuring undertaken since the revision of the enforcement decree. According to the FSC, three of the acquired banks were granted PCA (Prompt Corrective Action) waivers, while four had impaired capital at that time.

As these three examples illustrate, government intervention may be necessary, but it cannot be considered an effective crisis response by itself. In other words, governments must also take full advantage of market functions while maintaining confidence in the resilience of finance instead of artificially intervening in the market. The market, if left alone, has a way of correcting itself— much like the fire that broke out in Yellowstone National Park in 1988; despite its being allowed to burn, normalcy was eventually restored.

CAUTIONARY STANCE ON PROTECTIONISM IN FINANCE AND TRADE

One of the most important lessons of the recent financial crisis is in the way ordinary citizens, as much as financial authorities and policymakers, were given a painful lesson in the structure and characteristics of the global economy through economic hardship. In addition, the crisis witnessed the end of discussions on so-called "decoupling" with regard to EMEs. Up until the recent financial crisis, EMEs had been regarded as decoupled from developed economies. The crisis has shown, however, how the globalization of trade in goods and services, finance (in terms of the availability of credit and cost) and labor (in terms of direct/indirect demand for labor and transfers of labor income between nations) has linked individual countries around the world together in a historic and unprecedented way. Accordingly, the world has seen how a crisis occurring in the global economy or economic system and affecting major countries or groups of countries has immediate, adverse impacts on other nations as well.

Under these circumstances, some are of the opinion that the structure of the global economy, as represented by globalization. needs to be overhauled. It is true that a crisis, upon occurrence, grows to global proportions quite rapidly owing to increased integration of the world economy. It is equally true, however, that globalization brings with it benefits in economic terms to many nations and cannot be ignored, even though no decisive and quantitative evidence based on the cost-benefit model exists. Against this backdrop, any backlash against globalization may lead to a reversion to inwardly focused regionalism, self-seeking nationalism and overt protectionism. Many nations have revealed such tendencies in the form of policies in the areas of international trade and finance peppered with economic nationalism—albeit at a smaller scale—since going through the crisis.

A protectionist tendency in international trade manifests itself as a way of supporting domestic industries, which includes tariff hikes and foreign exchange policies. The "Buy America" measures adopted by the U.S. constitute one of the representative policies aimed at protecting domestic industries through expanded support for core industries. With tariffs, it seems the pendulum has swung the other way, as many nations find themselves tempted to raise them to compensate for their having been lowered to levels far below the maximum possible set by the WTO over the past decade. Furthermore, export policy based on the devaluation of local currency has been repeatedly raised as a problem. That is, some countries such as China and Japan are pursuing export growth by boosting price competitiveness through the devaluation of their currency.

As a protectionist tendency emerges in the domestic financial sector as well as in trade with other nations, the risk of holistic and economic nationalism continues to rise. Thus, credit availability to the financial sector and overseas has dwindled not only due to deleveraging and market-inherent risk aversion but also due to political considerations. For instance, some governments made it mandatory for local banks granted government aid to extend loans in their own domestic markets for the sake of injecting liquidity. If left to continue, this trend offers a dismal preview of the approaching situation for EMEs, as capital movement into the region is ultimately expected to decline drastically. Though these backlashes against globalization are likely to blow over with the revival of the global economy, they carry with them a lesson for overcoming future crises, namely that a crisis should be overcome at the global level.

Crises are inevitable. It also goes without saying that they are very likely to unfold at global proportions. Premised on these assumptions is the logical conclusion that pockets of protectionist policies adopted from a short-sighted perspective will only delay the pace of recovery. That is, the effort of an individual nation to extricate itself from a crisis under the structure of a global economy would act as a "negative externality" holding back the pace of recovery in other nations, which in turn would end up slackening the pace of recovery in that nation. This is a classic example of the kind of coordination failure and ensuing decline in overall welfare cited by economists.

In this respect, the G-20 summit efforts that have been under way since the crisis are proceeding in the right direction vis-à-vis international cooperation as a medium for realizing a turnaround in the crisis and banishing protectionism. Section 4 discusses this issue in more detail.

3. Strong Leadership for Inter-Agency Cooperation and Public Support

ON-THE-SCENE LEADERSHIP BY A NATIONAL LEADER

One of the important elements in tiding over an economic crisis lies in pulling together societal resources in a unified effort to overcome the crisis. It is important that policymakers use the harnessing of capabilities and the establishment of cohesion as a foundation for policy-making, and that they marshal government resources behind such policy-making as the starting point for pulling together social capital. Ultimately, only unified cohesion in policy-making can bring about a concentrated channeling of national capabilities toward such a daunting goal.

With this objective, the Korean government established an Emergency Economic Planning Committee under the direct control of President Lee Myung-bak in the immediate wake of the crisis. Its core members include the Minister of Strategy and Finance, FSC chairman, BOK governor, Presidential Special Advisor for Economic Affairs and Chief Presidential Economic Secretary. The composition of the committee speaks to the way the Korean government has strived to ensure inter-agency cooperation and maintain policy consistency, important elements in preventing market disturbances and sending a strong signal to the market. The Emergency Economic Planning Committee built a "war room" in an underground bunker containing four teams: the General Planning/Macro-Economy Team, Real Economy/SME Team, Financial/Restructuring Team, and Job Creation/Social Safety Net Team. As the names of the four teams suggest, these four assignments functioned as the Korean government's agenda for overcoming the crisis. Figure 3-4 illustrates the organization chart of the Emergency Economic Planning Committee.

The basic philosophy of the Emergency Economic Planning Committee boils down to "on-the-scene accommodation of the perceived economy." The formation of this committee attests to the national leader's strong determination to overcome the crisis. President Lee emphasized the importance of inter-agency cooperation and the measures that should be established to reflect accurately the "perceived economy," such as the difficulties experienced by SMEs, low-income households and other groups. That is, President Lee highlighted the importance of formulating "on-the-scene" measures without relying solely on statistics or other one-dimensional analytical methods in an effort to overcome the economic crisis.

With the benefit of hindsight, the prevention of market disturbances and the formulation of on-the-scene measures

Figure 3-4 **Schematics of Emergency Economic Planning Committee**

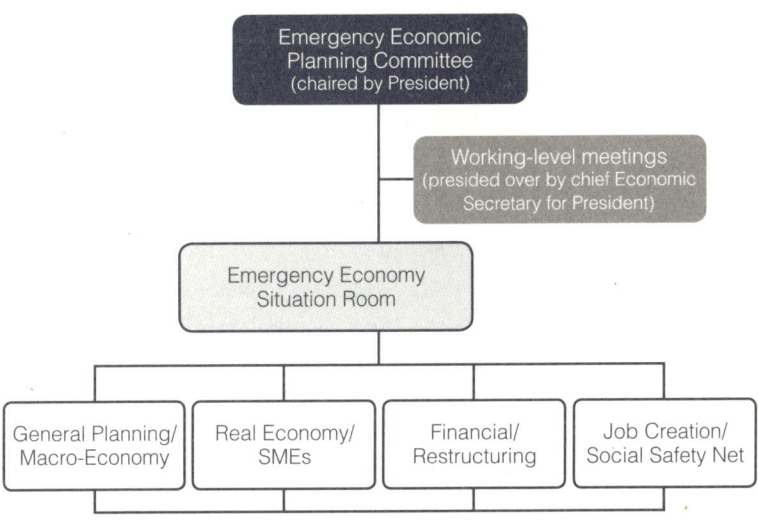

Source: Blue House

through inter-agency cooperation and coordination seem to have worked well as Korea's crisis recovery strategy, if one considers the pace of the nation's economic turnaround. The ultimate moral that we can draw from the Korean experience has to do with the cohesion of policymakers in bringing society together and the formulation of policy alternatives based on the perceived real economy as perhaps the most important imperatives in crisis management and remedying of the economy. .

STRONGER SUPPORT FOR THE LESS PRIVILEGED

Generally, a crisis of any kind is going to cause slower growth, leading to a shrinking job market and curtailment of wages and thus diminishing the consumption levels and welfare of society at large. The recent global financial crisis has generated the same outcome in many countries, irrespective of whether the country is a developed or emerging economy. According to ILO projections, some 30 million people are expected to lose their jobs by the end of 2009 in Asia alone. Reportedly, twenty million have already become unemployed in the Republic of China. However, these numbers are typically underestimated because of the trickle-down effect spreading through the value chain and then upstream to other industries—causing even more unemployment.

Adding to the severity of the situation is the fact that the intensity of the problem is more acute among EMEs than in developed economies. Whereas safeguard mechanisms are in place in developed economies in the form of long-standing social safety nets and welfare systems, poorer populations are more vulnerable in EME nations because they lack such buffers.

Before the crisis, EMEs had made great strides in poverty alleviation by maintaining continuous economic growth over a considerable period of time. This impressive run came to a

Figure 3-5 Ratio of the Poor and Vulnerable to Total Population in Asia

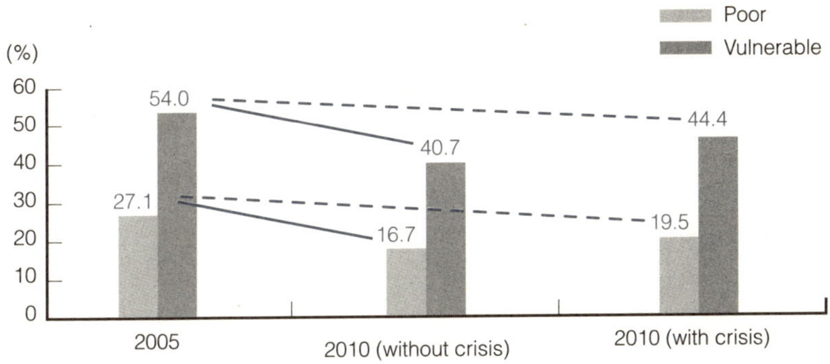

Source: ADB

virtual halt with the global financial crisis. According to research conducted by the Asian Development Bank (ADB), a total of 60 million people whose income would have soared over the poverty line—equivalent to a daily income of USD1.25—had the pace of economic growth prior to the financial crisis continued actually fell below the poverty line. If the current pace holds, the newly poor will increase to roughly 100 million by the end of 2010. If the impoverished population (daily income of less than USD2) is taken into account along with the poor, this number would be 80 million for 2009 and swell to 130 million in 2010.

Among the vulnerable groups, women laborers in particular are the most affected. Most of them are concentrated at the tip of the global supply chain in labor-intensive and export-oriented industries. Women workers are also two to five times more numerous than their male counterparts in the apparel, textile and electronics industries in Asia. Layoffs are most likely to begin with women workers as the first stratum of society to lose their jobs.

Under these circumstances, policymakers need to step up their efforts toward protecting the socially weak and strengthen social cohesion by providing support to the less privileged, who are the most vulnerable to a crisis upon its occurrence. As was reviewed in Chapter II, Korean policymakers have been implementing various financial and fiscal policies in a consistent fashion to achieve this goal. In particular, securing stable employment for these vulnerable groups was put forth as the most urgent priority. In Korea, the creation of jobs for young people was prioritized, and support for vulnerable industries and social strata such as SMEs, the self-employed, and agricultural workers was provided in a substantive fashion. Though it is important to protect the most vulnerable upon the occurrence of a crisis, the most vulnerable stratum of society may differ from country to country. Hence, there is a need to properly identify the stratum most in need, after which the most appropriate form of support can be provided.

4. Evolving Remedies for New Crises

NEED FOR INTERNATIONAL COOPERATION IN OVERCOMING CRISIS

One of the lessons learned in the wake of the global financial crisis is that policy coordination on a global scale is needed to cope with a crisis that arises under a global economic structure. The recent global financial crisis saw far more noticeable advances than in the past in terms of international cooperation in a crisis response. Namely, the G-20 meeting of finance ministers from different countries was elevated to a meeting of heads of state for the first time, clearly indicative of the level of awareness surrounding the important role of global cooperation.

Summit talks on the topic of international cooperation and a response to the crisis were held in Washington, D.C., and London in November 2008 and April 2009, respectively, with another round of talks held in September 2009 in Pennsylvania. As was reviewed in Section 3, Chapter II, the first two summit talks secured agreements on policy coordination, reconstitution of the international financial system, and a recognition of the importance of the basic principles of free trade and market economy, among other points.

Another fundamental lesson is that no substantive global response to a crisis can be achieved unless the agreements reached on agenda items at summit talks are binding. In this regard, the Philadelphia round of the summit talks seemed to be heading in the right direction. One of the agenda items was to review the progress of policies agreed upon in the previous talks. In lieu of any institutional authority, this kind of purposeful review constituted an enhancement in the binding power of future decisions reached at summit talks. Thus, the summit talks became one of the balancing factors in the stabilization of the global financial order. The other balancing factor is a new global regulatory agency, recreated from the global financial regime discussed in Chapter IV. Should the occurrence of future economic calamities be inevitable, much like the continuous roll of waves across the ocean, global coordination such as that witnessed during the recent financial crisis needs to be organized and solidified further to ensure global financial stability.

Apart from global coordination, the most significant lesson offered by the global financial crisis to EMEs is the significant change in the way the world views the usefulness of intra-regional cooperation—as attested to by the substantive advances made in this area. The multilateralization of the existing Chiang Mai Initiative (CMI) was the direct result of a unified global effort to emerge from the crisis. Despite a great deal of discussion regarding various long-term, intra-regional cooperative mechanisms to deal with exchange rate and currency policies, there have effectively been no substantive advances whatsoever except for the establishment of the CMI in the wake of the financial crisis in 1997-98. One of the primary reasons for this slow progress may be a low level of confidence over how much benefit a cooperative mechanism would actually offer, despite the increasingly compelling evidence surfacing on the need for creating such a mechanism.

It is both an irony and a blessing that many countries in the Asian region have learned this lesson through the financial crisis. This lesson should not be allowed to fade into oblivion once the world has extricated itself from the crisis. With the understanding that intra-regional cooperation is the only way to minimize the impact of the financial situation of developed countries on the rest of the world, it is essential to engage in steady and substantial efforts to create a more advanced intra-regional cooperative mechanism based on the lessons learned from this financial crisis.

It is important to understand that these various efforts toward intra-regional cooperation are not meant to deny the need for a cooperative mechanism between the EMEs and developed countries. Intra-regional cooperation is not about exclusive regionalism but about efforts in the broad context of international cooperation. Against this backdrop, considerable insights are offered by the establishment of diverse currency swap lines with the aim of breaking through the global financial crisis.

As was discussed in Chapter II, Korea strived to contribute to the establishment of an intra-regional cooperative mechanism by making the third largest contribution to the multilateralized CMI fund. Alongside this act, the Korean government also executed a currency swap agreement with the U.S. That is to say, Korea was able to dispel disturbances at home and abroad related to the liquidity risk in Korea's financial markets by executing this currency swap agreement immediately after the global financial crisis. In addition to their participation in intra-regional cooperative mechanisms, EMEs should strive to establish diverse cooperative schemes for liquidity enhancement alongside the U.S., EU and other countries in order to provide against a future crisis.

NEED TO RECONSTITUTE ROLE OF EMERGING MARKET

Another big lesson learned from the global financial crisis is an enhanced awareness of the status and role of the emerging market in the arena of the global economy. In particular, the growing role that the emerging market, with China at the forefront, played in overcoming a global financial crisis that was triggered in the U.S. and Eurozone and spread throughout the globe was an unexpected turn of events that prompted much thought regarding the role taken on by these nations.

Immediately after the crisis, China was regarded as the sole alternative for revitalizing the sagging global economy, given its size. As of 2008, it ranked third in the world in terms of GDP size and accounted for 6.4% of global GDP. Therefore, many economists and policymakers suggested that the Chinese market would provide a lift to the rapidly shrinking global demand—a scenario that to some extent did unfold as predicted.

A complete recovery from the global crisis can be achieved only after the economies of the U.S. and other developed nations have regained their footing. Nevertheless, it is indisputable that EMEs, with China at the forefront, were able to prevent a tailspin of the global economy and played a part in the current recovery. These economies are expected to pursue efforts to raise their stature and more accurately reflect their role in the process of reconstituting the global economy. In this context, it is easier to understand the objections China has been raising with regard to the debate over a global or leading hard currency. However, there is an important issue that should not be overlooked in this process, namely that EMEs can no longer push aside the concerns about "global imbalance" that were underscored by the financial crisis if they are to reposition themselves in the global economy.

Chapter I reviewed the issue of global imbalance as the biggest cause of the financial crisis. It is important to bear in mind the major lesson that global imbalance cannot be resolved without international cooperation, and that EMEs should therefore play a part in resolving problems in the process of reconstituting the global economic order. In this respect, EMEs, and most significantly China, should consider a drastic shift in their way of thinking on exchange rate policies and the current account. As is the case with any issue related to the international market, these problems are complex, particularly those applicable to China. Without establishing a more advanced cooperative mechanism for exchange rates and currency flows, the Asian region may not be able to end the foreign currency reserves cycle. That is, with the implementation of export-oriented economic policy based on exchange rate policy linked to the U.S. dollar, a surge in foreign reserves follows, potentially attracting another crisis back to the region. An important lesson to take away from this crisis is the need to move ahead based on a clear understanding of such risk and a strong determination to effect the necessary structural changes.

Chapter IV

LESSONS FOR CRISIS PREVENTION AND FUTURE AGENDA FOR SUSTAINABLE FINANCIAL DEVELOPMENT

It has been almost a year since the financial crisis touched off economic declines all over the world. Markets witnessed large investment banks like Citigroup and other seemingly untouchable institutions falling on hard times—to the point of having to receive government aid—as triggered by the bankruptcy of fellow financier Lehman Brothers in September 2008. As the crisis made its way through international financial systems, derivative instruments, which were once regarded as a means to ward off risk, became in themselves a risk factor that threatened the viability of financial institutions. Wall Street became less synonymous with top-notch talent, complex quantitative models, and generous compensation packages and more with greed, excess, and ultimately the epicenter of the financial crisis. Broadly speaking, the recent financial crisis should be traced back to the spread of financial capitalism vis-à-vis financial deregulation and globalization that began in the 1980s. Amid this backdrop, countries around the world put forth diverse emergency measures to tide over this financial crisis of unprecedented proportions and engaged in international efforts through concerted action.

There are many similarities between this crisis and previous ones, particularly in terms of causes and development patterns. The financial crisis this time around unfolded much like the one that followed the Great Depression—that is, it began with an asset bubble that formed in the wake of financial deregulation, followed by insufficient regulatory oversight and immoderate risk-taking, until the bubble finally burst. As economies evolve, however, so do their associated crises. Noteworthy is the fact that another financial crisis occurred despite the enormous efforts made by regulators in all countries to reform their financial systems and tighten regulations to prevent the recurrence of this very type of crisis. The lesson to take away from this experience is that it is not only important to have in place fundamental measures to prevent the occurrence of a crisis, but it is arguably even more important to know what measures to take to address a crisis outbreak promptly, decisively and effectively.

As long as immoderate greed for the quick accumulation of wealth exists in the minds of economic players, we cannot rule out the possibility of another financial crisis occurring. What is encouraging, however, is that this financial crisis affords us an opportunity to identify and review various issues either lurking below the surface or previously regarded as unproblematic prior to their emergence and to seek solutions to these issues. For example, some of the issues that have surfaced in the wake of this financial crisis and warrant further discussion include the dynamics between financial innovation and financial regulation, loss of confidence in the corporate and financial system, and uncertainties surrounding the future of financial capitalism and the global financial regime. Based on these discussions, this book puts forth five future agenda items aimed at minimizing the possibility of another financial crisis and contributing to the sustainable development of finance and economy.

1. Rebalancing Financial Innovation and Prudential Regulation

FINANCIAL CRISIS AND FINANCIAL INNOVATION

This financial crisis presents the challenge of killing two birds with one stone—that is, achieving financial innovation while at the same time maintaining the stability of the financial system via prudential regulation. More specifically, this financial crisis has been a testament to the critical need for proper regulation to accompany financial innovation. One of the consequences of the crisis has been the stigma that has formed in relation to the concept of financial innovation. Recent developments in innovative financial products like sub-prime mortgage loans, CDS and structured products have assumed a negative connotation as they have become symbols of the recent financial crisis. Once regarded as a solution to advancing financial development, these very products are now considered problems in need of resolution.

Nevertheless, no one can deny the role of financial innovation as a prime mover behind financial advancements. The U.S., despite being labeled the epicenter of the recent crisis, initially flourished as a pioneer in financial innovation. Deregulation began in earnest in the early 1970s when the scope of financial products provided to investors and competition among financial companies were tightly regulated. The abolition of the most representative regulations, such as Regulation Q regarding the interest rate ceiling and restrictions on branch opening, made possible the development and sale of diverse financial products and a greater supply of credit. Furthermore, the enactment of new government policies also set the stage for the creation of new financial products. One prime example is the development of the secondary mortgage market (asset-backed securitization market) through government-sponsored enterprises (GSE) such as Fannie Mae and Freddie Mac. Up until the early 1980s, the secondary mortgage market was so tiny that securitized transactions in the private sector were not recorded in the FRB's flow of funds accounts. As the OFHEO, a watchdog agency, tightened the capital requirements for GSEs in 2004, the issuance of residential mortgage-backed securities in the private sector surged rapidly. Thanks to the growth of the secondary mortgage market, lenders' access to funding and capacity for risk diversification improved, and the development of new financial products accelerated.

It should be noted, however, that, despite its positive effects, financial innovation, unless accompanied by appropriate regulation, can elicit a boomerang effect and come back in the form of a financial crisis. The recent financial crisis is a case in point. At the base of this crisis are changes in the business models of financial companies. Commercial banks in developed countries introduced the Originate-to-Distribute (OTD) model in response to global liquidity-related policies and other factors related to excessive liquidity that emerged in the 2000s and effectively made it impossible to generate adequate income based on interest margins. Unlike the conventional Lend and Hold (L&H) model of holding credit assets until maturity, this new model allowed banks to allocate (or transfer) credit risk to a variety of investors via asset securitization. The securitization of sub-prime mortgage loans that touched off the recent financial crisis also adopted this model. Ironically, the spread of the OTD model was driven by financial innovations such as the development of credit derivatives and the asset securitization market. In actuality, credit derivatives and asset securitization techniques allowed the creation of products with complex structures related to mortgage loans and afforded market participants higher rates of return and more frequent profit-generating opportunities. As shown in Figure 4-1, in the six years preceding the crisis the global volume of CDS transactions (based on ending balances) skyrocketed 6,666.3% from USD0.9 trillion in 2001 to USD62.2 trillion in 2007. Over the same period, the asset-backed securities issued and outstanding (including MBSs) in the U.S. (which accounts for roughly 70% of the global ABS market) increased 110.8% from USD5.4 trillion to USD11.4 trillion according to the Securities Industry and Financial Markets Association.

In spite of this, regulatory and supervisory regimes did not do enough to control the misuse and potential risk of these new financial products. In the case of the U.S., it became customary following the Great Depression for the government to establish

Figure 4-1 **Global Volume of Credit Derivatives (On the Basis of CDS)**

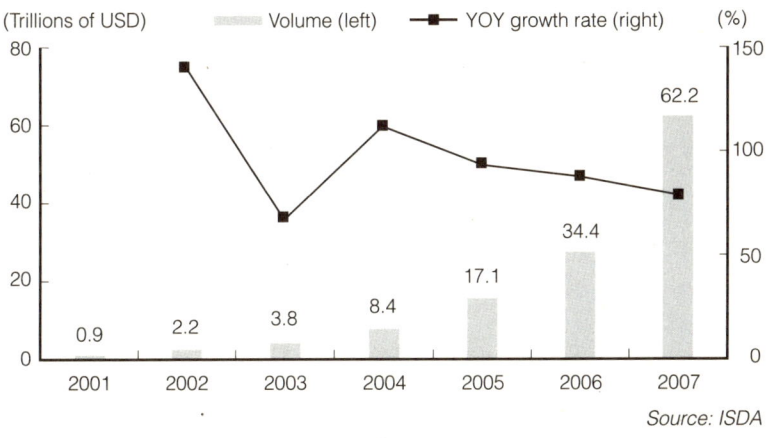

Source: ISDA

a new regulatory commission whenever a large-scale crisis called for one. As a result, various regulatory bodies ended up having overlapping responsibilities, leading to inefficiencies. Furthermore, oversight of major OTD model adopters such as hedge funds and mortgage companies was minimal at best. To make matters worse, the risks embedded in the complex structured products were not sufficiently appreciated amid the weak regulatory regime. Overall, the recent financial crisis was attributed mainly to the immoderate misuse of structured securities and financial derivatives under the overarching theme of inadequate oversight of innovative financial products.

However, this lack of oversight of financial innovation products does not necessarily justify the tightening of regulations. Ultimately, financial innovation has a positive impact on the further development of the financial system, the national economy, and consumers. Hence, supervision in the context of regulating financial innovation is not desirable. The bottom line is how well financial authorities understand and supervise the risk factors embedded in the process of financial innovation. A regulatory regime that takes into account the negative consequences as well as positive second- and third-order effects of financial innovation is necessary to help prevent a repeat of the recent crisis.

TOWARD BETTER (NOT NECESSARILY MORE) REGULATION

As mentioned in the preceding section, the purpose of regulation does not lie in obstructing financial innovation. Rather, the regulatory regime needs to be reconfigured to ensure that financial innovation can contribute to the transparency and further development of the financial system and the welfare of society. The danger is in misinterpreting the need to implement better regulation as a need to enact more regulation under the pretext of reconfiguring the regulatory regime. In other words, a regulatory regime that supports the stability of the financial system without restricting financial advancements and economic growth needs to be established. To that end, consideration should be given to raising the stability of the overall financial system and minimizing the side effects of financial innovation.

Raising Stability of Overall Financial System

The recent financial crisis suggests that macro-prudential regulation that takes systemic risk into account should be strengthened for the sake of stabilizing the overall financial system, although micro-prudential regulation is important as well. Most experts attribute the financial crisis to excessive risk-taking by market participants against the backdrop of a fragile regulatory regime. Particularly problematic was the failure of financial authorities, which focused on micro-prudential regulation, to oversee the so-called risk accumulation occurring at the macro level and across the entire financial system. The gap that existed between the regulatory scope of the financial authorities and the information necessary for such regulation was also a significant impediment to effective oversight.

One case in point is the failure to regulate the shadow banking system that encompasses investment banks (IB), special purpose companies, hedge funds and the like. In particular, regulatory gaps were formed when the Glass-Steagall Act, which was enacted in 1933 to separate the banking and securities businesses, was repealed and then replaced by the Gramm-Leach-Bliley Act in 1999. This act also gave rise to the concept of the financial holding company, which was allowed to operate diverse financial businesses such as banking, securities, and insurance indirectly in the form of operating subsidiaries. The act, however, did not clearly specify rules for large IBs such as Goldman Sachs, Lehman Brothers, and Bear Stearns, effectively allowing them to fall through the supervisory cracks of the SEC. Accordingly, the SEC set up a "consolidated supervised entities (CSE) program" on June 8, 2004, to patch up the regulatory loopholes. Being that it was a non-binding agreement premised on mutual cooperation between the SEC and large investment banks, the program was ineffective in terms of actual oversight. Under these circumstances, large IBs were able to obtain CSE qualification easily from the SEC and increase their assets via excessive and unrestricted leveraging activities.

The use of the structured investment vehicle (SIV), an off-balance SPC for securitization, was another primary factor in the insolvency of financial companies. SIVs also existed outside the purview of financial supervision. A prime example is Citigroup, which was effectively nationalized in February 2009 after expanding its assets aggressively via off-balance special purpose entities (SPEs) such as variable interest entities (VIEs) and qualifying special purpose entities (QSPEs). As of the end of 2007, prior to the occurrence of the financial crisis, the size of off-balance SPE assets, which was not accounted for in the consolidated balance sheet, stood at USD1.16 trillion, representing 53.2% of total assets. Part of the reason that Citigroup sought to expand its assets via these SPEs is that it wanted to capitalize on the regulatory arbitrage that arose in the transition of capital regulation from Basel I to Basel II.

Underlying the fragile regulation of the shadow financial system is the belief that only commercial banks that receive deposits need rigorous regulation, whereas the shadow financing engendered by financial innovation is not problematic as long as the market is able to function properly. The recent financial crisis, however, became a clear testament to how market discipline with regard to shadow financing did not function properly under loose regulation. Furthermore, as can be seen in the case of Citigroup, a regulatory regime that fully takes into account system risks stemming from the interaction between regulated and unregulated financial institutions was not in place. In the end, this failure to regulate translates into enormous moral hazard costs for taxpayers.

In addressing the problem of moral hazard—where private entities reap all of the profit while the public incurs the cost of all risk—the purview of regulation needs to be broadened to

* Use of SPE by Citigroup

Citigroup tried to expand its asset size while curtailing regulatory capital during the transitional phase from Basel I to Basel II, and this can be seen as an attempt to pursue regulatory arbitrage. From 2002 to June 2007, immediately before the spread of the financial crisis, the asset size of Citigroup had swelled by 102.6%. This increase was the result of the higher proportion of mortgage loans, which, under Basel II, enjoyed a lower risk weight. Accordingly, the proportion of mortgage loans to total loans, which had stood at 34.0% at the end of 2002, started to exceed 40% in 2005. Interestingly enough, the proportion of risk-weighted assets to total assets dropped to 52.6% as of the end of June 2007 from 63.5% in 2002 as the proportion of mortgage loans rose.

Citigroup employed two forms of SPEs to securitize its mortgage loans. As of the end of 2007, the asset size of VIEs stood at USD477.9 billion, up 211.3% from USD153.5 billion in 2003. Approximately 74.6% of VIE assets, or USD356.3 billion, was not included in the consolidated financial statements. Of the VIE assets not subject to consolidation, 42.7% (compared to non-consolidated VIE assets) constituted the maximum loss exposure that could impact Citigroup.

Asset Size of Citigroup's Off-Balance SPEs Related to Asset Securitization

(Units: Billions of USD)

	2003	2004	2005	2006	2007
SPEs (a+b+c)	807.4	1,143.3	1,445.3	971.6	1,286.1
VIEs (Consolidated, a)	36.9	35.6	50.4	42.1	121.6
VIEs (Important, Non-Consolidated, b)	116.6	135.8	191.4	388.3	356.3
˙ Portion of Max. Loss Exp.	**42.9**	**57.4**	**47.5**	**38.1**	**42.7**
QSPEs (Non-Consolidated, c)	653.9	971.9	1,203.5	541.2	808.2
Non-Consolidated SPEs (b+c)	770.5	1,107.7	1,394.9	929.5	1,164.5
Share in Total Assets	**61.0**	**74.6**	**93.4**	**49.3**	**53.2**

Source: Annual Report

incorporate factors that affect the stability of the overall financial system instead of focusing on soundness at the individual financial company level. In other words, though the soundness of individual financial companies is important, greater priority should be given to macro-prudential regulation to secure the stability of the overall financial system by preventing the system risk that might arise from changes in the macro-environment. In the end, the goal of macro-prudential regulation is to counter the tendency among companies to each take action, however reasonable, at the individual level, which ultimately impacts the overall system negatively.

According to the World Bank, macro-prudential regulation simultaneously takes into consideration business cycles (time-series aspect) and interconnectivity between individual financial companies (cross-section aspect). From the time-series perspective, the core issue of macro-prudential regulation is to ease the phenomenon of procyclicality. Especially in times of economic difficulty, as was seen recently, procyclicality of lending has a negative effect on the soundness of the real economy, which in turn triggers anxieties in the financial system. In order to head off this problem in advance, it is as important to maintain the level of capital in consideration of the business cycle as it is to secure a certain level of capital in absolute terms. Recently, policy means such as the introduction of the TTC (through-the-cycle) approach in determining minimum capital and the setting of the capital buffer in a manner contrary to business cycles have been discussed worldwide [Turner Review, Financial Stability Forum]. The TTC approach takes into account the business cycle instead of employing the credit rating at a certain point in time (PIT) when calculating the minimum capital requirement based on Basel II.

"Capital buffer" refers to the capital set aside in excess of the minimum required capital, and dynamic loan loss provisioning is one of the most representative examples of setting aside such a buffer. Dynamic loan loss provisioning is a mechanism according to which an additional loan loss provision, apart from general provisions and special provisions, is set aside depending on the stage of the business cycle. Under this approach, loan loss provisions increase during a boom period when the amount of bad debts decreases while the potential risk increases. Loan loss provisions decrease or become depleted in times of depression when the amount of bad debts increases and credit risk materializes. This approach was first adopted in Spain in July 2000 and is currently in operation there. Based on this approach, Spain's NPL coverage ratio has risen significantly since 2000 and stands at roughly 215% as of the end of 2007, far exceeding the ratios for the banks in other major advanced economies.

Figure 4-2 **NPL Coverage Ratios of Major Countries**

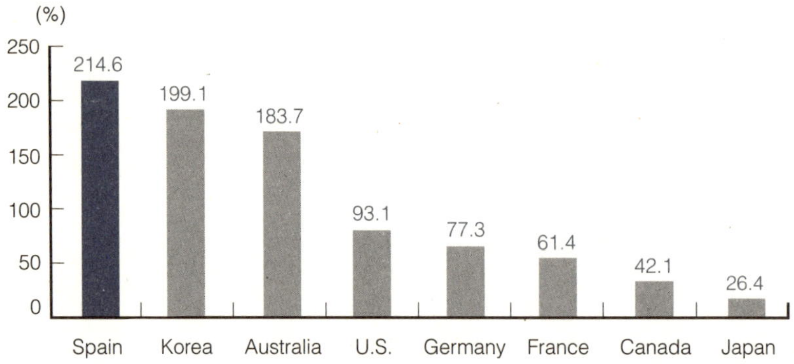

(%)

	Spain	Korea	Australia	U.S.	Germany	France	Canada	Japan
	214.6	199.1	183.7	93.1	77.3	61.4	42.1	26.4

Source: IMF

From the perspective of the cross-section, it is important to minimize the systemic risk that arises from the interaction between financial companies, financial products and financial markets instead of regulating liquidity, leverage, and other indicators at the individual company level. Measures that can be taken to that end include widening the regulation scope to incorporate financial companies, markets, and products that are important from the systemic standpoint; tighter regulation of liquidity; and mitigation of counterparty risk. Among these measures, the expansion of regulatory purview is absolutely necessary for preventing regulatory arbitrage, as was confirmed in the case of Citigroup. It is virtually impossible to prevent regulatory arbitrage entirely, since financial companies are always going to seek the means to get around regulations as they are newly enacted. Therefore, one alternative would be to enact regulations that would result in an absolute increase in cost or decrease in profit should financial companies try to get around them.

In the meantime, certain questions have yet to be resolved, including how macro-prudential regulation will proceed in actuality, and how this will apply to financial companies—in particular non-banking financial companies—that were outside the purview of supervision. In addition, the question of defining the relationship between macro-monetary policy and macro-prudential regulation remains. Establishing a macro-prudential regulatory regime will require specific designation of the discretionary rights of regulators, among other parameters.

Minimizing Side Effects of Financial Innovation

In order to strike a balance between financial innovation and financial regulation, there is a need for policy instruments alongside macro-prudential regulation that maximize the benefits of financial innovation and minimize its side effects. A close look at the recent financial crisis reveals that proper oversight functions and means of regulation did not exist to regulate the OTD model, which was used to transfer credit risk on a large scale. The reason for this absence has to do with the level of complexity involved in recently developed financial products such as structured products and CDS, as well as the financial services that use such products, making it difficult to value these products properly.

An analysis of this situation using informational economics reveals a conflict of interest among OTD model adopters and the limitations of imperfect information regarding new financial products. As shown in Figure 4-3, the main OTD model adopters can be categorized as originators, intermediaries, investors and third parties. Under the OTD model approach, originators can enjoy the benefit of transferring credit risk through securitization, whereas new types of information asymmetry and moral hazard prevention measures had previously been problematic.

Under the OTD model, originators that had a greater advantage in terms of information than their intermediaries had little incentive to monitor underlying assets and obligors, as they

Figure 4-3 **Basic OTD Model Structure**

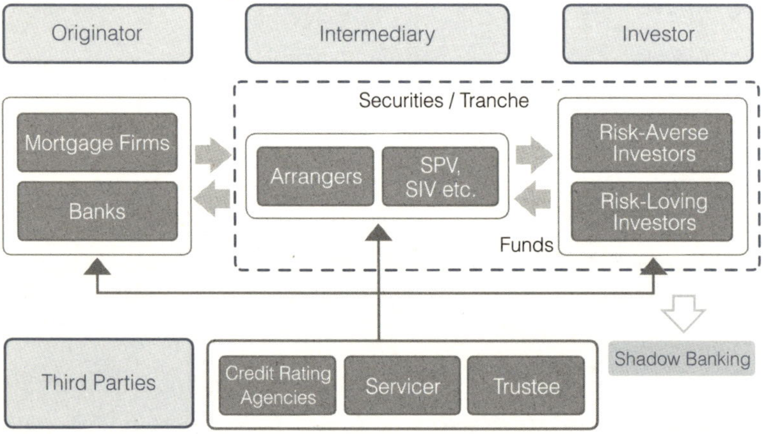

Note: Model has been simplified and is not an accurate illustration of the more complex OTD model.

Source: ECB, Chart 17, "The Incentive Structure of the 'Originate and Distribute' Model," 2008, edited for the purpose of this publication.

no longer held the assets on their balance sheets. Intermediaries designed products in accordance with what investors desired, or in riskier ways than were sustainable, in order to maximize profits, as opposed to simply providing services related to securitization. Credit rating agencies put the interest of intermediaries—from whom fees are received—before that of investors, who paid no fees. Furthermore, there was little information on the risks of new financial products such as structured products. Off-balance as well as on-balance items were not valued and reported, and the pricing process of structured products was not propounded in a transparent manner. On top of that, financial institutions were vulnerable to counterparty risk, as information on OTC derivatives was not sufficiently available.

Since new financial products are at the heart of the financial crisis, a regulatory regime needs to be established in such a way as to minimize conflicts of interest and information asymmetry. Tightening disclosure rules is an effective way to address these problems, as both stem from asymmetric information. Allowing investors themselves to assume some of the due diligence process that is currently carried out by credit rating agencies could alleviate information concerns to a certain extent. Managing an integrated database of market information for new financial products could also be a solution.

It is important to note, on the other hand, the possibility that tightened disclosure rules may lead to higher transaction costs, which could then cause shrinkage in the market for new financial products. In other words, the higher the level of bureaucracy in disclosure requirements and investment procedures, the lower the demand for such products. Accordingly, while it is imperative to head off systemic risk through tighter disclosure rules, policies aimed at encouraging transactions involving new financial products should also be put in place.

2. Rebuilding Trust in Corporate and Financial Systems

REDESIGNING COMPENSATION AND INCENTIVE STRUCTURE

Many experts point to the compensation and incentive structure of financial companies (IBs in particular) as one of the indirect causes of the financial crisis touched off by the U.S. sub-prime mortgage problem. In particular, the asymmetric compensation schemes of large IBs on Wall Street and the conflicts of interest arising from operating both CB and IB businesses speak directly to the weaknesses of the financial system.

First, the compensation scheme at most investment banks is identical to the typical profit and loss structure of a call option writer. That is, a fund manager or a trader who makes a big profit for the company is rewarded with a generous bonus or compensation. When this same individual incurs an enormous loss, however, he is not held accountable for the loss, other than perhaps losing his position with the company. Under this structure, an "agency problem" arises, as is the case with "risk incentives" on the part of shareholders—meaning that bank representatives will prefer short-term risky investments to long-term investments.

Actually, the management activities of the top five IBs in the U.S. immediately preceding the financial crisis can be characterized as "expanded investment in proprietary accounts through excessive leveraging." Previously, an IB had acted as an agent that earned fees and commissions in return for offering services such as underwriting of stocks and bonds and M&A consulting. Beginning in the 2000s, the top five IBs applied themselves to increasing their income through their own accounts through principal trading, principal investments (PI), and other services, made possible by excessive borrowing based on these investments banks' ample liquidity. Reflecting this trend, the leverage ratio (total assets/shareholders' equity) of the top five IBs surged to 29.0 times at the end of 2007 from 21.0 times at the end of 2001. As shown in Figure 4-4, the share of gains on trading through their own accounts to total income (an annual average of 31%) shot up to 42% in 2006 from 28% in 2001 before dropping back down to 27% in 2007, which still constitutes the biggest share in terms of type of revenue to total income. Excessive risk-taking on the part of IBs was partly attributed to a deregulation policy called the CSE program, referring to CSE-qualified companies that were allowed to increase their leverage ratios to 40 times, which the SEC implemented in 2004. The management behavior of IBs, which prioritized profit without proper regard for other factors, suggests excessive risk-taking arising from an asymmetric compensation structure as one of the main causes of the crisis for investment banks.

To prevent a recurrence of the financial crisis, it is therefore important to modify the compensation scheme that currently incentivizes excessive risk-taking. The asymmetric structure focusing excessively on earnings should be remodeled to promote better overall symmetry. Alternative incentives include a "restricted stocks" scheme wherein the sale of stocks given as an incentive is restricted for a considerable length of time. The "performance shares" program would delay the actual awarding of shares until the entire management target is achieved. A more fundamental solution would be to design a compensation scheme that ensures the long-term shareholder value is consistent with the enterprise

Figure 4-4 **Profit Structure of Top 5 IBs**

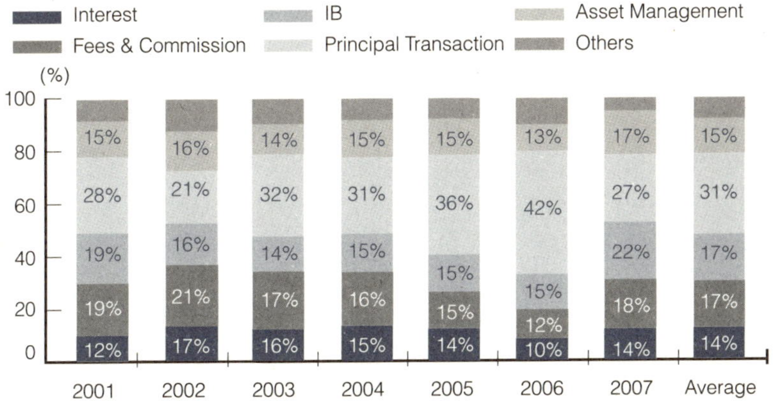

Note: Compared to total net revenue; average for 2001-2007.

Source: Bankscope

173

value. To that end, the level of compliance with risk management procedure and relative risk levels of business activities (e.g., risk-adjusted performance) should be incorporated into the compensation scheme in addition to each individual's financial performance. Without improving the compensation scheme, IBs will not be able to stave off the criticism that they benefit generously when times are good but rely on taxpayers to bail them out when they are faced with a crisis.

In addition to revising the compensation scheme for IBs, another task for policymakers involves addressing the conflict of interest arising from operating CBs and IBs together. It is difficult to define in one sweeping policy whether and how the operation of CBs and IBs should be separated, given the different phases of historical development in which these businesses exist in various countries. However, what has been evident is that simultaneous operation of these different businesses without clearer lines separating their modus operandi can breed conditions for a serious crisis. In particular, running these two types of business within a single corporate entity could engender a graver form of moral hazard characterized by immoderate risk-taking. This is because banks will naturally gravitate toward higher rates of return as long as the "too big to fail" myth persists, under the pretext of minimizing the social cost of an actual bank bankruptcy.

UBS is a case in point illustrating the problem of conflicts of interest stemming from the simultaneous operation of a CB and IB under one roof. Prior to the financial crisis, UBS increased its investments in high-risk, high-return structured securities such as CDOs for fear of lagging behind its major competitors like Goldman Sachs and Citigroup in the fixed-income area. As UBS took on a growth-oriented strategy, potential conflicts of interest between its CB and IB operations, as well as risk management issues, were put on the back burner. More specifically, the bank

replaced risk managers—or risk management practitioners—
with sales experts as a way to drive this new strategy. Despite the
existence of a centralized funding system, each business unit could
obtain funding at a price lower than market prices as the internal
transfer price (ITP) used for allocating capital to each business unit
was set at a level below LIBOR. Furthermore, the UBS internal
funding model was in itself asymmetrical. That is, business units
could obtain funding internally at a low price if the asset that
the business units acquired carried sufficient value as collateral,
and the business units with assets of lower value did not need to
pay a correspondingly higher price for funding. Compensation
schemes for senior management were also exclusively focused on
the achievement of performance targets, and not on performance
appraisal in consideration of funding cost. These structural
problems led to an increased risk appetite in pursuit of higher
growth. In the end, UBS accepted bailout funds worth USD59.2
billion in 2008 on account of losses stemming from its CB and IB
activities.

As can be seen in the cases illustrated, while the intended goal
of dual IB and CB operations may have been a synergy effect,
financial institutions must also be concerned about a possible
contagion effect. Not securing a proper level of separation between
CB and IB activities can jeopardize the entire organization. In
other words, instead of the CB side of the house assisting its IB
sibling during a crisis, and the IB profiting when the CB's income
drops, the IB's poor performance can spill over into the CB side,
resulting in a company-wide deterioration that could in turn mar
the stability of an entire financial system.

The recent financial crisis revealed a need to explore in more
depth the co-existence of CB and IB operations within a single
entity. It would be difficult to prohibit the practice altogether, with
financial services becoming more diverse and competition among

financial companies growing fiercer. The bottom line, then, is to minimize the problems arising from joint CB-IB operation. To this end, dissolving conflicts of interest by installing a "Great Wall" between the CB and the IB is one option. Another alternative would be to pursue CB and IB operations using the form of a holding company. In addition, there is a need to establish a group-level integrated risk management process that cuts through CBs and IBs and takes into consideration contagion risk, concentration levels and other factors arising from a CB-IB operation. For example, it is necessary to manage leverage and liquidity at the group level.

This chapter has reviewed schemes for compensation and incentivisation. To recap briefly, the key point is to establish an institutional regime that ensures that costs commensurate with the level of risk taken are covered. It is also important to instill a risk management culture to prevent overconfidence with respect to high-risk activities. Only then can excessively risky behavior be controlled, enabling responsible management and mitigating the problem of moral hazard in relation to private profit and community loss. Lost confidence can also be regained when these efforts are combined.

IMPROVING ACCOUNTING STANDARDS AND CREDIT ASSESSMENTS

Preparing a Unified and Flexible Accounting Standard

The need for improved accounting standards was raised by many in the wake of the financial crisis. Fair value accounting, mitigation of procyclicality, loan loss provisioning, and consolidation of off-balance exposure were the primary objects of criticism. Fair value accounting in particular was a major bone of contention.

Fair value accounting is one of the most important IFRS

principles, as well as the most likely method to become the global accounting standard. This method is based on the valuation of a financial asset at its market value. If a market price does not exist, the basis is then the market value of a similar product or simulated pricing model. Amid the financial crisis, however, this accounting approach was criticized as having effectively deepened the insolvency of financial companies by undervaluing financial assets to an unrealistic extent. Thus, the International Accounting Standards Board (IASB) and Financial Accounting Standards Board (FASB) eased the accounting method for market valuation by allowing the reclassification of financial assets as defined according to fair value accounting standards when specific requirements are met. Thanks to this measure, banks were able to value the assets on their books in a more flexible fashion based on their own valuation methods. This practice gave rise to concerns that the transparency of financial statements would be compromised, thus shaking investor confidence. Some people claimed that the seemingly improved earnings of U.S. banks in 2009 were merely an illusion created by the easing of accounting standards.

Another issue related to the accounting standard has to do with loan loss provisioning as set forth in the IFRS. There have been issues raised throughout the world over the practice of loan loss provisioning contrary to the business cycle. While the IFRS requires provisions to be set aside for incurred losses, business cycle-contrary loan loss provisioning requires provisioning for expected losses. Having a different accounting standard for the same accounting item is a factor that casts a pall over the transparency of accounting information.

When considering these examples, clearly the most urgent priority is to formulate a unified standard by reconciling conflicting accounting criteria. In doing so, there are two primary factors to take into account: transparency of accounting information and economic substance. The latter refers to the understanding that market prices are subject to sharp declines during an economic crisis.

The views of emerging economies, including Korea, should be reflected in the discussions on enacting and revising the IFRS with the aim of tiding over the global financial crisis. The accounting treatment of foreign currency translation, for instance, would have a particular impact on companies in Brazil, Russia, India and China (the so-called BRICs) in addition to Korea. Their high volume of foreign trade renders them particularly vulnerable to exchange rate fluctuations—much more so than entities like the U.S. and EU that trade in their own currencies. More specifically, despite the fact that Korean shipbuilders hedge exchange rates by executing FX forward contracts upon receiving orders, they still experience funding difficulties as their debt-to-equity ratio increases with their assets and liabilities accounted for on a gross amount basis. Korean banks also have difficulties with new foreign-currency funding, since their BIS capital adequacy ratio dropped with the increase in the amount of KRW-equivalent liabilities denominated in foreign currency. Accordingly, when preparing unified accounting criteria, it is important to consider whether or not it is desirable to apply the current currency translation accounting treatment across the board, considering the possible shocks that could arise from abnormal variations of exchange rates caused by the global financial crisis.

Preparing a unified accounting standard is also an urgent imperative from the regulatory perspective. Typically, financial authorities use processed data based on financial statements to regulate financial companies. Currently, there is a paucity of uniformity in the international accounting standard with regard to the use of processed data. One case in point involves the way foreign media took issue with the LDR (loan-to-deposit ratio) compiled by Korean banks in the wake of the financial crisis. Emerging economies will remain at a greater disadvantage until a unified standard is put in place—ideally as quickly as possible.

Tightening Regulation of Credit Rating Agencies

The OTD model that many advanced financial companies used for transferring credit risk and earning a high return has been accompanied by various "agency problems." The agency problem between credit rating agencies and investors was considered particularly severe during the crisis. A cohort of companies deemed creditworthy by credit rating agencies saw downgrades in their credit ratings or even defaulted on their bonds.

What is the fundamental cause of the agency problem? As many experts have already pointed out, the heart of the problem is the fact that the profit-generating model used by credit rating agencies is based on fee-based compensation. Credit rating agencies earn their income from the fees paid by intermediaries— and not from investors or regulatory agencies. Given the nature of this profit-making model, credit rating agencies were predisposed to focus on the maximization of their fees rather than that of investor profits.

Under this "issuer pays" model, credit rating agencies had little choice but to reflect the views of intermediaries such as arrangers in their credit rating process and found it difficult to make downward adjustments of ratings. A study by the SEC found that the staff of a credit rating agency not only was involved in fee negotiations but took part in the credit analysis as well.

Aggravating the agency problem was the fact that the bulk of fees received by credit rating agencies came from structured products. According to Portes (2008), forty percent of Moody's fee income in 2006 was earned by providing advisory services on the design of structured products [Portes, R., "Ratings Agency Reform," VOX website, 2008]. Under these circumstances, credit rating agencies needed an incentive to include structured products that were difficult to assess, owing either to a paucity of past data or the complexity of their structure, in a bid to expand their fee income. The reliability of the assessment by credit rating agencies was in doubt as well. The assessment findings as provided by credit rating agencies could only serve as ex post indicators. As a consequence, their assessment results were of no use in the recently witnessed financial crisis.

Policy attempts were made to resolve these issues. Though various measures were proposed, they mostly addressed the inadequate assessment of structured products or oversight of credit rating agencies but did not contain fundamental solutions. The time to discuss fundamental reforms for credit rating agencies is now. Above all, the priority should be to draw up measures to resolve the proxy issue that arises under the "issuer pays" model and raise the transparency of the credit rating process. To this end, one idea would be to require that credit rating agencies provide additional information or to hold them legally accountable for any misapplied credit ratings.

In terms of market structure, there is a need to introduce an element of competition into the credit rating market, which is currently characterized as a monopoly. Ironically, the heavy dependence of regulators on information provided by credit rating agencies was a factor that further aggravated this monopoly. One prime example is the introduction of the Nationally Recognized Statistical Ratings Organization (NRSRO) by the SEC in 1975. In the U.S., there are about 130 credit rating agencies, but only seven agencies were accorded NRSRO certification. In actuality, however, only three credit rating agencies around the world are recognized as NRSRO-certified, and these dominate more than

90% of the world credit rating market. In this context, it can be said that NRSRO certification effectively acts as a market entry barrier. In order to reduce this heavy dependence on a handful of credit rating agencies, certain measures need to be adopted, including the abolition of the NRSRO.

3. Resetting Modern Financial Capitalism

In the two preceding sections, an agenda was proposed and discussed pertaining to financial market reforms aimed at raising the stability of financial markets and curtailing the possibility of another financial crisis. This section explores these fundamental issues in greater detail.

The past few decades have seen the financial services industry evolve—particularly with respect to the fundamental framework that financial economists have put forth in an effort to predict market behaviors. When assessing the recent financial crisis, it is necessary to look into its economic and econo-philosophical roots. . As the Machiavellian once observed, the world should learn and wisely capitalize on the opportunities presented by the recent turn of events. And financial economists have in fact been making a concerted intellectual effort to provide insight into the operation of the financial market through the lens of the crisis.

In connection with this intellectual effort, this section discusses the problems raised in the debate between the behavioral economy and finance camp versus those who embrace the efficient market hypothesis. This hypothesis has formed the bedrock for the analysis of financial markets as well as the discussion on the future direction of financial economics raised amid the global financial crisis. Lastly, the issue of financial capitalism and its future direction will be briefly discussed.

OVERVIEW OF EFFICIENT MARKET HYPOTHESIS

It is widely known that the efficient market hypothesis has long served as a fundamental tool in the analysis of financial markets. The theory is based on the idea that the financial market is "informationally efficient," and that the prices of assets traded in the market reflect all the information available at the time. Furthermore, the theory posits that prices change instantaneously to reflect new information.

The theoretical background presupposes that market participants have rational expectations on top of the fact that they pursue the "maximization of utility," as is well known in microeconomics. The amazing connotation of this hypothesis is that the population (market) is correct on average under the circumstances, and that each individual is wrong. Market participants fine-tune their expectations as new relevant information becomes available.

This hypothesis leads to the powerful conclusion that the market evaluates financial assets correctly. If the price of a certain asset deviates from the equilibrium, this situation cannot last long. For instance, if the price of a stock is too low, well-informed investors will jump at the stock and drive up its price. Conversely, if a price runs too high, investors will sell the stock to make a profit. Furthermore, this hypothesis does not allow for the occurrence of a bubble. If formed at all, the bubble will be short-lived because savvy investors will recognize and puncture it. Based on this theory, it would be impossible to beat the market continuously with information already available in the market, except by coincidence.

According to The Economist, these theories, combined with some complicated mathematics, set the foundation for the financial engineering of Wall Street. Financial engineers came up with derivatives and securitized products, and these products ranged from the simple interest rate option to far more complex products such as the credit default swap (CDS) and collateralized debt obligation (CDO). Confident of the theoretical foundation that supported the financial products these engineers created, they argued that these financial activities were intended to make the financial system safer and the economy more robust rather than to increase bank earnings.

Such confidence was the reason why the financial crisis in 2007 constituted such a disastrous blow not only to the banking industry but to the entire financial economic framework. As Roger Lowenstein, a financial journalist, observed, "The emergence of the recent great depression [global financial crisis] might be tantamount to driving a wedge into the heart of the academic economic panacea known as the efficient market hypothesis."

BEHAVIORAL ECONOMICS OR NITPICKY FINANCE?

Even in times when the efficient market hypothesis enjoyed wide appeal, certain economists sought to find fault with it. Financial engineers busily set about designing the most ingenious financial products under the supposition that the market was efficient, but certain scholars continued to conduct research to disprove the hypothesis and show that markets could go awry. For instance, in 1980, Sanford Grossman and Joseph Stiglitz, a future Nobel laureate for economics, pointed out one paradox: if prices were set to reflect all the information, no one would take the trouble to glean information, since such an effort would produce no gains. However, in order to incentivize sophisticated investors to effect the setting of an "efficient price" in the market, Grossman and Stiglitz concluded that some inefficiency was necessity. Furthermore, Andrei Shleifer pointed out that it would be too costly for informed investors to borrow sufficient funds to bet on noise traders. The efficient market hypothesis posits that informed investors can overwhelm noise traders, prodding the market to reflect the real price by engaging in trades with less sophisticated noise traders. It is clear, however, that there is a limit to engaging in arbitrage transactions against noise traders in terms of cost. If it is recognized that prices formed in the market show movements deviating from the intrinsic prices for a long period of time, informed investors (as assumed by the efficient market hypothesis) would prefer capitalizing on the trend rather than fighting it.

Apart from this peripheral criticism, what is positioned as an alternative to efficient market hypothesis is behavioral economics, which can be dubbed the second line of financial economics. Behavioral economics has grown increasingly popular over the last decade. As events transpired that were not in line with the efficient market hypothesis, behavioral economists tried to broaden their understanding of how consumers, borrowers and investors arrived at decisions, as well as how these decisions affected price, income, and resource allocation, by capitalizing on scientific research into human, social, perceptual and emotional factors. Fundamentally, behavioral economists are skeptical about the idea of immanent rationality existing in the market. Instead, they try to explain the market outcomes that contradict rational expectations and market efficiency, including incorrect pricing, irrational decision-making, abnormal rates of return, and other market anomalies.

Ultimately, their main argument is directly opposed to the premises of the rational market hypothesis. Their evidence is based on trends such as price movements and the continuation of bubbles. For instance, they believe market participants are overconfident and have the tendency to project the current trend into the future. Combined, these two predispositions create a bubble. In addition, there is evidence that the occurrence of losses makes investors so extremely irrational that their behavior actually expedites price declines when a bubble bursts.

ALTERNATIVE DIRECTIONS AND CHALLENGE OF FINANCIAL ECONOMICS

Despite the fundamental skepticism brought about by the global financial crisis and the criticisms presented by behavioral economics/finance, many financial economists are not ready to dismiss the efficient market paradigm. Myron Scholes, a Nobel laureate in economics, was quoted as saying, "To say something has failed you is to have to have something to replace it, and so far we don't have a new paradigm to replace efficient markets." In his view, behavioral economics/finance has not convincingly explained how prices in the markets are set.

One positive development since the crisis has been a movement toward a dialectic between the principles of the efficient market hypothesis and those of behavioral economics and finance. Proponents of the efficient market hypothesis and behaviorists are increasingly asking questions and finding common ground— ultimately incorporating each other's ideas into their own analytic framework. For example, Richard Thaler, a renowned advocate of behavioral economics, has come forward saying that the economic phenomena witnessed over the past several years have actually lent increasing support to the efficient market hypothesis.

In a sense, it is neither natural nor surprising to see the distinction between the two camps blurring and a new paradigm emerging, with the recent bubble and near-collapse of the financial market serving as the catalyst. The following sections will take a closer look at the Adaptive Expectation Hypothesis emerging from this synthesis of economic theories, in addition to two major issues facing the changing world of financial economics and global financial markets in general.

Emergence of Adaptive Expectation Hypothesis

Andrew Lo, an economist with the Massachusetts Institute of Technology working on the establishment of a new economic paradigm, identifies strengths in both the efficient market hypothesis and behavioral economics. He has worked on reconciling the two camps within the purview of the adaptive expectation hypothesis, which presupposes that humans are neither perfectly rational (as assumed by the rational market hypothesis) nor perfectly confused (as assumed by behavioral economics). According to the adaptive expectation hypothesis, a theory symbiotic with the behavioristic model in an intellectually consistent fashion can be elicited by applying the principles of evolution (conceptual frameworks such as competition, adaptation, and natural selection) to the efficient market hypothesis, which is a conventional theory of modern financial economics. That is, examples propounded by behaviorists as contrary to economic rationality, such as loss aversion, overconfidence, overreaction and behavioral biases, can be consistent with the evolutionary model if simple heuristics are considered, which means that individuals continuously adapt to their ever-changing environments.

Lo, who was originally a proponent of the efficient market hypothesis, does not regard the market as an efficient mechanism according to the perspective of Eugene Fama, but rather as a fairly competitive mechanism. Naturally, people make mistakes in the adaptation process as the ecosystem changes over time. Nevertheless, people make efforts to draw the best inference through trial and error. For instance, if one investment strategy fails, the investor tries a different strategy. If the strategy works, he sticks with it. Worn-out strategies become obsolete, and new ones are called in as replacements. Based on the discussion above, distinctions can be drawn between the efficient market hypothesis and adaptive market hypothesis. The following fall under the adaptive market hypothesis:

- Arbitrage opportunities occasionally exist, unlike in the classical efficient market hypothesis.
- Investment strategies continuously wax and wane. That is, the strategy may perform well in some environments and perform poorly in others.
- Survival is the sole objective of the market participants, and profit or maximum utilization is incidental to survival.
- Innovation is the core element of survival. The best way to consistently achieve a certain level of expected returns is to adapt to the changing market environment, since the relationship between risk and compensation changes over time.

According to these views, human rationality is limited, and people are understood as being capable of error. Still, decision-making is regarded as reflecting rationality to the utmost extent amid a changing environment. This perspective provides much insight to regulators, policymakers and investors.

Reappraisal of Risk Management Models of Financial Institutions
One of the tasks facing financial economists involves a theoretical reappraisal of the risk management models of financial institutions. Up to now, the value-at-risk (VAR) model has been

used mostly by institutional investors in the financial markets to calculate the capital set aside as insurance against potential loss of risk assets. The glaring error of this model, however, is that it assumes consistency between volatile prices of assets and the real value of assets. If it is accepted that there is a correlation between the two different movements of assets, investors, assuming that a loss would not occur on both sides simultaneously, would think that a single unit of capital could be used as a buffer against the potential losses of the two different assets (instead of different units of capital set aside against the loss of each asset). However, as the entire financial services industry is currently learning from the global financial crisis, the two asset groups no longer correlate in their fluctuations, and what was once expected to be a downswing phase is suddenly appearing to move in the opposite direction. Hence, the amount of buffer capital as calculated by the VAR model has fallen gravely short of covering the losses.

Therefore, it would be better to rely less on the VAR model when calculating the amount of capital needed to provide against potential losses. For instance, one alternative would be to set aside capital separately to cover each group of assets and ensure that the same unit of capital is not shared for the coverage of another asset group, even if the pricing of the two groups may have correlated in the past. Financial economics should set a theoretical foundation for risk management techniques along these lines.

Another problem that is immanent when applying the VAR methodology has to do with its fundamental structure. That is, because VAR relies on historical data, it carries with it the so-called "black swan risk." Hence, this model may lead to a situation in which it is not applicable to an unprecedented incident (e.g., drastic declines in U.S. housing prices), as such a phenomenon would not have been previously reflected in the model. It is precisely this kind of risk that has threatened the viability of major financial institutions amid the current financial crisis. It is important that banks come up with a way of determining whether or not they have sufficient capital to withstand a material loss. By the same token, in order to resolve the problem of capital adequacy in financial institutions raised from the perspective of risk management, it is perhaps a greater priority to lay a theoretical foundation for this issue than for banks to develop their own respective risk management models.

A Better Understanding of Systemic Risk

Another pressing issue for financial economics is to further theoretical understanding of systemic risk. Both camps—those embracing the efficient market hypothesis and supporters of behavioral economics—admit to underestimating the significant implications of systemic risk. According to Myron Scholes, though many risk managers working in financial companies believe that the risks in their organizations are adequately controlled, it is important that they understand how risk managers in other companies are doing their jobs if they are to gain a holistic understanding of overall market risk. Previous outcomes have made it clear that all risk managers work in a similar fashion. For example, if the VAR model that they use requires them to sell an asset, this causes the price of the asset in a downswing market to drop even further as everyone sells at the same time. Accordingly, the model demands that they sell even more assets.

This situation is a typical example of how common exposure touches off systemic risk. Common exposure creates the potential for all of the financial institutions to generate a problem simultaneously. Typically, correlation among financial institutions stems from the ownership of similar portfolios or correlative counterparty exposure. The total risk of the whole financial system is not the sum of all risks generated at individual financial institutions. Rather, total risk depends on the level of correlation between the balance sheets of the financial institutions. This implies that a financial market comprised of many small financial institutions with similar balance sheet content is as risky as a market comprised of a small number of large-scale financial institutions.

Externalities arising from this common exposure provide important insight with regard to capital adequacy. That is, individual institutions will measure their own risk separately and will not take into account the incremental risk that they add to the overall financial system. Therefore, the sum of the capital held by all of the individual institutions will be far lower than the amount of capital required by the overall market.

Currently, several countries are trying to introduce a systemic risk regulator, a task for which financial economists could offer some advice. Discussion is currently under way on how to collate and use information from the regulatory perspective. Most financial economists agree that information is important. Accordingly, data should be collated, totaled, and made available to the public. Financial economists are of the opinion that this method is better than micro-managing individual financial institutions.

The job for financial economists is thus to identify ways to measure, as precisely as possible, the amount of risk that externalities pose to the overall system; to analyze the causes of these risks; and to formulate possible countermeasures to ward off systemic risk. These important agenda points in turn give rise to related issues that also stand to challenge economists. In particular, markets require better theories to explain why a liquid market suddenly becomes illiquid, as well as how to better manage moral hazard. Sholes, whose work has largely focused on long-term capital management, has also delved into the question of the surprising swiftness with which seemingly normal, liquid markets have been known to dry up.

Moral hazard can be defined as follows: a situation that arises when market participants take on a risk far greater than they would normally incur if not for government regulations and safety nets in place to protect them from these very risks. The collapse of Lehman Brothers, which was intended to address the moral hazard issue, illustrated how the midway point in a crisis was not the right time to take a hardball approach. This observation brings up the other issue of "time point" for economists to grapple with in their search for an adequate risk management model.

Soul Searching in Financial Capitalism

The global financial crisis also triggered discussions about financial capitalism. These discussions had been spearheaded mostly by liberal and non-mainstream economists, and now more than ever, there is a need to explore their views.

The issues that they raise are captured in the word "financialization," which has been taking place since the 1980s. Simply put, financialization refers to the phenomenon in which finance makes every sphere of the economy an investment product and, in so doing, remains deviant from the real economy.

As widely recognized, capitalism would not have advanced as it has without the development of finance. Richard Thaler ventured that financial markets are the best mechanism for capital allocation. However, the developments that have unfolded over the past two decades are characterized not so much by the mere advancement of finance, but rather by the dominance of financial logic over everything else. As faster movement of capital became possible, shareholders began to seek short-term, high rates of return. Furthermore, as the regulation of M&As eased up, corporations curtailed long-term investments, which led to deterioration in the long-term productive capacity of corporations and the national economy. It therefore becomes apparent that not every sphere of the real economy should be financialized, and that finance should reinforce the function of supporting the healthy development of the economy—that is, improvement in the efficiency and productive capacity of the overall economy.

In addition, increasing the economic welfare of society in general should be taken into consideration. As has been pointed out, a predisposition toward short-term performance under financial capitalism led to a lack of job security, which in turn touched off anxieties in household income. Furthermore, financialization compelled the redirection of household savings into investment products, compromising the soundness of household assets.

For the sake of more solid development in global capitalism, in-depth discussion is needed to set a future direction for capitalism that takes into account the balanced enhancement of the household welfare, corporate structure, and national economy in a holistic way.

4. Reshaping International Financial Regime

One of the big lessons learned in the wake of the global financial crisis is that the global nature of the current financial system has become ingrained in the minds of ordinary people as well as policymakers in all nations. In addition, the perception developed that a crisis in any form is inevitable and far-reaching under today's global financial structure. This lesson carries an important meaning in terms of the reconfiguration of the global financial system. Ultimately, the reconfiguration of the financial structure can gain momentum only when it enjoys policy consensus among all nation-states.

Given the global nature of the financial structure, the adoption of self-insurance, which has been discussed intermittently as a means to prevent a crisis, can be considered a convenient, though not completely reliable, expedient. Consider Korea as an example. After the 1997-98 Asian financial crisis, Korea strived to amass enormous foreign reserves as a form of self-insurance. Obviously, this measure was not enough to protect Korea from the tumultuous economic and financial shocks of the recent crisis. It is noteworthy that discussions of decoupling have died down compared to the time before the global financial crisis.

Furthermore, the accumulation of foreign reserves by emerging countries and the resultant global imbalances, an issue of much debate, cannot last for long. Over the course of the global financial crisis, it has become evident that mankind is at a crossroads in the reconfiguration of the overall global financial structure and must now address the issue in earnest.

This chapter begins by discussing future directions for reconstituting the IMF to function as a lender of last resort. The discussion will then move on to the topics of methods for promoting regional cooperation, which directly impacts EMEs; the creation of a mechanism to stabilize regional foreign exchange markets; and, lastly, the G-20 agenda as part of the effort to strengthen the global cooperative framework.

INTERNATIONAL LENDER OF LAST RESORT

The creation of the "international lender of last resort" as a crisis lender and crisis manager is not a new theoretical proposition. In actuality, there has been much dialogue about the idea from the perspectives of theory and policy. Instead of delving into the theoretical background and historical developments of these discussions, this chapter will focus on the roles of the international lender of last resort and what would be needed to turn the IMF into an organization well-equipped to perform such a role.

Generally, the role of the international lender of last resort is related to the deterrence of a financial crisis or the mitigation of its fallout. More specifically, this role is tied to the supply of liquidity to the markets as a way of managing liquidity risk. According to Jeffrey Sachs, liquidity risk has three distinct dimensions: financial panic, debt overhang and public sector collapse. The international lender of last resort is expected to address the three dimensions in the event of a liquidity crisis.

First, the existence of an international lender of last resort presupposes "panic"; the lender supplies liquidity in circumstances under which "financial panic" is taking place. Financial panic occurs when a debtor is not able to make payment when asked to pay back a short-term debt, and the debtor's short-term debt exceeds his short-term liquid assets. This situation especially applies to EMEs, which tend to hold significant amounts of short-term debt denominated in foreign currencies. EMEs face serious liquidity shortages as demand for repayment of these debts heighten due to deleveraging of the financial institutions in the developed countries. Under these circumstances, the existence of an international lender of last resort eliminates panic among market participants.

Second, the IMF could provide liquidity to address debt overhang. By its nature, debt overhang has to do with the legal system for supplying working capital to companies upon bankruptcy in the context of U.S. bankruptcy law. The possibility of sovereign bankruptcy is very relevant because the government concerned would need working capital as its liquidity shrinks, bringing the international lender of last resort into play.

Third, the lender can provide liquidity upon the collapse of the public sector. When revolution, civil war, an independence movement or any other similar situation occurs, basic public order such as the ability to levy and collect taxes and supply public goods breaks down. The country in question will then face a shortage of liquidity alongside the market, consequently relying upon the international lender of last resort to provide much-needed liquidity and ultimately help the country recover public order.

When addressing the question of what form the international lender of last resort should take, it would be logical to start with an existing organization like the IMF. Since its establishment, the IMF has naturally evolved through international cooperation, economic history and changing financial systems and global paradigms. Based on its own experience of providing liquidity during times of crisis all over the world, the IMF has been the de facto lender of last resort and is in an ideal position to progress naturally to the next step of an expanded and more official role.

However, there has been much criticism about this transition, in particular pertaining to the fact that the IMF does not have the power to issue international currencies or their equivalents. Without such power, the IMF may not be able to secure sufficient funds to act as the international lender of last resort. Other issues that have been raised are the lengthy decision-making process and the potential of moral hazard due to the lack of transparency in the decision-making process. In particular, an international lender of last resort should make decisions promptly, but the IMF's current process takes too much time in putting together reform programs and the terms of bailout funds. In addition, expedient decision-making is contingent upon the lender of last resort having readily available information regarding the various financial systems around the world. But such a database would take a long time to build, and it would be difficult for the IMF to take on tasks without such information.

Transparency in the decision-making process is possible only when the procedures are already in place. Moreover, moral hazard can be circumvented when the procedures are formulated and made publicly available. As for the issue of sufficient funding, there are alternative practical solutions to ensure that the IMF has enough funds even if it does not have the authority to print money.

Regarding this last point, Barry Eichengreen has introduced proposals for garnering funds to sustain a viable crisis response system. The first method is referred to as reverse-cycle funding. Eichengreen explains that contributions to the IMF by each country should be indexed and made annually. Funding should be cycle-contrary. For instance, if the global GDP is 4%, the IMF increases its funding by 5%, whereas IMF funding is adjusted downward to 1% if the global GDP declines to 2%. One variation has the funding linked to the GDP growth rate of each country rather than the global GDP. In addition, imposing higher contributions for those nations that record a surplus would adjust for global imbalances. For example, countries with a surplus exceeding 3% of global GDP would make additional contributions to the IMF at the end of each year. Alternatively, countries that currently have foreign reserves exceeding 3% of GDP and have increased their foreign reserves in the last three consecutive years could also make higher contributions. These proposals would serve as effective funding methods to ensure that the lender of last resort has the necessary means to overcome financial crises.

Eichengreen argues that special drawing rights (SDRs) should be commercialized. There has been much debate over the role of SDRs and their practical application. The focal point of the criticism is the fact that since the failure of commercialization in 1975, the issue size of SDRs has been limited and therefore cannot function as reserves any time soon. According to Eichengreen, SDRs should have liquidity and a rate of return comparable to those of securities denominated in U.S. dollars if they are to function effectively as a key international currency. For this to be possible, an organization should function as a market-maker and support the operation of the market until the SDRs reach a certain level of size and liquidity. Eichengreen says that the IMF should take on this role.

Much effort is being made to improve the promptness and transparency of the decision-making process as well, including specific discussions on the topic at the G-20 summit talks. These discussions are likely to continue. The operational structure of the IMF was also discussed, and some argued that its crisis response capacity should be strengthened, including its early warning programs. To this end, a consensus was formed that the policies of each nation should be assessed on a regular basis, and that a plan for resolving the information issue pointed out earlier should be formulated.

There has been a lively debate about the competence of the IMF as an international lender of last resort in the wake of the global financial crisis, and one concern is the strong possibility that skepticism about its stature may spread as the negative economic and financial effects brought on by the crisis ease up. In the end, the establishment of the IMF as the international lender of last resort depends on whether or not this skepticism can be overcome.

G-20 AGENDA

The global financial crisis led to the perception that the globalization of the world economy was irreversible. The crisis also showed that international cooperation based on trust is essential to stabilizing and advancing the world economy in the future. Chapter II briefly reviewed the G-20 summit talks and how they served as a pivotal means for international cooperation in coping with the global financial crisis. This chapter outlines the achievements of theose talks and go over the discussion topics covered at the third G-20 meeting in Pittsburgh, Pennsylvania, from the standpoint of Korea, which now serves as the chair nation in 2010. At the third meeting, participants reviewed the progress of the implementation of the agreements reached at the previous London summit talks (e.g., additional funding by international financial institutions and financial regulatory reforms), recovery of growth, a future growth strategy, and other agenda points.

Additional Funding Efforts by International Financial Institutions

The London summit talks produced a consensus about the need for additional funding for international financial institutions such as the IMF and MDB. A brief summary of the agreements reached is as follows.

With regard to the progress of these agreements, there was some improvement in terms of the additional funding needed to overcome the crisis, the reform of lending policies, additional SDR allocation and other agenda items, although governance reform is regarded as somewhat deficient overall. Additional funding in the amount of USD411.5 billion, out of the target of USD500 billion, was secured as of September 2009. In the meantime, Mexico (USD47 billion), Poland (USD20.6 billion), and Colombia (USD10.5 billion) also made use of FCL. The special allocation of SDRs worth USD21.4 billion met the requirements for effectuation through ratification by U.S. Congress on June 18, and an additional allocation of USD250 billion is planned for August 28, 2009. However, quota reform as part of governance reform had not met the requirements for

> ### * Agreements on IMF Funding
>
> 1. Increase IMF funding by USD500 billion
>   (Total funds: USD250 → USD750 billion)
> 2. Introduce a Flexible Credit Line (FCL), which is a form of crisis
>   prevention lending
> 3. Effect the allocation of SDRs equivalent to USD21.4 billion and
>   an additional allocation of USD250 billion
> 4. Implement the quota reform agreed upon in April 2008 and complete
>   the next GRQ ahead of schedule (Jan 2013 → Jan 2011)
> 5. Garner funds for aiding impoverished nations by securing additional
>   funds through the sale of gold and other means (USD6 billion over 2-3 years)

effectuation, and the next round of discussions on quota reform was slated to begin in September 2009.

Prompt ratification of the quota reform was expected at the third Summit Meeting. Ultimately, quota reform should be implemented within the promised period in such a way that it reflects the improved situation of the EMEs. In addition, the government of Korea, as a chair nation, should kick off its roles and responsibilities by formulating measures such as diverting the SDRs newly allocated from the advanced economies, or those economies with excessive amounts of foreign reserves, into impoverished nations via the IMF Trust Fund.

The details of increased lending by the MDB and governance reform at the World Bank have not yet been determined but are expected to proceed as scheduled. Lending volume is expected to increase to USD165 billion in 2009 on account of a capital increase and an expansion in available capital. With regard to governance reform at the World Bank, various ideas are being discussed, including balancing the proportion of voting rights between developed and developing countries, which currently stands at 44:55. Recently, the U.S. has suggested improving MDB governance, dividing up various responsibilities within the MDB,

* Agreements on MDB Funding

1. The MDB and other funding institutions will provide additional loans worth USD100 billion over three years to cope with crises and review capital adequacy.

2. The WB will move up the timeline for the second round reform (2011 → April 2010).

and improving capital adequacy through an analysis of demand for a capital increase by the MDB. Discussions on these items are under way, and the Korean government in particular is expected to be consistent in its support for implementation of the agreements.

Enhancement of Financial Regulation

The most pressing initiative of the G-20 summit talks involved strengthening financial regulation and resulted in a specific agreement.

Regulatory reform in international institutions is proceeding without a hitch, and the COP (communication of progress) report was slated for submission to the Finance Ministers' meeting and summit talks in September. Against this backdrop, regulation of uncooperative regions and additional reform measures were discussed as part of the main agenda. The main discussion points for the regulation of uncooperative regions were sanctions,

* Agreements Regarding Enhancement of Financial Regulation

1. Eight-point agreement [establishment of the FSB, closer international cooperation, prudential regulation, scope of regulation, compensation scheme, uncooperative regions, enhancement of accounting standards, and regulation of credit rating agencies]

2. International institutions such as the FSB and BCBS to provide a detailed report at the G-20 ministerial or summit talks.

tax havens, money laundering, terrorist funding, and prudent regulation. Prudent regulation will mostly be undertaken by the FSB, as this issue has not received much exposure. In addition, further regulation of larger banks, reduction of the risks of OTC derivatives, and further enhancement of compensation schemes will be discussed. The Korean government should actively conduct checks on the progress of implementation of these reforms, lest the momentum for enhancing financial regulation abate with the stabilization of the economy.

Recovery of Growth: Macroeconomic Policy and Exit Strategy

In recognition of the fact that the global financial crisis can be overcome through globally coordinated economic policies, the London summit reached an agreement on the need for the coordination of macroeconomic policies to revive global economic growth. Issues related to the recovery of growth, as well as a detailed "exit strategy," are discussed below and in the following section.

According to the IMF's analysis released at the London summit, actual fiscal spending appears to have exceeded planned fiscal spending. While fiscal spending helped to slow economic declines throughout the world, downside risks such as volatility in raw material prices and uncertainties in the financial sector are expected to remain, as is the tight labor market.

---

* Agreements on Recovery of Growth

1. Execute budget of USD5 trillion by 2010 through active fiscal expansion policy and make use of monetary policies, including non-conventional measures (GDP is expected to increase by 4%p).

2. Have IMF conduct a regular assessment of the action steps taken and to be taken

3. Formulate "credible exit strategy" to ensure long-term financial soundness and price stability.

Discussion of an exit strategy will soon emerge as the economy rebounds. The timing of such a strategy will be particularly critical to its success, while recovery of GDP growth will also become a major focus for international forums. The Korean government, while recognizing the importance of preparing an exit strategy for the sake of easing market uncertainties, should work at engaging in discussion to produce an agreement on the need for an internationally coordinated exit strategy. Furthermore, in an extension of the discussion regarding recovery of the potential GDP growth rate, the Korean government is expected to raise the issue of how to rebalance consumption at home and abroad for sustainable growth, as well as the current account imbalances among various nations, and to take the lead in such discussions.

Future Growth Strategy

With respect to a future growth strategy, three agenda points are expected to surface: sustainable and balanced economic growth, reform of international financial institutions, and sustainable economic charters. Perceptions regarding sustainable and balanced economic growth are somewhat different between developed and developing economies. The U.S. and U.K. prioritize declining world demand and deteriorating growth as issues in need of international cooperation, whereas China maintains that economic imbalances, such as the widening development gap between developed and developing nations, constitute a more pressing topic.

Given these different opinions, the paucity of world demand is expected to become a short-term issue, and the developmental divide between the two camps a long-term focus. The position of the Korean government is that rebalancing of the world economy at the national and industry levels is essential to pursuing sustainable growth. Positioned somewhere between the two camps, Korea should refrain from thinking that the global imbalance is attributable to a saving glut or excessive self-insurance on the part of EMEs. Instead, it needs to promote balance in the discussion by encouraging increased savings and the construction of a global safety net on the part of developed nations.

The shared global task of reforming international financial institutions will be discussed in the long-term perspective. The U.S. expressed the opinion that there has been relatively little discussion on the issue of reforms aimed at enhancing the effectiveness of the IMF. Therefore, the heads of the G-20 member countries should provide directions and take a decisive lead in these discussions. The U.K. believes that discussion of the mission and structure of the international financial institutions is necessary for the sustainable growth of the world economy. As such, the setting of basic principles and long-term initiatives such as a strong role for the IMF and governance reform were discussed at the third Summit Meeting. The Korean government should support these initiatives while sharing in the perception that the missions and governance of the IMF need to be improved for it to carry out a rebalancing act for the sustainable growth of the world economy. As for the MDB, its roles should be expanded to cope with new issues such as climate change. Expanding the role of the IMF as the international lender of last resort would have been another worthwhile topic of discussion.

Countries differ in their positions on the establishment of a Charter for a Sustainable Economy. Germany is planning to review specific principles and action steps after agreeing upon a basic charter framework and principles in the form of a task force that would include several countries (e.g., Germany, the U.S. and South Africa). Many countries support this idea of a charter task force, while certain countries like China, Saudi Arabia, Turkey,

India, Indonesia and Japan have suggested that the issue be put before the UN, arguing that the content of the charter is still vague and not appropriate for discussion by the heads of G-20 nations. Should the Korean government agree to the U.K.'s approach, this would help secure the support of Europe, and in particular Germany, and maintain the momentum of the G-20.

PROMOTING INTRA-REGIONAL COOPERATION AND STABILIZING FX MARKETS OF EMES

Even prior to the occurrence of the global financial crisis, there was much discussion about intra-regional cooperation in exchange rate and currency policy. These discussions basically stemmed from efforts to overcome the Asian financial crisis of 1997-1998 and provide against the recurrence of similar situations. There are several reasons why exchange rate and currency cooperation are critical issues in Asia.

First, Asian nations are characterized by a heavy dependence on exports and a high level of regional economic interdependency. This export dependence is problematic, since most Asian nations do not have a proper economic system in place for stabilizing exchange rates. Most Asian nations have historically pursued export-oriented economic growth. Under these circumstances, a drastic change in a country's exchange rate adversely affects trade between these nations, with grave consequences for their economies. Furthermore, intra-regional economic interdependency has continued to deepen, exacerbating the contagion effect in the event of a crisis outbreak.

Second, it is well known that imbalances in the current account between the U.S. and Asia (especially East Asia) have been widening. That is, the U.S. has been amassing a current account deficit whereas the countries in the Asian region have been accumulating large current account surpluses. Accordingly, the dominance of the U.S. dollar as a key currency has been gradually eroding. In the end, if the current account imbalances continue or increase, the resultant uncertainties may potentially have a negative impact on the world economy. A cooperative mechanism for exchange rates and currencies could offer one solution for stabilizing exchange rates and alleviating global imbalances.

Third, repetitive and excessively short-term capital movements in environments where banks are not fully developed have led to frequent bouts of economic anxiety. Controlling the excessive inflow of international short-term capital and resolving the shortage of liquidity arising from a sudden capital outflow are beyond the abilities of an individual country. However, if these issues are dealt with by a regional cooperative regime for exchange rates and currencies, more desirable results can be achieved.

Fourth, as was shown in the Asian financial crisis in 1997-1998 and the recent global financial crisis, a regional cooperative regime for exchange rates and currencies will be able to function as a direct crisis-prevention mechanism. Without such an agreement in place, the Asian region will continue to be exposed to the contagion effect of external shocks as its economic and financial relations with the international community continue to grow.

In addition, the Chiang Mai Framework and attempts to promote the Asia Bond Market, as discussed in Section 2, will not be able to gain sufficient momentum without international cooperation. Along this line of reasoning, proposals of every stripe surfaced in the name of intra-regional (financial) cooperation and stabilization of the foreign exchange market. To continue where Section 2 left off, there is much in the way of potential and developmental prospects for the Asia Monetary Fund (AMF) as a regional institutional mechanism.

Section 2 discussed how the Chiang Mai Initiative revealed

many of its limitations amid the global financial crisis, ultimately evolving into the Multilateral Chiang Mai Initiative (MCMI). However, the MCMI also has its limits. First, the total swap amount is not enough to prevent a liquidity crisis. Second, and perhaps more importantly, the MCMI is not connected with an intra-regional mechanism for stabilizing exchange rates. For these reasons, the initiative is not regarded as a practical crisis management mechanism within the region, as it fails to prevent both the occurrence and spread of a crisis.

Because of these factors, the CMI scheme should ultimately evolve into the AMF. The general perception is that the AMF should function as a permanent organization equipped with three main capabilities: functioning as lender of last resort, carrying out surveillance and enforcing conditions. The lender feature is a tool that ensures an independent and holistic response to a financial crisis. The second and third features help to establish the criteria for convergence toward a regional cooperative mechanism.

In the end, Asian nations need to make more of an effort to advance the CMI scheme instead of settling for the current ad hoc cooperative framework that was put together in response to the global financial crisis. As mentioned earlier, the AMF is also likely to reveal its own limitations without a regional exchange rate mechanism in place. Still, the region should seek to advance the AMF via agreed-upon channels until a regional exchange rate mechanism is established. For example, the surveillance function of the Economic Review and Policy Dialogue (ERPD), which was devised for the exchange of information and capital movement in 2000 when the CMI was created, could be further developed as a separate effort.

Although there has been much theoretical discussion about the regional exchange rate mechanism (and key currency) necessary to complete the AMF, little has materialized in reality or in specific terms. Coordinated policies to promote the creation of this mechanism would help build a stronger regional cooperative arrangement.

First, the integration of the real economy needs to be accelerated through the expansion of intra-regional FTAs and multilateralism. Such integration carries important insights into intra-regional policy coordination and currency integration. In particular, the increase in intra-industry trade volume will align the business cycles of the countries in the region. The heightened correlation in economic activities will lead to a reduction in the occurrence of asymmetrical shocks and become a prerequisite for entering into a regional exchange rate agreement that will help unify intra-regional currency policy. In addition, this expansion of FTAs and multilateralism will promote the economic growth and mutual understanding of countries in the region, thus contributing to the reduction of political and social conflicts.

Second, since Asian nations differ in terms of economic development levels as well as political and cultural traditions, one strategy would be to pursue exchange rate cooperation on a smaller scale. That is, countries would initially be grouped into sub-level currency and exchange rate mechanisms according to economic development level and cultural characteristics, with more countries gradually added on over time. This is typically referred to as a "multi-track" or "multi-speed" approach, according to which the countries that first engage in in-depth mutual cooperation effectively jump-start the integration process. Each group intensifies the level of coordination in its respective currency and exchange rate policies. These groups conduct negotiations with one another over time in order to evolve into a bigger monetary union.

Third, there is a need for gradual deregulation of intra-regional capital markets. Up until now, intra-regional capital markets have been integrated to a great extent thanks to the deregulation of the local financial system, openness of financial services, relaxed controls on capital and exchange rates, and other liberalization measures. Nevertheless, the level of integration in these areas is actually quite meager compared to the extent to which activities such as trade and foreign direct investment have been integrated. This is attributable to rigorous regulation and control of capital movements by China and low-income ASEAN countries. However, measures undertaken in Asia such as FTAs, the CMI, and the Asian Bond Market Initiative (ABMI) will ultimately redirect the course of these policies in a direction that will mitigate capital controls in the region.

5. Rethinking Transition from Stimulus to Exit Strategy

DISCUSSION OF EXIT STRATEGY

As the global financial crisis subsides and economic indices improve, expectations of an economic revival are high. This optimism is reflected in the recent OECD forecast for quarterly GDP growth in each major country, which is expected to rise and maintain positive figures throughout 2010. In the updated World Economic Outlook released on July 8, 2009, the IMF estimated that world GDP would grow 2.5% in 2010, up 0.6%p from the previous forecast of 1.9% released in April. The growth estimate for advanced economies was revised upward from 0.0% to 0.6%, and EMEs and developing nations also saw an upward adjustment from 4.0% to 4.7%.

As expectations of an economic turnaround increase, so have

Table 4-1 **World GDP Growth Estimates**

(Unit: %, %p)

	Actual		July 2009 Estimates		Change from April 2009 Estimates	
	2007	2008	2009	2010	2009	2010
World	5.1	3.1	-1.4	2.5	-0.1	0.6
(Advanced)	2.7	0.8	-3.8	0.6	0.0	0.6
US	2.0	1.1	-2.6	0.8	0.2	0.8
Euro Zone	2.7	0.8	-4.8	-0.3	-0.6	0.1
Japan	2.3	-0.7	-6.0	1.7	0.2	1.2
(EMEs and Developing)	8.3	6.0	1.5	4.7	-0.1	0.7

Source: IMF

calls for an exit strategy. An exit strategy refers to an effort to pull out from atypical policies undertaken to cope with the financial crisis. Some have argued that expansionist policies should be dropped as another asset bubble forms. On the other hand, others claim that the recent signs of recovery are merely a transient phenomenon stemming from increased liquidity. However, all seem to agree that now is not the time to implement an exit strategy, as the world continues to exhibit signs of economic weakness, downside risks such as rising unemployment rates, and lingering uncertainties in the financial sector, although the pace of declines in the world economy has decelerated.

Nevertheless, international institutions continue to discuss an exit strategy. For instance, at the G-8 ministerial talks on June 12-13, 2009, several European financial ministers, including Germany's, commented that an exit strategy should be implemented to prepare for the post-crisis era and ward off inflationary pressures resulting from fiscal spending and the increased supply of liquidity undertaken to boost the economy and stabilize the financial markets. At the same time, the BIS argued at the annual general meeting of the world's central banks on June 29, 2009, that delays in interest rate hikes by the central banks of major economies, together with a belated recall of the liquidity previously supplied, could touch off inflation. In an updated version of its Global Financial Stability Report released on July 8, 2009, the IMF stated that an exit strategy needed to be implemented in consideration of previous fiscal policies to address lingering uncertainties in the markets. It argued that the financial situation was improving as the risk of a systemic collapse declined, necessitating an exit strategy.

In an observation on the U.S. economy, the epicenter of the financial crisis, the FRB stated at an FOMC meeting on August 12, 2009, that given the way U.S. economic activities were leveling off, this trend would gradually slow the purchase of treasury bonds worth USD300 billion, bringing the market to a close by the end of October and thereby heralding a change in the expansionist policy. Many experts are interpreting this as an effective reversal in policy toward shrinking liquidity supply and a reference to implementation of an exit strategy. However, it was decided that the target Fed funds rate would be kept in the 0-0.25% range for a considerable period of time, and that an exit strategy would be implemented on a gradual basis.

The signs of inflationary pressure typically brought about by a cycle of relaxed lending criteria, which then leads to more lending and a surge in currency circulation, have not yet surfaced. As shown in Table 4-2, the FRB survey on bank lending practices in July 2009 revealed that most U.S. banks would apply more rigorous lending criteria compared to the average of the past 10 years at least until the end of 2010. In the real economy, inflationary pressure has increased as employment, consumption and other indicators have maintained solid growth.

However, consumer sentiment has not recovered as much since sharply declining in the early stages of the crisis. Apparently, the prerequisites for implementing an exit strategy in earnest have not been fully met.

Table 4-2 **Results of Survey of U.S. Banks on Lending Practices By Type of Borrower**

(Unit: %)

Response to Lending Terms	Revert to Long-Term Average in 2010[1]	Revert to Long-Term Average in 2011	Maintain Strict Terms During the Foreseeable Economic Future	Current Lending Criteria Less Strict Than Long-Term Average
❖ **Investment Grade**				
Loans	50.1	4.5	20.5	25.0
Commercial Mortgage	24.4	20.0	40.0	15.6
❖ **Speculative Grade**				
Loans	33.4	31.3	22.9	12.5
Commercial Mortgage	10.2	28.6	53.1	8.2
❖ **Good Credit Households**				
Residential Real Estate	35.5	12.5	41.7	10.4
Credit Card	25.8	25.8	32.3	16.1
❖ **Bad Credit Households**				
Residential Real Estate	15.3	15.4	57.7	11.5
Credit Card	11.2	11.1	66.7	11.1

Note 1) Includes those respondents who said they would revert to the long-term average at the end of 2009 and in 1Q 2010.

Source: FRB

PRINCIPLES FOR ESTABLISHING EXIT STRATEGY

Though it will take some time, each country's government will have to implement an exit strategy that scales back the crisis-specific measures undertaken so far if signs of economic stabilization appear. Before implementation, however, much thought should be given to ways of mapping out the strategy and the timing for implementing it. With the FRB effectively setting about liquidity control, it is highly likely that the monetary authorities of major countries will engage in lively discussion of an exit strategy. There are a few considerations to take into account while mapping out such a strategy.

Notwithstanding the numerous views and postulations about an exit strategy, the most pivotal principle lies not in the speed of its implementation but in how well the strategy can be designed and implemented. In other words, though the initial response to a crisis should be prompt and bold, an exit strategy should be implemented meticulously and circumspectly. Hastily switching over to different policies upon signs of economic recovery could bring about serious consequences such as the prolongation of economic recession.

Two prime examples are the Great Depression of the U.S. in the 1930s and the long economic depression of Japan in the 1990s. During the boom years following World War I in the U.S., bubbles began to form in the housing and stock markets. The FRB launched a tight monetary policy out of fears of inflation. In particular, the FRB raised the rediscount rate from 5.0% to 5.74% in August 1929, and then to 6.0% the very next month, rapidly adopting an even tighter policy. These decisions, however, punctured the bubbles, leading to a stock market crash and pulling the U.S. economy down into a depression that endured until March 1933. In total, some 9,755 banks went bankrupt during

Figure 4-5 Major U.S. Economic Indices During Great Depression

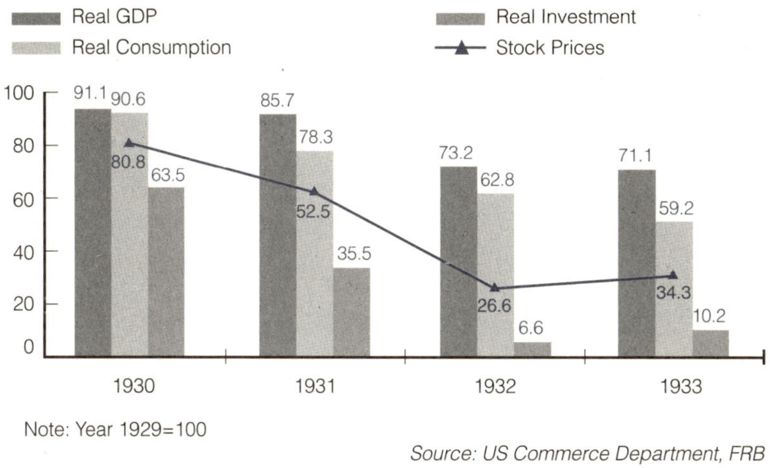

Legend:
- Real GDP
- Real Consumption
- Real Investment
- Stock Prices

Chart data (Year 1929=100):

Index	1930	1931	1932	1933
Real GDP	91.1	85.7	73.2	71.1
Real Consumption	90.6	78.3	62.8	59.2
Real Investment	63.5	35.5	6.6	10.2
Stock Prices	80.8	52.5	26.6	34.3

Note: Year 1929=100

Source: US Commerce Department, FRB

the Great Depression of 1929-1933, and real GDP in 1933 had plummeted 28.9% from its 1929 level. The jobless rate soared to 26.6%, and stock prices plummeted 65.7%.

After the Plaza Agreement in September 1985, Japan implemented monetary easing to protect itself from deterioration in its economy due to the rapid appreciation of the JPY. Furthermore, asset bubbles developed as stock and home prices rose sharply due to lending competition among financial institutions based on low interest rates. In response, the Japanese government quickly turned to monetary tightening after 1989, triggering a bubble burst and the abrupt downswing of the real economy from its peak in February 1991. Eventually, Japan experienced a protracted economic decline that lasted until January 2002 (the so-called "lost decade"). Consequently, the real GDP growth rate dropped to 1.0% in the post-bubble era (1992-2002) from an annual average of 3.9% in 1981-1991.

The IMF's analysis of the occurrence of slowdowns or recessions in the wake of financial stress in advanced economies reveals that more discretion needs to be applied in dealing with the signs of a global economic comeback. According to the IMF, a total of 113 cases of financial distress occurred in 17 advanced economies over the past 30 years, and the ensuing slowdown or recession was longer than those not preceded by financial distress. Moreover, a slowdown or a recession following financial distress triggered by the banking sector turned out to be longer than those triggered by other factors.

Table 4-3 **Duration of Financial Distress, Slowdown and Recession in 17 Advanced Economies**

(Unit: %)

	Frequency	Period (Quarter)		Output Loss	
		Financial Distress	Slowdown/ Recession	Cumulative	Quarterly Average
Overall Financial Distress	113	2.4			
Financial Distress→Slowdown	29	2.7	7.6	-7.6	-0.7
(By banking sector)	18	3.2	8.4	-9.3	-0.8
Financial Distress→Recession	29	3.0	6.8	-13.8	-1.2
(By Banking Sector)	17	4.0	7.6	-19.8	-1.5
Other	55	2.0			
Slowdown without Financial Distress	109		5.1	-4.1	-0.6
Recession without Financial Distress	31		3.1	-5.4	-0.9

Note: 1) Output loss is a percentage relative to GDP.
2) The 17 advanced economies are Australia, Austria, Belgium, Canada, Denmark, Finland, France, Germany, Italy, Japan, the Netherlands, Norway, Spain, Sweden, Switzerland, the U.K. and the U.S.

Source: IMF, World Economic Outlook

The survey results above suggest that the establishment of an exit strategy amid ever-present downside risks to the world economy needs to take into account the possibility of a "W" economic cycle. That is, the economy can experience a temporary recovery before sliding back into a slowdown or recession, and the timing and sequence of an exit strategy should reflect this analogy when interpreting economic rebound trends.

There are varying opinions about what a well-executed exit strategy looks like. What is clear, however, is that an exit strategy is not merely limited to recovering liquidity that was abnormally funneled into the markets to cope with a financial crisis. Though it is necessary to recollect liquidity, a more fundamental approach is required. This means that the purpose of an exit strategy lies in enabling long-term, sustainable economic revival. An exit strategy cannot be disconnected from the task of preventing the occurrence of another financial crisis. To this end, an exit strategy should be designed from a long-term perspective along the lines of the future tasks mentioned in the section titled *Reshaping International Financial Regime*, such as proper balancing between financial innovation and prudential regulation and the rebuilding of confidence in the corporate and financial systems.

The details of an exit strategy need to be determined based on a proportionate equilibrium of financial, monetary and fiscal policy, lest the process of policy normalization trigger overly ambitious deleveraging and easing of lending restrictions, which could then affect the economy adversely in the short term. That being said, the first priority should be to discuss how to normalize the situation that arose from having implemented atypical policies such as large fiscal deficits, enormous government and bank loans funneled into the credit market, guarantee support, and nationalization of banks. When the right balance is reached between short-term and long-term objectives, market confidence

Table 4-4 **Fiscal Condition of Major Economies**

(Unit: %)

		2007	2008	2009	2010
US	Fiscal deficit	2.9	5.8	10.2	11.9
	Total Liabilities	62.9	71.9	88.1	100.0
Japan	Fiscal Deficit	2.5	2.6	6.8	8.4
	Total Liabilities	167.1	172.1	186.2	197.3
Eurozone	Fiscal Deficit	0.7	1.8	5.4	7.0
	Total Liabilities	71.2	71.0	77.7	84.4
OECD	Fiscal Deficit	1.4	3.0	7.2	8.7
	Total Liabilities	74.5	78.8	90.6	99.9

Note: Percentage (%) relative to nominal GDP

Source: OECD, OECD Interim Economic Outlook

can be regained and reinforced. Furthermore, only then can there be an end to the vicious boom-bust cycle wherein the end of a crisis leads to the beginning of another.

Finally, it is important to recall that nations differ in terms of economic damage sustained and level of recovery achieved. Subsequently, the elements of an exit strategy, such as timing and sequence, may differ among nations depending on their circumstances and should be customized accordingly. In this regard, cooperation among nations is an issue that requires an international platform. It is imperative to formulate a globally consistent exit strategy via active collaboration as the world economy becomes more interconnected and more susceptible to negative contagion effects and regulatory arbitrage arising from globalization. International cooperation will more effectively dispel lingering global uncertainties.

Conclusion

It has not been long since pessimistic views prevailed in light of the unprecedented global financial crisis. At first, some were predicting a long and painful road to recovery; indeed, a few commentators even talked about the end of financial capitalism itself. Although the story is still unfolding and it is certainly too early to declare victory, the situation has clearly brightened within a relatively short period of time. It must be said that the emergence of an economic recovery is a truly welcome development.

From the chaos generated by the events leading up to the crisis, opportunities have been created for reform within the broad global financial system. If conscious efforts are made to learn from the mistakes made pre-crisis and the manner in which the crisis was successfully handled by certain countries, players on the world scene can move forward with positive, deliberate steps to ensure a financially sustainable future.

Importantly, there has been a realization that regulatory authorities can no longer think and act in term of nation-specific guidelines and rules. Even sector-specific rules have proved troublesome as corporations increasingly operate across market sectors and national boundaries. The ramifications of institutional financial failure are far-reaching and have the potential for negative effects far greater than their direct liability assumes. From this latest crisis, it has become undeniably clear how greatly regulatory authorities underestimated risk based on the faulty premises of nation-specific analysis.

Indeed, when global economic considerations were taken into

account and regulations were altered within the U.S. financial system, this was done in an effort to allow U.S. primary lenders the ability to compete with their European counterparts in terms of profitability and share gains, rather than to pursue the long-term stability of the U.S. financial system. Competition is, of course, essential in a healthy free market system. However, in creating a fair playing field for financial institutions to compete, nations must acknowledge the key importance of the sustainability of all primary lenders and the need for cooperation among nations in order to prevent failure of the entire global system.

In view of this, the importance of certain international organizations, especially the G-20, has come to light. Once this crisis was acknowledged as being global in scope, the G-20 played a key role in coordinating cooperation and bridging the interests of advanced and emerging economies. In the future, the roles of the G-20 and other more regional organizations will be increasingly emphasized by all their members, and especially by the nations holding chairmanship. Korea assumes the chairmanship in 2010, and as the nation with the fastest rebounding economy among the OECD states, it has valuable insights into how to rapidly revive an economy after crisis.

LESSONS FROM KOREAN TURNAROUND

When I first assumed the chairmanship of the Korean Financial Services Commission, I knew that the position held great responsibility and required keen supervision of the Korean market and the external factors affecting it. Although signs of turbulence were clear in the lead-up to the crisis, what took me and most everyone else by surprise was the severity and pervasiveness of the crisis. It very quickly became clear that this latest crisis required an equally comprehensive preemptive response to the potential attack on all fronts of our financial system. Armed with the weaponry the FSC had at its disposal, my team and I set out to devise an aggressive counterattack to head off the impending financial disaster.

The immediate implementation of steps to create a number of massive public funds in order to fend off the anxiety created by the looming cloud of credit unavailability had a marked effect. In particular, the Bond Market Stabilization Fund and Bank Recapitalization Fund in the early phase, among others, enabled us to significantly increase confidence in the availability of capital to the market. Although the introduction of these funds and trusts was essential to provide relief, it was also necessary to closely monitor their appropriateness and effectiveness from the time of their implementation and, should the need for increases in available capital become apparent, to act accordingly. We found that in addition to making public funds available, it was imperative to encourage all lending institutions to raise capital in order to put a decisive halt to the deterioration of solvency ratios.

The much-needed capital supplied to primary and non-banking lending institutions was geared to providing support at the front lines. However, in order to target support for corporations, the FSC needed to be more specific in producing available capital. To this end, loans with state bank funding were significantly increased for the use of industries identified as being core to Korea's growth engine in the present and future; exports, high technology, green growth and start-ups were chosen as such industry sectors and given key support during the crisis.

Although pumping life back into the large players in the economy was of extreme importance, it was also necessary to protect individual smaller economic contributors, as their effect as a whole has a huge role in the sustained success of the economy. As part of the overall strategy of strength through support to every link in the chain, the Korean government needed to continually identify those areas most at risk and skillfully adjust investment priorities so as to not let one link falter.

Through the successful implementation of policy measures undertaken to provide financial stimulus and stability in the economy, useful lessons for crisis management emerged. It became evident that the critical importance of preemptive and decisive stimulus packages delivered in the early phases of crisis had a profound effect on the ability to produce a solid turnaround. And in the course of putting such measures into practice, the imperative of maintaining principles and discipline throughout the crisis and beyond also proved itself to be entirely critical. Another lesson learned is the need for strong leadership and inter-agency cooperation, and the need to garnish public support for policy implementation. It must be noted that while these lessons are of great usefulness in order to combat new crises in the future, there must be a sense of constant financial regulatory evolution to meet the ever changing needs of future economies.

I am reminded of a quote from Niccolo Machiavelli: "Never waste the opportunities offered by a (good) crisis." Inspired by this, I have suggested that there is a set of principles and tasks that all nations can follow in order to better control the sustainability and stability of the global financial system.

In the spirit of learning from the past to act on the future, we should consider the "Five Rs":

1. "Rebalancing financial innovation and prudential regulation": Striking a balance between mitigating the risks of recurring financial crisis and promoting the virtues of market innovation and creativity.
2. "Rebuilding trust in corporate and financial systems": Redesigning compensation and incentive structures and

further improving accounting standards, credit assessment and the oversight of rating agencies.

3. "Resetting modern financial capitalism": Reassessing the true value of the sophisticated quantitative models used in financial decision-making and exploring more dependable and pragmatic alternatives.

4. "Reshaping international financial architecture": Creating an international lender of last resort, harmonizing prudential standards, and improving governance structure at IFIs through more equitable representation between advanced and emerging economies.

5. "Rethinking the transition from stimulus to exit strategy": Coordinating implementation of exit strategies through deliberation at the G-20 level, leading to more sustainable and balanced growth in the world.

It is with great belief in the future that we glean lessons from the failings of the past and change our actions and understanding to improve on the system as it exists now. Shortsightedness and a limited scope of vision led the financial industry, and thus every person in the world, down a path of uncertainty; while a path has emerged from the shadows, we have yet to see the sun on the horizon. The view has become much clearer through our new understanding of the interconnectedness of the global system and the need for a dynamic, flexible approach to financial policy measures, as was shown by the Korean government. With increased cooperation and assistance between different actors on the global stage and a renewed sense of cautious optimism and discipline, the world will proceed beyond crisis.